Lecture Notes in Computer Science 8996

More information about this series at http://www.springer.com/series/7407

Teijiro Isokawa · Katsunobu Imai
Nobuyuki Matsui · Ferdinand Peper
Hiroshi Umeo (Eds.)

Cellular Automata and Discrete Complex Systems

20th International Workshop, AUTOMATA 2014
Himeji, Japan, July 7–9, 2014
Revised Selected Papers

Editors
Teijiro Isokawa
University of Hyogo
Himeji
Japan

Katsunobu Imai
Hiroshima University
Hiroshima
Japan

Nobuyuki Matsui
University of Hyogo
Himeji
Japan

Ferdinand Peper
National Institute of Information
and Communications Technology
Osaka
Japan

Hiroshi Umeo
Osaka Electro-Communication University
Osaka
Japan

ISSN 0302-9743 ISSN 1611-3349 (electronic)
Lecture Notes in Computer Science
ISBN 978-3-319-18811-9 ISBN 978-3-319-18812-6 (eBook)
DOI 10.1007/978-3-319-18812-6

Library of Congress Control Number: 2015938087

Springer Cham Heidelberg New York Dordrecht London

Printed on acid-free paper

Springer International Publishing AG Switzerland is part of Springer Science+Business Media
(www.springer.com)

Preface

AUTOMATA 2014 is the 20th International Workshop on Cellular Automata and Discrete Complex Systems and continues a series of events established in 1995. AUTOMATA is an annual workshop and aims of the workshop are:

- To establish and maintain a permanent, international, multidisciplinary forum for the collaboration of researchers in the field of Cellular Automata (CA) and Discrete Complex Systems (DCS).
- To provide a platform for presenting and discussing new ideas and results.
- To support the development of theory and applications of CA and DCS (e.g. parallel computing, physics, biology, social sciences, and others) as long as fundamental aspects and their relations are concerned.
- To identify and study within an inter- and multidisciplinary context, the important fundamental aspects, concepts, notions, and problems concerning CA and DCS.

AUTOMATA 2014, held in Himeji, Japan, from July 7 to 9, 2014, is the result of cooperation of the institutions of the members of the Organizing Committee, i.e., Hiroshima University, the National Institute of Information and Communications Technology (NICT), Osaka Electro-Communication University, and University of Hyogo, Himeji.

The volume contains papers for three invited talks and ten accepted papers of AUTOMATA 2014. We thank all authors for their contributions. We are grateful to all members of the Program Committee for selecting the accepted papers.

We would also like to express our sincere thanks to the invited speakers, Jarkko Kari, University of Turku (Finland), Satoshi Murata, Tohoku University (Japan), and Martin Kutrib, Universität Gießen (Germany), for presenting their works.

We are indebted to all participants for making this workshop a successful and fruitful meeting.

Finally, the organization of AUTOMATA 2014 was made possible, thanks to financial and technical support of Osaka Electro-Communication University, University of Hyogo in Himeji, the city of Himeji, the Himeji Convention & Visitors Bureau, the Support Center for Advanced Telecommunications Technology Research (SCAT), and the Society of Instrument and Control Engineers (SICE).

March 2015

Teijiro Isokawa
Katsunobu Imai
Nobuyuki Matsui
Ferdinand Peper
Hiroshi Umeo

Organization

AUTOMATA 2014 was organized by University of Hyogo, Osaka Electro-Communication University, and Hiroshima University, Japan. The conference took place at Egret Himeji (Himeji Cultural and International Exchange Foundation), Himeji, Hyogo, Japan.

Steering Committee

Enrico Formenti	University of Nice Sophia Antipolis, France
Eric Goles	Adolfo Ibáñez University, Chile
Jarkko Kari	University of Turku, Finland
Andreas Malcher	Universität Gießen, Germany
Thomas Worsch	Karlsruhe University, Germany

Program Committee

Paola Flocchini	University of Ottawa, Ottawa, Canada
Enrico Formenti	University of Nice Sophia Antipolis, Nice, France
Anahí Gajardo	Universidad de Concepción, Concepción, Chile
Eric Goles	Adolfo Ibáñez University, Chile
Pierre Guillon	University of Aix-Marseille, Marseille, France
Katsunobu Imai	Hiroshima University, Japan
Teijiro Isokawa	University of Hyogo, Japan
Jarkko Kari	University of Turku, Turku, Finland
Martin Kutrib	Universität Gießen, Gießen, Germany
Jia Lee	Chongqing University, Chongqing, China
Genaro Martínez	National Polytechnic Institute, Mexico city, Mexico
Andreas Malcher	Universität Gießen, Germany
Bruno Martin	University of Nice Sophia Antipolis, Nice, France
Kenichi Morita	ex. Hiroshima University, Japan
Hidenosuke Nishio	ex. Kyoto University, Japan
Ferdinand Peper	National Institute of Information and Communications Technology, Osaka, Japan
Kai Salomaa	Queen's University, Kingston, Canada
Klaus Sutner	Carnegie Mellon University, Pittsburgh, USA
Veronique Terrier	University of Caen, Caen, France
Hiroshi Umeo	Osaka Electro-Communication University, Japan
Thomas Worsch	Karlsruhe University, Karlsruhe, Germany

Organizing Committee

Chair

Teijiro Isokawa	University of Hyogo, Japan

Co-chairs

Katsunobu Imai	Hiroshima University, Japan
Nobuyuki Matsui	University of Hyogo, Japan
Ferdinand Peper	National Institute of Information and Communications Technology, Japan
Hiroshi Umeo	Osaka Electro-Communication University, Japan

Sponsoring Institutions

Osaka Electro-Communication University
University of Hyogo
Himeji City, Japan
Support Center for Advanced Telecommunications Technology Research
The Society of Instrument and Control Engineers

Invited Papers

On a Cellular Automaton and Powers of 3/2

Jarkko Kari

Department of Mathematics and Statistics, University of Turku, 20014, Finland
jkari@utu.fi

In this talk we begin with a question asked by Stanislaw Ulam about generating all patterns from a single finite seed [4, p. 30]. The problem is to design a cellular automaton rule and an initial configuration with all but finitely many cells in null states such that in the evolution that follows all finite patterns over the state alphabet will appear.

We use two simple facts to design such a rule [2]: (i) the powers of a number n written in base b contain all finite digit sequences if n is not a rational power of b, and (ii) the multiplication of numbers by n in base b is a cellular automaton if all prime factors of n also divide b. Smallest such example is the cellular automaton $F_{\times 3}$ that multiplies by $n = 3$ in base $b = 6$. The existence of this simple solution raises other interesting questions to investigate:

- Do there exist analogous universal pattern generators also in two- and higher dimensional cellular spaces?
- Does there exist a solution with fewer than six states? In particular: is there a universal pattern generator over the binary alphabet?
- Does there exist a solution that generates all patterns at all positions?

A candidate to solve the last problem is obtained by combining $F_{\times 3}$ with a suitable right shift. This suggests the automaton $F_{\times 3/2}$ that multiplies numbers in base 6 by constant 3/2. Whether it is able to generate all patterns everywhere depends on some difficult open problems in number theory. Namely, for such universal pattern generation to happen one needs an integer m such that the fractional parts of $m(3/2)^i$ are dense in the interval [0, 1]. Also Mahler's problem on *Z-numbers* [3] can be rephrased in terms of $F_{\times 3/2}$. Finally, by adding a new state to represent a floating radix point, we modify $F_{\times 3}$ to simulate the Collatz-function on base 6 representations of positive integers [1].

References

1. Kari, J.: Cellular automata, the collatz conjecture and powers of 3/2. In: Yen, H.-C., Ibarra, O.H. (eds.) DLT 2012. LNCS, vol. 7410, pp. 40–49. Springer, Heidelberg (2012)
2. Kari, J.: Universal pattern generation by cellular automata. Theoret. Comput. Sci. **429**, 180–184 (2012)
3. Mahler, K.: An unsolved problem on the powers of 3/2. J. Aust. Math. Soc. **8**, 313–321 (1968)
4. Ulam, S.: A Collection of Mathematical Problems. Interscience, New York (1960)

Introduction to Molecular Robotics: Computation to Control Chemical Systems

Satoshi Murata

Department of Bioengineering and Robotics, Graduate School of Engineering, Tohoku University

Abstract. Molecular robotics is an emerging area of research aiming at building robots made of components such as sensors, computers, and actuators, which are all implemented as molecular devices. The molecular robot is supposed to react autonomously to its environment by receiving chemical/physical signals and decides behavior by molecular computation [1–3].

Firstly, I would like to introduce some basic principles of molecular computation based on hybridization reactions of DNA molecules. Various computational methods ranging from signal amplification, logic operation to reaction-diffusion-like computation have been proposed so far, will be implemented as computational components for the molecular robots. Despite extensive efforts, however, systems having all three functions (sensing, computation, and actuation) are still difficult to realize, because integrating different chemical components in the same spatio-temporal space causes a lot of undesired spurious interactions among them. How to integrate chemical devices into a consistent network is the central issue of molecular robotics indeed. I think new architectures are necessary to cope with this intrinsic difficulty. Proposed models of computation for molecular robots such as single-molecular computing, computing in liposomes and computing in gel will be introduced to show the current level of research in this field.

References

1. Murata, S., Konagaya, A., Kobayashi, S., Saito, H., Hagiya, M.: Molecular robotics: a new paradigm for artifacts. New Gener. Comput. **31**, 27–45 (2013)
2. Hagiya, M., Konagaya, A., Kobayashi, S., Saito, H., Murata, S.: Molecular robots with sensors and intelligence. Acc. Chem. Res., ACS **47**(6), 1681–1690 (2014)
3. Molecular Robotics Project: Grant-in-Aid for Scientific Research on Innovative Areas. MEXT, Japan (2012–2016). http://www.molecular-robotics.org/en/

Complexity of One-Way Cellular Automata

Martin Kutrib

Institut für Informatik, Universität Giessen
Arndtstr. 2, 35392 Giessen, Germany
kutrib@informatik.uni-giessen.de

Abstract. Among the different types of cellular automata the onedimensional one-way variant with fixed boundary conditions is one of the simplest. Here we consider these devices as massively parallel computing model. The formal investigations of their properties and capacities began in the sixties. Though a lot of results have been found over the years, there are still several open problems. The survey addresses the basic hierarchy of induced language classes. Aspects of computational complexity are discussed in connection with classical complexity theory. Hard open problems give rise to consider one-way cellular automata also from the structural complexity point of view. Adding (limited) nondeterminism to the model yields structurally more complex and computationally more powerful devices. Finally, the capabilities of one-way cellular automata to time-compute functions are considered. This means that given an input of length n a distinguished cell has to enter a distinguished state exactly after $f(n)$ time steps. We present some selected results on these topics and want to draw attention to the overall picture and to some of the main ideas involved.

Contents

Invited Paper

Complexity of One-Way Cellular Automata

Martin Kutrib(✉)

Institut für Informatik, Universität Giessen,
Arndtstr. 2, 35392 Giessen, Germany
kutrib@informatik.uni-giessen.de

Abstract. Among the different types of cellular automata the one-dimensional one-way variant with fixed boundary conditions is one of the simplest. Here we consider these devices as massively parallel computing model. The formal investigations of their properties and capacities began in the sixties. Though a lot of results have been found over the years, there are still several open problems. The survey addresses the basic hierarchy of induced language classes. Aspects of computational complexity are discussed in connection with classical complexity theory. Hard open problems give rise to consider one-way cellular automata also from the structural complexity point of view. Adding (limited) nondeterminism to the model yields structurally more complex and computationally more powerful devices. Finally, the capabilities of one-way cellular automata to time-compute functions are considered. This means that given an input of length n a distinguished cell has to enter a distinguished state exactly after $f(n)$ time steps. We present some selected results on these topics and want to draw attention to the overall picture and to some of the main ideas involved.

1 Introduction

The advantages of homogeneous arrays of interacting processing elements are simplicity and uniformity. It turned out that a large array of not very powerful elements operating in parallel can be programmed to be very powerful. One of the simplest types of such systems are cellular automata, whose homogeneously interconnected finite automata (the cells) work synchronously at discrete time steps obeying one common transition function. Cellular automata have extensively been investigated from different points of view. Here we consider them as massively parallel computing model. Instances of problems to solve can be encoded as strings of symbols which are the data supplied to the devices. If (one piece of) the answer to the problems is binary, the set of possible inputs is split into two sets associated with the binary outcome. From this point of view, the computational capabilities of cellular automata are studied in terms of string acceptance, that is, the determination to which of the two sets a given string belongs. These investigations are with respect to and with the methods of language theory.

The object of the survey is one of the simplest and best studied types of cellular language acceptors, so-called one-way cellular automata (OCA). The formal

T. Isokawa et al. (Eds.): AUTOMATA 2014, LNCS 8996, pp. 3–18, 2015.
DOI: 10.1007/978-3-319-18812-6_1

investigations of their properties and computational capacity began in the sixties. Over the decades a lot of results have been explored, but there are still some basic unanswered questions. The presented survey is, of course, far from being complete. We have been motivated in choosing topics based on our knowledge and interest.

The survey addresses the basic hierarchy of induced language classes. It turned out that only little is known about the properness of inclusions in the time hierarchy ranging from real time to unrestricted, that is, exponential time. Surprisingly, the only inclusions known to be strict are between real time and linear time. This might be one of the reasons why there is a particular interest in these fast computations.

Aspects of computational complexity are discussed in connection with sequential computational complexity. The open problems of cellular automata classes are related to hard open problems of the classical theory. This gives rise to consider cellular automata also from the structural complexity point of view. Adding (limited) nondeterminism to the model yields structurally more complex and computationally more powerful devices, that are related to the deterministic classes.

An important concept for constructing cellular automata algorithms are signals. Since signals can encode and propagate information through the array, their realizability can show us the computation power and the limitations of the model. Moreover, we can regard signals as a higher programming concept which allows modularization techniques at algorithm design. For one-way information flow the capability of OCA to time-compute functions f is considered. This means that given an input of length n a distinguished cell has to enter a distinguished state exactly after $f(n)$ time steps.

2 One-Way Cellular Language Acceptors

We denote the set of non-negative integers by $\mathbb{N}$. In general, we write 2^S for the powerset of a set S. Let A denote a finite set of letters. Then we write A^* for the set of all finite words (strings) built with letters from A. The empty word is denoted by λ, the reversal of a word w by w^R, and for the length of w we write $|w|$. For the number of occurrences of a subword x in w we use the notation $|w|_x$. A subset of A^* is called a language over A. We use $\subseteq$ for set inclusion and $\subset$ for strict set inclusion. For a function $f\colon \mathbb{N} \to \mathbb{N}$ we denote its i-fold composition by $f^{[i]}$, $i \geq 1$. In order to avoid technical overloading in writing, two languages L and L' are considered to be equal, if they differ at most by the empty word, that is, $L \setminus \{\lambda\} = L' \setminus \{\lambda\}$. Throughout the article two devices are said to be *equivalent* if and only if they accept the same language.

A (non)deterministic one-way cellular automaton is a linear array of identical (non)deterministic finite state machines, sometimes called cells, that are identified by positive integers. Except for the rightmost cell each one is connected to its nearest neighbor to the right. The state transition depends on the current state of a cell itself and the current state of its neighbor, where the rightmost cell receives information associated with a boundary symbol on its free input line. The state changes take place simultaneously at discrete time steps. The input mode for cellular automata is called parallel. One can suppose that all cells fetch their input symbol during a pre-initial step.

Definition 1. *A nondeterministic one-way cellular automaton (NOCA) M is a system $\langle S, F, A, \#, \delta\rangle$, where S is the finite, nonempty set of* cell states, *$F \subseteq S$ is the set of* accepting states, *$A \subseteq S$ is the nonempty set of* input symbols, *$\# \notin S$ is the permanent* boundary symbol, *and $\delta\colon S \times (S \cup \{\#\}) \to (2^S \setminus \emptyset)$ is the* local transition function.

A configuration *of M at time $t \geq 0$ is a mapping $c_t\colon \{1, 2, \ldots, n\} \to S$, for $n \geq 1$, that assigns a state to each cell. The computation starts at time 0 in a so-called* initial configuration, *which is defined by the input $w = a_1a_2 \cdots a_n \in A^+$. We set $c_0(i) = a_i$, for $1 \leq i \leq n$. Successor configurations are computed according to the global transition function Δ. Let c_t, $t \geq 0$, be a configuration with $n \geq 1$, then its successor c_{t+1} is defined as follows:*

$$c_{t+1} = \Delta(c_t) \iff \begin{cases} c_{t+1}(i) \in \delta(c_t(i), c_t(i+1)), i \in \{1, 2, \ldots, n-1\} \\ c_{t+1}(n) \in \delta(c_t(n), \#) \end{cases}$$

Thus, Δ is induced by δ.

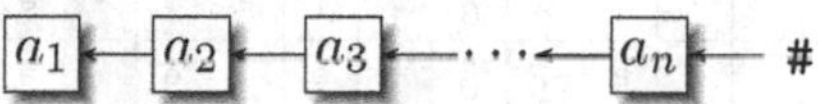

Fig. 1. A one-way cellular automaton.

An NOCA is *deterministic* if $\delta(s_1, s_2)$ is a singleton for all $s_1, s_2 \in S \cup \{\#\}$. Deterministic cellular automata are denoted by OCA (Fig. 1).

An input w is accepted by an NOCA M if at some time step during its course of computation the leftmost cell, that is cell 1, enters an accepting state. The *language accepted by M* is denoted by $L(M)$. Let $t\colon \mathbb{N} \to \mathbb{N}$ be a mapping. If all $w \in L(M)$ are accepted with at most $t(|w|)$ time steps, then M is said to be of time complexity t (cf. [20] for a discussion of this general treatment of time complexity functions). In particular, an input w is accepted if the leftmost cell enters an accepting state at some time $i \leq t(|w|)$. Subsequent states of the leftmost cell are not relevant.

In general, the family of languages accepted by some device X with time complexity t is denoted by $\mathscr{L}_t(X)$. The index is omitted for arbitrary time. Actually, arbitrary time is exponential time due to the space bound. If t is the identity function n, acceptance is said to be in *real time* and we write $\mathscr{L}_{rt}(X)$. The *linear-time* languages $\mathscr{L}_{lt}(X)$ are defined according to $\mathscr{L}_{lt}(X) = \bigcup_{k\in\mathbb{Q},\, k\geq 1} \mathscr{L}_{k\cdot n}(X)$.

Example 2. The unary language $\{a^{2^n} \mid n \geq 1\}$ is accepted by some OCA with time complexity $t(n) = n + \log(n)$.

The basic idea of the construction is to generate a binary counter in the rightmost cell with one step delay (cf. Fig. 2). The counter moves to the left whereby the cells passed through are counted. The length of the counter is increased when necessary. In addition, cells which are passed through by the counter have to check whether all bits are 1. In this case the value of the counter is $2^n - 1$, for some $n \geq 1$. Due to the delayed generation this indicates a correct input length and the cell enters the final state. Clearly, the desired time complexity is obeyed. A formal construction can be found in [19]. □

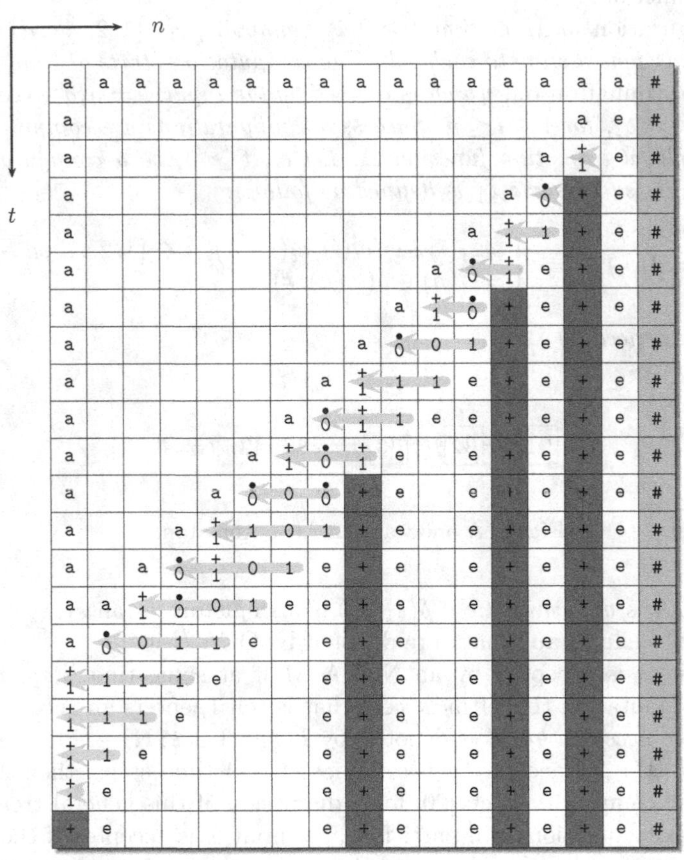

Fig. 2. Space-time diagram of an OCA accepting an input from the unary language $\{a^{2^n} \mid n \geq 1\}$ in $n+\log(n)$ time. The arrows mark the moving counter, whose digits are 0, 1, or $\overset{\bullet}{0}$. The latter is a 0 reporting a carry-over. A $\overset{+}{1}$ indicates that, so far, the cell has been passed through by 1 only.

The non-regular unary language $\{a^{2^n} \mid n \geq 1\}$ of Example 2 cannot be accepted by any OCA with time complexity $t(n) \in o(n + \log(n))$ [19,25]. So, the example is optimal with respect to the time complexity. Moreover, it shows the proper inclusion $\mathscr{L}_{rt}(\text{OCA}) \subset \mathscr{L}_{rt+\log}(\text{OCA})$.

3 A Basic Hierarchy

The computational capacity of different types of cellular automata is a natural and well-investigated field. The relations between basic language families are depicted in Fig. 3.

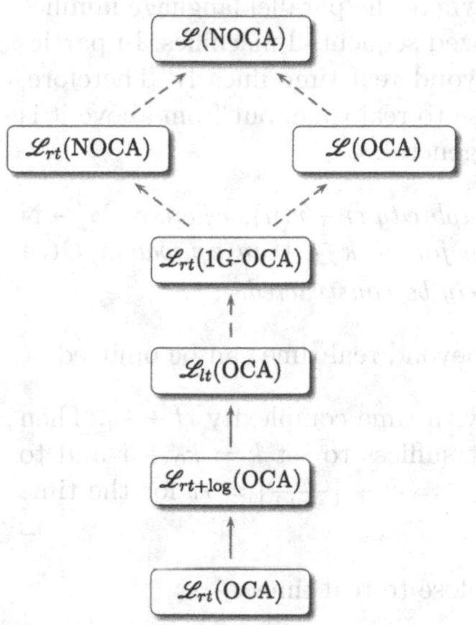

Fig. 3. A basic hierarchy of one-way cellular automata language families. Solid arrows indicate proper inclusions, dashed arrows indicate inclusions that are not known to be proper.

The weakest class at the bottom of the hierarchy is given by cellular automata with only one-way information flow and a time constraint at the limit to trivial computations, that is, real time. As mentioned before, it is known that the family $\mathscr{L}_{rt}$(OCA) is properly included in $\mathscr{L}_{rt+\log}$(OCA) [18]. The latter is in turn a proper sub-family of the linear-time OCA languages. This proper inclusion follows from results in [8,32]. Unfortunately, beyond linear time none of the levels of the hierarchy is separated. To emphasize this fact even more, the class at the top of the hierarchy is defined by nondeterministic one-way cellular automata without time limit, that is, exponential time due to the space bound. Since for nondeterministic devices the question whether one-way information flow is weaker than two-way information flow has been solved negatively in [10], the family $\mathscr{L}$(NOCA) is equal to the complexity class $\mathsf{NSPACE}(n)$, that is, the context-sensitive languages. By 1G-OCA one-way cellular automata with limited nondeterminism are denoted. Basically, in such devices all cells are allowed to perform just one nondeterministic step at the very beginning of the computation. A more detailed discussion of this topic follows in Sect. 5 below. However, the family $\mathscr{L}_{rt}$(1G-OCA) fits very well into the hierarchy [2,3]. While the inclusion $\mathscr{L}_{rt}(\text{1G-OCA}) \subseteq \mathscr{L}_{rt}(\text{NOCA})$ follows for structural reasons, the inclusion $\mathscr{L}_{rt}(\text{1G-OCA}) \subseteq \mathscr{L}(\text{OCA})$ follows from the equality $\mathscr{L}(\text{1G-OCA}) = \mathscr{L}(\text{OCA})$. Moreover, the computing power of real-time OCA is, in fact, strictly increased by adding one nondeterministic step. This result can be strengthened, whereby the strictness of the inclusion is lost: $\mathscr{L}_{lt}(\text{OCA}) \subseteq \mathscr{L}_{rt}(\text{1G-OCA})$.

4 Between Real Time and Linear Time

The levels of the basic hierarchy of language families accepted by several types of one-way cellular automata are separated up to linear time only. Beyond linear time the edge of knowledge about the properness of inclusions has been crossed. This section is devoted to a more closer look at several aspects, in particular, in the range between real time and linear time.

Speed-Up. Helpful tools in connection with time complexities are speed-up theorems. Strong results are obtained in [13,14], where the parallel language families are characterized by certain types of customized sequential machines. In particular, it is possible to speed up the time beyond real time linearly. Therefore, linear-time computations can be sped up close to real time, but from above it is known that real time cannot be achieved in general.

Theorem. *Let M be an OCA with time complexity $rt + r(n)$, where $r : \mathbb{N} \to \mathbb{N}$ is a mapping and rt denotes real time. Then for all $k \geq 1$ an equivalent OCA with time complexity $rt + \lfloor \frac{r(n)}{k} \rfloor$ can effectively be constructed.*

The next example shows that any constant beyond real time can be omitted.

Example 3. Let $k_0 \geq 1$ and M be an OCA with time complexity $rt + k_0$. Then there is an equivalent real-time OCA M'. It suffices to set $k = k_0 + 1$ and to apply Theorem 4 in order to obtain $rt + \lfloor \frac{k_0}{k} \rfloor = rt + \lfloor \frac{k_0}{k_0+1} \rfloor = rt$ for the time complexity of M'. □

Next, a linear-time computation is sped up close to real time.

Example 4. Let $k_0 \geq 1$ and M be an OCA with time complexity $rt + k_0 \cdot rt$. Then for all rational numbers $\varepsilon > 0$ there is an equivalent OCA M' with time complexity $\lfloor (1+\varepsilon) \cdot rt \rfloor$. We set $k = \lceil \frac{k_0}{\varepsilon} \rceil$ and apply Theorem 4 in order to obtain $rt + \left\lfloor \frac{k_0 \cdot rt}{\lceil k_0/\varepsilon \rceil} \right\rfloor \leq rt + \left\lfloor \frac{k_0 \cdot rt}{k_0/\varepsilon} \right\rfloor = rt + \lfloor \varepsilon \cdot rt \rfloor = \lfloor (1+\varepsilon) \cdot rt \rfloor$. □

Unary Languages. Already in [25] is has been shown that any unary real-time OCA language is regular. As mentioned before, language $\{a^{2^n} \mid n \geq 1\}$ of Example 2 is a witness for the proper inclusion $\mathscr{L}_{rt}(\text{OCA}) \subset \mathscr{L}_{rt+\log}(\text{OCA})$ [18].

Disproving Real-Time Recognizability. Until 1995 the regularity of unary real-time OCA languages was the only source to show that a language does not belong to $\mathscr{L}_{rt}(\text{OCA})$. Then, in [27,28] a method based on equivalence classes has been developed. Basically, an equivalence relation can be defined such that the number of equivalence classes distinguishable by real-time OCA is bounded:

Theorem. *Let $L \subseteq A^*$ be a language and $X \subseteq A^*$ and $Y \subseteq A^*$ be two sets of words. Two words $w \in A^*$ and $w' \in A^*$ are (L, X, Y)*-equivalent *if and only if $xwy \in L \iff xw'y \in L$, for all $x \in X$ and $y \in Y$.*

The upper bound for the number of equivalence classes which can be distinguished by some real-time OCA is as follows.

Theorem. *Let $L \subseteq A^*$ be a real-time OCA language and $X = A^{m_1}, Y = A^{m_2}$ be two sets of words for positive integers m_1 and m_2. Then there exists a constant $p \geq 1$ such that the number N of (L, X, Y)-equivalence classes is bounded by $N \leq p^{|X|}p^{(m_2+1)|Y|}$.*

In order to apply that method to a witness language L, one has to determine such an equivalence relation so that the number of equivalence classes induced by L exceeds the number of equivalence classes distinguishable by any real-time OCA.

Example 5. Consider the linear context-free language

$$L = \{a^n b^n \mid n \geq 1\} \cup \{a^n bvab^n \mid n \geq 1, v \in \{a, b\}^*\}.$$

By applying the equivalence relation method, in [28] it has been shown that the two-linear concatenation $L \cdot L$ is not accepted by any real-time OCA. □

The next tool which allows us to show that languages do not belong to the family $\mathscr{L}_{rt}(\text{OCA})$ is based on pumping arguments for cyclic strings [23]:

Theorem. *Let L be a real-time OCA language. Then there exists a constant $p \geq 1$ such that any pair of a word w and an integer k that meets the condition $w^k \in L$ and $k > p^{|w|}$ implies that there is some $1 \leq q \leq p^{|w|}$ such that $w^{k+jq} \in L$, for all $j \geq 0$.*

Example 6. The language $L = \{a^{2^n} \mid n \geq 1\}$ is not accepted by any real-time OCA.

Contrarily assume there is a real-time OCA accepting L. Then we set $w = a$, $k = 2^p$ and derive that a^{2^p+q} as well as a^{2^p+2q} belong to L. If $2^p + q$ is not a power of two, we obtain a contradiction. So, let $2^p + q = 2^{p+r}$, for some $r \geq 1$. We derive $2^{p+r} < 2^{p+r} + q = 2^{p+r} + 2^{p+r} - 2^p = 2^{p+r+1} - 2^p < 2^{p+r+1}$, and conclude that $2^p + 2q$ is strictly in between two consecutive powers of two. Hence, a^{2^p+2q} does not belong to L. □

An Infinite Proper Hierarchy of Language Families. So far, there is one language family known to be in between the real-time and linear-time OCA languages. In fact, there is an infinite proper hierarchy of families in this range [17]. For the proof it is necessary to control the lengths of words with respect to some internal substructures. The following notion of constructibility expresses the idea that the length of a word relative to the length of a subword should be computable. To this end, a function $f : \mathbb{N} \to \mathbb{N}$ is said to be OCA-*constructible*, if there exist an λ-free homomorphism h and a language $L \in \mathscr{L}_{rt}(\text{OCA})$ such that $h(L) = \{a^{f(n)-n}b^n \mid n \geq 1\}$. At a glance this notion of constructibility might look somehow unusual or restrictive. But λ-free homomorphisms are very powerful so that the family of (in this sense) constructible functions is very rich. Examples and the next theorem are presented in [17].

Theorem. *Let $r_1, r_2 : \mathbb{N} \to \mathbb{N}$ be two increasing functions. If $r_2 \cdot \log(r_2) \in o(r_1)$ and r_1^{-1} is OCA-constructible, then $\mathscr{L}_{rt+r_2}(OCA) \subset \mathscr{L}_{rt+r_1}(OCA)$.*

Example 7. Let $0 \leq p < q \leq 1$ be two rational numbers. Clearly, $n^p \cdot \log(n^p)$ is of order $o(n^q)$. Moreover, the inverse of n^q is OCA-constructible. Thus, we have the strict inclusion $\mathscr{L}_{rt+n^p}(\text{OCA}) \subset \mathscr{L}_{rt+n^q}(\text{OCA})$. □

Example 8. Let $i < j$ be two positive integers, then $\log^{[j]}(n) \cdot \log^{[j+1]}(n)$ is of order $o(\log^{[i]}(n))$. Since the inverse of $\log^{[i]}(n)$ is OCA-constructible, we obtain the strict inclusion $\mathscr{L}_{rt+\log^{[j]}}(\text{OCA}) \subset \mathscr{L}_{rt+\log^{[i]}}(\text{OCA})$. □

Beyond Real Time? We conclude this section with an open problem: Does the copy language $\{\, ww \mid w \in \{a,b\}^* \,\}$ belong to $\mathscr{L}_{rt}(\text{OCA})$?

5 Limited Nondeterminism

Before we turn to discuss the basic hierarchy beyond linear time, we take a closer look at the role played by the family $\mathscr{L}_{rt}(\text{1G-OCA})$ based on limited nondeterminism. Why is there no corresponding linear-time family in the hierarchy? How about more than one nondeterministic step?

Traditionally, nondeterministic devices have been viewed as having as many nondeterministic guesses as time steps. The studies of this concept of unlimited nondeterminism led, for example, to the famous open LBA-problem or the unsolved question whether or not P equals NP. In order to gain further understanding of the nature of nondeterminism, in [11, 16] it has been viewed as an additional limited resource at the disposal of time or space bounded computations.

Exemplarily, here we consider one-way cellular automata with time-bounded nondeterminism, that is, the number of nondeterministic state transitions is a limited resource which depends on the length of the input (see [21] for further details, variants, and references). In order to distinguish between deterministic and nondeterministic steps a *deterministic* as well as a *nondeterministic* transition function is provided. Let $k \geq 0$ be an integer. The global transition induced is such that the cells of a *kG-OCA* perform initially k nondeterministic transitions that are followed by only deterministic transitions.

Guess Reduction. A result obtained in [3] shows that $k+1$ guesses per cell are not better than k guesses. Moreover, it allows to reduce the number of nondeterministic transitions by a constant as long as one remains.

Theorem. *Let $k \geq 1$ be an integer. Then $\mathscr{L}_t(k\text{G-OCA}) = \mathscr{L}_t(1\text{G-OCA})$, for all time complexities $t\colon \mathbb{N} \to \mathbb{N}$.*

The idea of the guess reduction is shown in Fig. 4. Basically, in its first nondeterministic step the 1G-OCA simulates the first step of the kG-OCA and, additionally, $k-1$ further nondeterministic steps of the kG-OCA for all possible pairs of states, that is, $k-1$ finite mappings from $S \times (S \cup \{\#\})$ to S. These mappings are stored in additional registers. The deterministic transition of the 1G-OCA applies these mappings to the current situations, thus, simulating further guesses of the kG-OCA. Afterwards it simulates the deterministic transition of the kG-OCA.

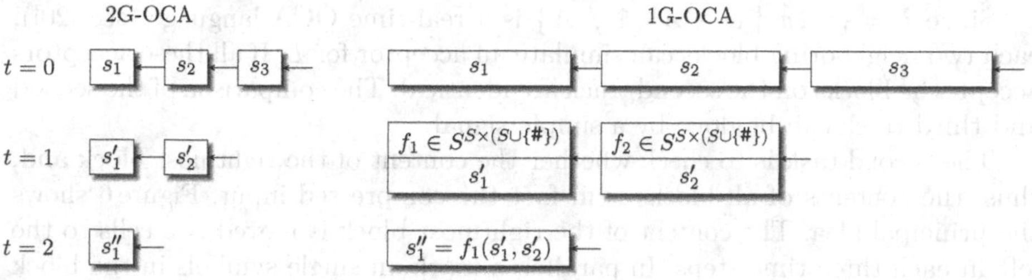

Fig. 4. Idea of the guess reduction. $S^{S\times(S\cup\{\#\})}$ denotes the set of mappings from $S \times (S \cup \{\#\})$ to S.

In general, the number of nondeterministic transitions cannot be reduced to 0. It will turn out that $\mathscr{L}_{rt}(\text{OCA}) = \mathscr{L}_{rt}(\text{0G-OCA})$ is a proper subfamily of $\mathscr{L}_{rt}(\text{1G-OCA})$.

Speed-Up. From above it is known that deterministic OCA can be sped-up from $(rt + r(n))$-time to $(rt + \lfloor \frac{r(n)}{k} \rfloor)$-time. Thus, linear-time is close to but not real-time. For kG-OCA a stronger result has been obtained in [3]. It says that real-time is as powerful as linear-time.

Theorem. *Let $i, k \geq 1$ be integers. Then $\mathscr{L}_{i\cdot t}(k\text{G-OCA}) = \mathscr{L}_t(k\text{G-OCA})$, for all time complexities $t\colon \mathbb{N} \to \mathbb{N}$ with $t(n) \geq n$.*

Due to the guess reduction, it is sufficient to show the speed-up for 1G-OCA. The technique used for the construction is referred to as *packing-and-checking.* The basic idea is to guess the input in a packed form on the left of the array. The verification of the guess can then be done by a deterministic OCA in real time. Figure 5 shows the situation after a correct guess in the first step. Subsequently, the simulation of the given 1G-OCA takes place on the compressed input on the third track. Due to the compression, each i of the original steps can be simulated in one step.

Besides the simulation on the third track, the simulating 1G-OCA has to verify whether the initial guesses were correct. To this end, two tasks are performed. The first task is to check whether all blocks on the second track, and whether the leftmost blocks on the second and third track are identical.

a	b	c	d	e	f	g	h	i	j	k	l	
abc	def	ghi	jkl	abc	def	ghi	jkl	abc	def	ghi	jkl	#
abc	def	ghi	jkl									

Fig. 5. Packing-and-checking: Configuration after a first step with correct guesses. The input is kept on the first track. It appears in i-fold compressed and repeated form with center markers on the second track. The leftmost block is additionally written on the third track.

Since $L = \{ w\$w \mid w \in A^+, \$ \notin A \}$ is a real-time OCA language (see [20]), each two neighboring blocks can simulate an acceptor for L. If all these acceptors accept, the blocks on the second track are identical. The comparison of the second and third track can be done by a simple signal.

The second task is to check whether the content of the rightmost block and, thus, the contents of all blocks is in fact the compressed input. Figure 6 shows the principal idea. The content of the rightmost block is moved two cells to the left in each three time steps. In parallel, a mark on single symbols in the block is moved from right to left in every time step. Finally, in every time step the marked symbol is compared with the original input. If all comparisons match the block has correctly been guessed.

a	b	c	d	e	f	g	h	i	j	k	l	
								abc	def	ghi	! jkl	#
							abc	def	ghi	! jkl		#
						abc	def	ghi	! jkl			#
						abc	def	! ghi	jkl			#
					abc	def	! ghi	jkl				#
				abc	def	! ghi	jkl					#
				abc	! def	ghi	jkl					#
			abc	! def	ghi	jkl						#
		abc	! def	ghi	jkl							#
		! abc	def	ghi	jkl							#
	! abc	def	ghi	jkl								#
! abc	def	ghi	jkl									#

Fig. 6. Packing-and-checking: Comparing the compressed with the original input.

Relations to Other Types of Automata. Here we turn to adjust the family $\mathscr{L}_{rt}$(1G-OCA) in the basic hierarchy.

For structural reasons we have the inclusion $\mathscr{L}_{lt}(\text{OCA}) \subseteq \mathscr{L}_{lt}(\text{1G-OCA})$. The strong speed-up results revealed $\mathscr{L}_{rt}(\text{1G-OCA}) = \mathscr{L}_{lt}(\text{1G-OCA})$ and, thus, the next theorem follows.

Theorem. *The family $\mathscr{L}_{lt}$(OCA) is included in $\mathscr{L}_{rt}$(1G-OCA).*

Again structural reasons yield the inclusion $\mathscr{L}_{rt}(\text{1G-OCA}) \subseteq \mathscr{L}_{rt}(\text{NOCA})$. The proof of the remaining inclusion $\mathscr{L}_{rt}(\text{1G-OCA}) \subseteq \mathscr{L}(\text{OCA})$ is more involved.

In [12] the equivalence of OCA and a restricted online single-tape Turing machine has been shown. This characterization is utilized for the construction [3]. In particular, it shows that the increase of computing power gained in adding one nondeterministic transition to real-time OCA cannot be achieved in general, that is, for automata without time limits. On the other hand, one can avoid the nondeterministic transition without reducing the computing power.

Theorem. *The family $\mathscr{L}_{rt}(1G\text{-}OCA)$ is included in $\mathscr{L}_{rt}(NOCA)$ as well as in $\mathscr{L}(OCA)$.*

6 Relations to Computational Complexity

Here we consider the part of the basic hierarchy beyond linear-time OCA languages, where none of the inclusions is known to be proper. This fact is astonishing at a first glance, since deterministic linear time is in opposite to nondeterministic exponential time. However, in the following open problems concerning the properness of the inclusions are related to hard open problems of the classical complexity theory. In particular, we consider the chain of inclusions

$$\mathscr{L}_{lt}(\text{OCA}) \subseteq \mathscr{L}_{rt}(\text{1G-OCA}) \subseteq \mathscr{L}(\text{OCA}) \subseteq \mathscr{L}(\text{CA}) \subseteq \mathscr{L}(\text{NOCA})$$

where CA denotes two-way cellular automata, that is, each cell is connected to its immediate neighbor to the right as well as to its immediate neighbor to the left. The inclusion $\mathscr{L}(\text{OCA}) \subseteq \mathscr{L}(\text{CA})$ follows for structural reasons and the inclusion $\mathscr{L}(\text{CA}) \subseteq \mathscr{L}(\text{NOCA})$ for structural reasons and the know equality $\mathscr{L}(\text{NOCA}) = \mathscr{L}(\text{NCA})$ [10].

A straightforward observation is that a Turing machine sweeping back and forth over the nonempty part of the tape can simulate a cellular automaton. For example, a $t(n)$-time bounded (N)OCA is simulated by a (non)deterministic Turing machine in $n \cdot t(n)$ time. The space bound of cellular automata even reveals, for example, $\mathscr{L}_{rt}(\text{N(O)CA}) \subseteq \mathsf{NSPACE\text{-}TIME}(n, n^2)$. Together with the famous result $\mathsf{NSPACE\text{-}TIME}(s(n), t(n)) \subseteq \mathsf{DSPACE}(O(s(n) \cdot \log(t(n))))$ of [24] this implies immediately $\mathscr{L}_{rt}(\text{N(O)CA}) \subseteq \mathsf{DSPACE}(O(n \cdot \log(n)))$.

In [26] the Turing machine simulation by cellular automata has been shown.

Theorem. *The family $\mathscr{L}(CA)$ is identical with the deterministic context-sensitive languages, that is, $\mathscr{L}(CA) = \mathsf{DSPACE}(n)$. Similarly, $\mathscr{L}(N(O)CA)$ equals the family of context-sensitive languages, that is, $\mathscr{L}(N(O)CA) = \mathsf{NSPACE}(n)$.*

Why is it so hard to (dis)prove the strictness of the inclusions?

$\mathscr{L}(\text{CA})$ versus $\mathscr{L}(\text{NOCA})$. At the right end of the chain we directly derive $\mathscr{L}(\text{CA}) = \mathscr{L}(\text{NOCA})$ if and only if $\mathsf{DSPACE}(n) = \mathsf{NSPACE}(n)$. So, solving the properness of the inclusion would solve the famous open LBA-problem.

$\mathscr{L}(\text{OCA})$ versus $\mathscr{L}(\text{CA})$. Concerning the next inclusion $\mathscr{L}(\text{OCA}) \subseteq \mathscr{L}(\text{CA})$, in [7] it has been shown that the complexity class $\mathsf{ATIME}(O(n))$ of linear-time alternating Turing machine languages is a subset of $\mathscr{L}(\text{OCA})$. In turn, the inclusion $\mathsf{NSPACE}(\sqrt{n}) \subseteq \mathsf{ATIME}(O(n))$ is well known. Thus, we have the inclusion $\mathsf{NSPACE}(\sqrt{n}) \subseteq \mathscr{L}(\text{OCA})$ and, on the other hand, $\mathscr{L}(\text{CA}) = \mathsf{DSPACE}(n)$. So, showing the properness of the inclusion in question would improve Savitch's famous result $\mathsf{NSPACE}(s(n)) \subseteq \mathsf{DSPACE}(s(n)^2)$ [24].

$\mathscr{L}_{rt}(\text{1G-OCA})$ versus $\mathscr{L}(\text{OCA})$. The family $\mathscr{L}(\text{OCA})$ is still very powerful. It contains the context-free languages and a PSPACE-complete language [7,12]. Since we have $\mathscr{L}_{rt}(\text{1G-OCA}) \subseteq \mathsf{NSPACE} - \mathsf{TIME}(n, n^2) \subseteq \mathsf{NP}$, showing the equality $\mathscr{L}_{rt}(\text{1G-OCA}) = \mathscr{L}(\text{OCA})$ would imply $\mathsf{NP} = \mathsf{PSPACE}$.

$\mathscr{L}_{lt}(\text{OCA})$ versus $\mathscr{L}_{rt}(\text{1G-OCA})$. Real-time 1G-CA can simulate nondeterministic real-time multitape Turing machines. To this end, basically, the leftmost cell simulates the state control of the Turing machine as well as the top of some finite number of stacks that are simulated by the other cells in real time [19]. Nondeterministic real-time multitape Turing machines define the so-called *quasi-real-time languages* [1], that include an NP-complete language. Moreover, $\mathscr{L}_{rt}(\text{1G-CA})$ is equal to $\mathscr{L}_{rt}(\text{1G-OCA})$ [3] and $\mathscr{L}_{lt}(\text{OCA}) \subseteq \mathsf{DSPACE} - \mathsf{TIME}(n, n^2) \subseteq \mathsf{P}$. So, showing the equality $\mathscr{L}_{lt}(\text{OCA}) = \mathscr{L}_{rt}(\text{1G-OCA})$ would imply $\mathsf{P} = \mathsf{NP}$.

7 Time-Computable Functions

So far, the complexity of cellular automata has been considered from the formal language point of view. Now we turn to a slightly different approach. The capability of OCA to time-compute functions is considered. That means, given an input of length n and a function f, a distinguished (the leftmost) cell has to enter am accepting state exactly after $f(n)$ time steps (see [6] for details on the following examples and results).

Definition 9. *A function $f : \mathbb{N} \to \mathbb{N}$, $f(n) \geq 1$, is OCA-*time-computable *if and only if there exists an OCA with unary input alphabet $A = \{\sqcup\}$ that accepts any non-empty input w exactly at time $\lfloor f(|w|) \rfloor$.*

The family of all *OCA*-time-computable functions *is denoted $\mathscr{C}(OCA)$.*

Example 10. For all bases $b \geq 2$, the function $f(n) = n + \log_b(n)$ belongs to the family $\mathscr{C}(\text{OCA})$.

The idea of the construction for $b = 2$ is depicted in Fig. 7. At initial time the OCA generates a signal in the rightmost cell (which can identify itself). The signal moves to the left and strikes out each other cell passed through. Moreover, in the first cell which is not struck out it generates a new signal. This one is one time step delayed and behaves as the first one. It proceeds to the left and strikes out each other non struck out cell. If it passes through a cell which will not be struck out it generates again a new signal which behaves identical and so on. The unique signal which does not find any cell to strike out sets the left border cell into a final state for the first time.

The number $s(n)$ of signals on input length n is $s(n) = \lfloor 1 + \log_2(n) \rfloor$. Since the first signal arrives at the left border at time n and every new signal is delayed by one time step, the total computation time and, hence, $f(n)$ is $n + \lfloor \log_2(n) \rfloor$.□

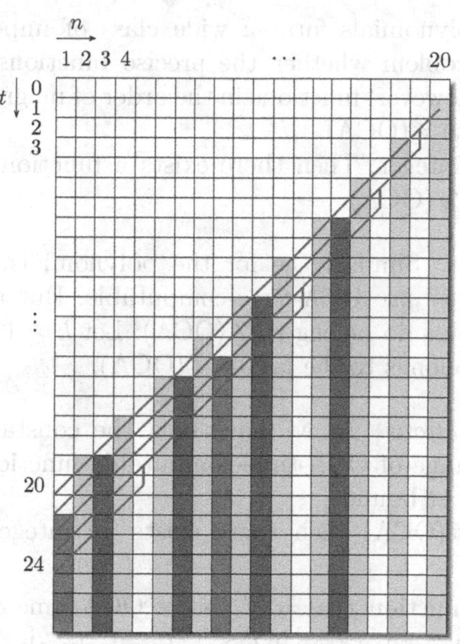

Fig. 7. OCA-time-computation of the function $f(n) = n + \log_2(n)$; $n = 20$, $f(n) = 24$.

Next we explore the structure of $\mathscr{C}$(OCA) in more detail. While all constants and linear functions belong to $\mathscr{C}$(OCA), the world below the identity is sparse.

Constants and Linear Functions. Let $k \geq 1$ be an integer. Then the functions $f(n) = k$ and $f(n) = k \cdot n$ belong to $\mathscr{C}$(OCA).

All OCA-time-computable functions below the identity are ultimately constant.

Roots. Functions involving roots have to be greater than the identity. The following result has been shown in [22] for $k \geq 2$, and in [29] for $k = 1$ in terms of signals for two-way unbounded CA. However, the constructions use only leftward signals such that they can easily be adapted.

Let $k \geq 1$ be an integer. Then the function $f(n) = k \cdot n + \sqrt{n}$ belongs to the family $\mathscr{C}$(OCA).

Logarithms. Example 10 already shows that the functions $f(n) = n + \log_b(n)$ belong to the family $\mathscr{C}$(OCA), for all $b \geq 2$.

Furthermore, for all bases $b_1 \geq 2$ and $b_2 \geq 2$ it is known that the function $f(n) = 2 \cdot n + \log_{b_1}(\log_{b_2}(n))$ for $n \geq b_2$, and $f(n) = 2 \cdot n$ otherwise belongs to

$\mathscr{C}$(OCA). Here the factor 2 is necessary, since there is another gap between the identity and $n + \log(n)$: Let $f(n) \geq n$ be an OCA-time-computable function so that for all bases $b \geq 2$, $f(n) \not\geq n + \lfloor \log_b(n) \rfloor$. Then there exists a constant $k \geq 0$ such that $f(n) = n + k$ for infinitely many $n \geq 1$.

Polynomials. The polynomials form a wide class of important and interesting functions. The problem whether the precise functions n^k are OCA-time-computable is open. However, functions in the order of magnitude of polynomials are known to belong to $\mathscr{C}$(OCA).

Let $k \geq 1$ be an integer. Then there exists a function $f(n) \in \Theta(n^k)$ that belongs to the family $\mathscr{C}$(OCA).

Exponential Functions. Similarly as for the polynomials, it is open whether the precise functions k^n are OCA-time-computable. But after adding n more time steps, the functions do belong to $\mathscr{C}$(OCA): Let $k \geq 1$ be an integer. Then the function $k^n + n$ belongs to the family $\mathscr{C}$(OCA).

Superexponential Functions. As we have seen the constant functions form a lower bound of the range of OCA-time-computable functions. The exponential functions form an upper bound:

If f belongs to $\mathscr{C}$(OCA) then there exists an integer $k \geq 1$ such that $\lim_{n\to\infty} \frac{f(n)}{k^n} = 0$.

For example, the function $f(n) = 2^{2^n}$ is not OCA-time-computable since the series $\{\frac{2^{2^n}}{k^n}\}_{n\geq 1}$ is unbounded for all $k \geq 1$. Similarly, the factorial function $n!$ does not belong to $\mathscr{C}$(OCA).

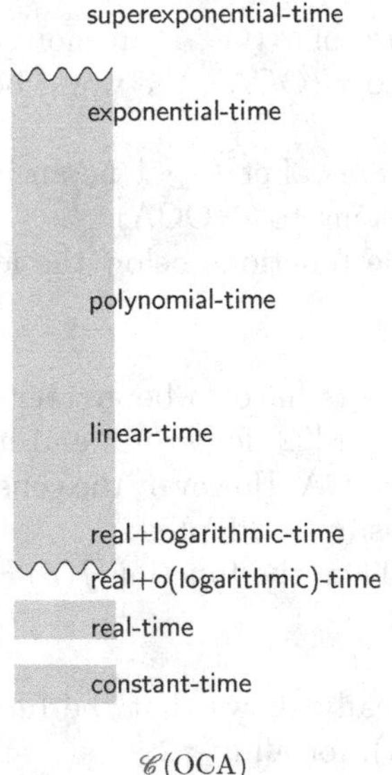

Fig. 8. Structure of the family $\mathscr{C}$(OCA).

The structure of the family $\mathscr{C}(\text{OCA})$ is depicted in Fig. 8.

More details and further results on the family of OCA-time-computable functions can be found in [6]. For example, several closure properties are derived that – in the positive case – can be used to construct new OCA-time-computable functions from given ones. Additionally, $\mathscr{C}(\text{OCA})$ is characterized in terms of formal languages. That is, $f(n) \geq n$ belongs to $\mathscr{C}(\text{OCA})$ if and only if $L_f = \{ a^n b^{f(n)-n} \mid n \geq 1 \}$ belongs to $\mathscr{L}_{rt}(\text{OCA})$.

The time-computation at some points is concerned with the concepts of signals and time-constructibility. Further results on these topics can be found, for example, in [4–6,9,15,30,31].

References

1. Book, R.V., Greibach, S.A.: Quasi-realtime languages. Math. Syst. Theor. **4**, 97–111 (1970)
2. Buchholz, T., Klein, A., Kutrib, M.: One guess one-way cellular arrays. In: Brim, L., Gruska, J., Zlatuška, J. (eds.) MFCS 1998. LNCS, vol. 1450, pp. 807–815. Springer, Heidelberg (1998)
3. Buchholz, T., Klein, A., Kutrib, M.: On interacting automata with limited nondeterminism. Fund. Inform. **52**, 15–38 (2002)
4. Buchholz, T., Kutrib, M.: On the power of one-way bounded cellular time computers. In: Bozapalidis, S. (ed.) Developments in Language Theory (DLT 1997), pp. 365–375. Aristotle University of Thessaloniki, Thessaloniki (1997)
5. Buchholz, T., Kutrib, M.: Some relations between massively parallel arrays. Parall. Comput. **23**, 1643–1662 (1997)
6. Buchholz, T., Kutrib, M.: On time computability of functions in one-way cellular automata. Acta Inform. **35**, 329–352 (1998)
7. Chang, J.H., Ibarra, O.H., Vergis, A.: On the power of one-way communication. J. ACM **35**, 697–726 (1988)
8. Choffrut, C., Čulik II, K.: On real-time cellular automata and trellis automata. Acta Inform. **21**, 393–407 (1984)
9. Dubacq, J.-C., Terrier, V.: Signals for cellular automata in dimension 2 or higher. In: Rajsbaum, S. (ed.) LATIN 2002. LNCS, vol. 2286, p. 451. Springer, Heidelberg (2002)
10. Dyer, C.R.: One-way bounded cellular automata. Inform Control **44**, 261–281 (1980)
11. Fischer, P.C., Kintala, C.M.R.: Real-time computations with restricted nondeterminism. Math. Syst. Theor. **12**, 219–231 (1979)
12. Ibarra, O.H., Jiang, T.: On one-way cellular arrays. SIAM J. Comput. **16**, 1135–1154 (1987)
13. Ibarra, O.H., Kim, S.M., Moran, S.: Sequential machine characterizations of trellis and cellular automata and applications. SIAM J. Comput. **14**, 426–447 (1985)
14. Ibarra, O.H., Palis, M.A.: Some results concerning linear iterative (systolic) arrays. J. Parallel Distrib. Comput. **2**, 182–218 (1985)
15. Iwamoto, C., Hatsuyama, T., Morita, K., Imai, K.: Constructible functions in cellular automata and their applications to hierarchy results. Theor. Comput. Sci. **270**, 797–809 (2002)
16. Kintala, C.M.R.: Computations with a Restricted Number of Nondeterministic Steps. Ph.D. thesis, Pennsylvania State University (1977)

17. Klein, A., Kutrib, M.: Fast one-way cellular automata. Theor. Comput. Sci. **1–3**, 233–250 (2003)
18. Klein, A., Kutrib, M.: Cellular devices and unary languages. Fund. Inform. **78**, 343–368 (2007)
19. Kutrib, M.: Cellular automata - a computational point of view. In: Bel-Enguix, G., Jiménez-López, M.D., Martín-Vide, C. (eds.) New Developments in Formal Languages and Applications, Chap. 6, pp. 183–227. Springer, Heidelberg (2008)
20. Kutrib, M.: Cellular automata and language theory. In: Meyers, R. (ed.) Encyclopedia of Complexity and System Science, pp. 800–823. Springer, New York (2009)
21. Kutrib, M.: Non-deterministic cellular automata and languages. Int. J. Gen. Syst. **41**, 555–568 (2012)
22. Mazoyer, J., Terrier, V.: Signals in one-dimensional cellular automata. Theor. Comput. Sci. **217**, 53–80 (1999)
23. Nakamura, K.: Real-time language recognition by one-way and two-way. In: Kutyłowski, M., Wierzbicki, T.M., Pacholski, L. (eds.) MFCS 1999. LNCS, vol. 1672, pp. 220–230. Springer, Heidelberg (1999)
24. Savitch, W.J.: Relationships between nondeterministic and deterministic tape complexities. J. Comput. Syst. Sci. **4**, 177–192 (1970)
25. Seidel, S.R.: Language recognition and the synchronization of cellular automata. Technical report 79–02, Department of Computer Science, University of Iowa (1979)
26. Smith III, A.R.: Real-time language recognition by one-dimensional cellular automata. J. Comput. Syst. Sci. **6**, 233–253 (1972)
27. Terrier, V.: On real time one-way cellular array. Theor. Comput. Sci. **141**, 331–335 (1995)
28. Terrier, V.: Language not recognizable in real time by one-way cellular automata. Theor. Comput. Sci. **156**, 281–287 (1996)
29. Terrier, V.: Construction of a signal of ratio $n + \lfloor\sqrt{n}\rfloor$ (2002) (unpublished manuscript)
30. Umeo, H., Kamikawa, N.: A design of real-time non-regular sequence generation algorithms and their implementations on cellular automata with 1-bit inter-cell communications. Fund. Inform. **52**, 257–275 (2002)
31. Umeo, H., Kamikawa, N.: Real-time generation of primes by a 1-bit-communication cellular automaton. Fund. Inform. **58**, 421–435 (2003)
32. Umeo, H., Morita, K., Sugata, K.: Deterministic one-way simulation of two-way real-time cellular automata and its related problems. Inform. Process. Lett. **14**, 158–161 (1982)

Regular Papers

Computational Complexity of the Avalanche Problem on One Dimensional Kadanoff Sandpiles

Enrico Formenti[1], Kévin Perrot[1,2,3(✉)], and Éric Rémila[4]

[1] Laboratoire I3S (UMR 6070 - CNRS), Université Nice Sophia Antipolis, 2000 Route des Lucioles, BP 121, F-06903 Sophia Antipolis Cedex, France
enrico.formenti@unice.fr

[2] Université de Lyon - LIP (UMR 5668 - CNRS - ENS de Lyon - Université Lyon 1), 46 allé d'Italie, 69364 Lyon Cedex 7, France

[3] Universidad de Chile - DII - DIM - CMM (UMR 2807 - CNRS), 2120 Blanco Encalada, Santiago, Chile
kperrot@dim.uchile.cl

[4] Université de Lyon - GATE LSE (UMR 5824 - CNRS - Université Lyon 2) , Site stéphanois, 6 Rue Basse des Rives, 42 023 Saint-etienne Cedex 2, France
eric.remila@univ-st-etienne.fr

Abstract. In this paper we prove that the general *avalanche problem* **AP** is in NC for the Kadanoff sandpile model in one dimension, answering an open problem of [2]. Thus adding one more item to the (slowly) growing list of dimension sensitive problems since in higher dimensions the problem is P-complete (for monotone sandpiles).

Keywords: Sandpile models · Discrete dynamical systems · Computational complexity · Dimension sensitive problems

1 Introduction

This paper is about cubic sand grains moving around on nicely packed columns in one dimension (the physical sandpile is two dimensional, but the support of sand columns is one dimensional). The Kadanoff Sandpile Model is a discrete dynamical system describing the evolution of sand grains. Grains move according to the repeated application of a simple local rule until reaching a fixed point.

We focus on the avalanche problem (**AP**), namely the problem of deciding if adding a single grain of sand in the first column of a sandpile given as an input causes a series of topples which hit some position (also given as a parameter).

This is an interesting problem from several points of view. First of all, it is dimension sensitive. Indeed, it is proved to be P-complete for sandpiles in dimension 2 or higher [2] and we proved it in NC^1 in this paper. Roughly speaking the problem is highly parallelisable in dimension 1 but not in higher dimensions (unless P=NC, of course). Second, an efficient solution to this problem could be useful for practical applications. Indeed, one can use sandpile models for

T. Isokawa et al. (Eds.): AUTOMATA 2014, LNCS 8996, pp. 21–30, 2015.
DOI: 10.1007/978-3-319-18812-6_2

implementing load schedulers in parallel computers [9]. In this context, answering to **AP** helps in forecasting the number of supplementary processors that are needed to satisfy one more load which is submitted to the system.

The paper is structured as follows. Next section introduces the basic notions and results about Kadanoff sandpiles. Section 3 gives the formal statement of **AP** and recalls known results about it. In Sect. 4, main lemma and notions that are necessary for the proof of the main result are introduced and proved. Section 5 contains the main result. Section 6 draws our conclusions and give some perspectives.

2 Kadanoff Sandpile Model

We present the definition of the model in dimension one. A *configuration* is a decreasing sequence of integers $h = {}^{\omega}h_1, h_2, \ldots, h_n^{\omega}$, where h_i is the number of stacked grains (*height*) on column i, and such that all the heights on the left of h_1 equal h_1, and on the right of h_n equal h_n. Note that all the configurations we consider are *finite*. According to a fixed parameter p, the transition rule is the following: if the difference of heights between two columns i and $i+1$ is strictly greater than p, then p grains can fall from column i and one of them land on each of the p adjacent columns on the right (see Fig. 1).

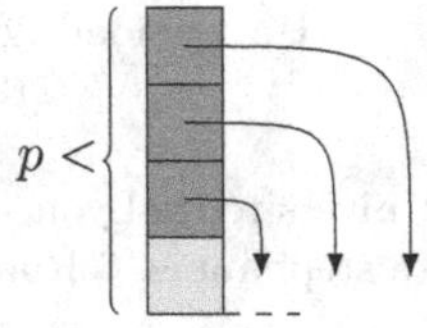

Fig. 1. Transition rule with parameter $p = 3$.

A more uniform and convenient representation of a configuration uses *slopes*. The *slope* at i is the height difference $s_i = h_i - h_{i+1}$. The transition rule thus becomes: if $s_i > p$, then

$$\begin{aligned} s_{i-1} &\mapsto s_{i-1} + p \\ s_i &\mapsto s_i - (p+1) \\ s_{i+p} &\mapsto s_{i+p} + 1. \end{aligned}$$

$|h| = |s| = n - 1$ is the *length* of the configuration, and the slope of an index i such that $i < 1$ or $n - 1 < i$ equals 0. The transition rule may be applied using different update policies (sequential, parallel, *etc.*), however we know from [8] that for any initial configuration, the orbit graph is a lattice, hence the stable configuration reached is unique and independent of the update policy. When, from the configuration s to s', the rule is applied on column i, we say that i is *fired* and we denote $s \xrightarrow{i} s'$ or simply $s \rightarrow s'$.

Notation 1. We denote ${}^{\omega}s_i$ (*resp.* s_i^{ω}) to say that all the slopes on the left (*resp.* right) of column i are equal to s_i.

Notation 2. For any $a, b \in \mathbb{Z}$ with $a \leq b$, let $[\![a, b]\!] = [a, b] \cap \mathbb{N}$ and $[\![a, b) = [a, b) \cap \mathbb{N}$. Finally, $s_{[\![a,b]\!]}$ denotes the subsequence $(s_a, s_{a+1}, \ldots, s_b)$.

A configuration s represented as a sequence of slopes is *monotone* if $s_i \geq 0$ for all $i \in [\![1, |s|)$. A configuration is *stable* if all its columns are *stable*, *i.e.*, $s_i \leq p$ for all $i \in [\![1, |s|)$. A stable monotone configuration is therefore a finite configuration s of the form

$$^{\omega}0, s_1, s_2, \ldots, s_{n-1}, 0^{\omega}$$

Let $\mathbf{gSM}(n)$ be the set of all stable monotone configurations of length n (note that in [2], the authors added the restrictive condition $s_i > 0$ for all i, whereas we let $s_i \geq 0$ for all i and add the letter **g** standing for *general*). Finally, Let $\mathbf{gSM} = \bigcup_{n \in \mathbb{N}} \mathbf{gSM}(n)$.

3 Avalanche Problem AP

An *avalanche* is informally the process triggered by a single grain addition on column 1 (a formal definition is given at the beginning of Sect. 4). The size of an avalanche may be very small, or quite long, and is sensible to the tiniest change on the configuration. We are interested in the computational complexity of avalanches.

> **Avalanche Problem AP**
> A parameter $p \in \mathbb{N}$, with $p \geq 1$, is fixed.
> *Instance:* a configuration $s \in \mathbf{gSM}$
> a column $k \in (|s|, |s| + p]\!]$
> *Question:* does adding a grain on column 1 trigger a grain addition on column k?

For a fixed parameter p, the size of the input is in $\Theta(|s|)$. Thanks to the convergence, the answer to this question is well defined and independent of the chosen update strategy.

Let us give some examples. For $p = 2$, consider the instance

$$^{\omega}0, \underline{2}, 0, 2, 1, 1, 2, 1, 0, 2, 0^{\omega},$$

where the slope of column 1 is underlined. The question is "does adding a grain on column 1 increases the slope of column k equal to 10 or 11?" And the answer is negative in both cases. Here is a sequential evolution:

$$\begin{aligned} ^{\omega}0, \underline{\mathbf{3}}, 0, 2, 1, 1, 2, 1, 0, 2, 0^{\omega} &\rightarrow {}^{\omega}0, 2, \underline{0}, 0, 3, 1, 1, 2, 1, 0, 2, 0^{\omega} \\ &\rightarrow {}^{\omega}0, 2, \underline{0}, 2, 0, 1, 2, 2, 1, 0, 2, 0^{\omega} \end{aligned}$$

For $p = 3$, consider the instance $0^{\omega}, \underline{3}, 0, 2, 3, 1, 3, 1, 0^{\omega}$. We have to decide if column k equal to 8, 9 or 10 ends up with a strictly positive slope after a grain is added on column 1. The answer is positive, positive and negative, respectively. Here is a sequential evolution:

$$\begin{aligned} &{}^{\omega}0, \underline{\mathbf{4}}, 0, 2, 3, 1, 3, 1, 0^{\omega} \rightarrow {}^{\omega}0, 3, \underline{0}, 0, 2, 4, 1, 3, 1, {}^{\omega}0 \\ &\rightarrow {}^{\omega}0, 3, \underline{0}, 0, 5, 0, 1, 3, 2, 0^{\omega} \rightarrow {}^{\omega}0, 3, \underline{0}, 3, 1, 0, 1, 4, 2, 0^{\omega} \\ &\rightarrow {}^{\omega}0, 3, \underline{0}, 3, 1, 0, 4, 0, 2, 0, 1, 0^{\omega} \rightarrow {}^{\omega}0, 3, \underline{0}, 3, 1, 3, 0, 0, 2, 1, 1, 0^{\omega} \end{aligned}$$

Known results on the dimension sensitive complexity of **AP** are the followings.

- In dimension one: the restriction of **AP** to the set of configurations s satisfying $s_i > 0$ for all i is known to be in NC^1 [2]. The key simplification induced by this restriction is the following: an avalanche goes forward if and only if it encounters a slope of value p at distance at most p from the previous one, and thus stops when there are p consecutive slopes strictly smaller than p. This condition is not sufficient anymore when we allow slopes of value 0, as shown for example by the instance ${}^{\omega}0, \underline{2}, 0, 2, 2, 1, 2, 2, 0^{\omega}$ and $p = 2$:

$$\begin{aligned} {}^{\omega}0, \underline{\mathbf{3}}, 0, 2, 2, 1, 2, 2, 0^{\omega} &\rightarrow {}^{\omega}0, 2, \underline{0}, 0, 3, 2, 1, 2, 2, 0^{\omega} \\ &\rightarrow {}^{\omega}0, 2, \underline{0}, 2, 0, 2, 2, 2, 2, 0^{\omega} \end{aligned}$$

- In dimension two: there are two possible definitions of the model. One has two directions of grain fall, and a configuration is a tabular of sand content that is decreasing with respect to those two directions. In this model **AP** is P-complete for all parameter $p > 1$ [2]. The second definition follows the original model of Bak, Tang and Wiesenfeld [1], and it has been proved that information cannot cross (under reasonable conditions) when $p = 1$, a strong obstacle for a reduction to a P-complete circuit value problem [6].
- In dimension three or greater: sandpiles are capable of universal computation [7].

4 Avalanches, Peaks and Cols

This subsection partly intersects with the study presented in [11], but follows a new and hopefully clearer formulation. For a configuration $s \in \mathbf{gSM}$, an avalanche is the process following a single grain addition on column 1, until stabilization. We will consider avalanches according to the sequential update policy, and prove that it is formed by the repetition (not necessarily alternated) of the following two basic mechanisms:

- fire a column greater than all the previously fired columns;
- fire the immediate left neighbor of the last fired column.

An *avalanche strategy* for s is a sequence $a = (a_1, \ldots, a_T)$ of columns such that $s^+ \stackrel{a_1}{\rightarrow} \ldots \stackrel{a_T}{\rightarrow} s'$, where s^+ denotes the configuration $s \in \mathbf{gSM}$ on which a grain has been added on column 1, and s' is stable. Such a strategy is not unique, therefore we distinguish a particular one which we think is the simplest.

Definition 1. *The* avalanche *for s is the minimal avalanche strategy for s according to the lexicographic order, which means that at each step the leftmost column is fired.*

For example, let us consider $p = 2$ and the configuration $s = {}^{\omega}0, \underline{2}, 2, 2, 2, 2, 0^{\omega}$, then $(0, 2, 4, 1, 3)$ is an avalanche strategy, but *the* avalanche for s is $(0, 2, 1, 3, 4)$ and leads to the same final configuration thanks to the lattice structure of the model [8].

Let us give two terms corresponding to the two basic mechanisms underlying the avalanche process, and prove the above mentioned description.

- a_t is a *peak* $\iff a_t > \max a_{[1,t[}$;
- a_t is a *col* $\iff a_t = a_{t-1} - 1$.

First, a simple Lemma.

Lemma 1. *An avalanche fires at most once every column.*

Proof. It is straightforward to notice that in order for a column to receive enough units of slope to be fired twice, another column must have been fired twice before, which leads to the impossibility of this situation when adding a single grain on column 1 of a stable configuration. □

Now, the intended description.

Lemma 2. *The avalanche of a configuration $s \in$ **gSM** is a concatenation of peaks and cols.*

Proof. Let $a = (a_1, \ldots, a_T)$ be the avalanche for s. We prove the lemma by induction on the avalanche size. The first fired column is necessarily $a_1 = 1$, and we take as a convention that $\max \emptyset = 0$ thus a_1 is a peak. Suppose that the result is true until time t, we'll prove that a_{t+1} is either a peak or a col. It follows from Lemma 1 that $a_{t+1} \neq a_t$, and let us denote a_{t-j} with $j \geq 0$ the largest (rightmost) peak before time $t+1$. The induction hypothesis implies that columns a_t to $a_{t-j} - 1$ are cols.

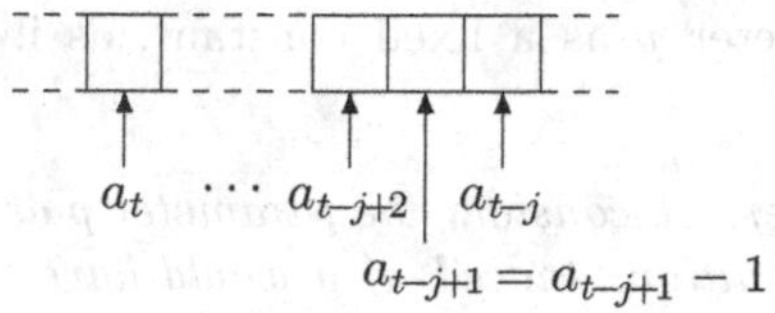

- If $a_{t+1} > a_t$, by induction on i from 0 to $j-1$, we have $a_{t+1} > a_t + i$ because $a_t + i$ has already been fired by hypothesis and a column cannot be fired twice (Lemma 1). As a consequence $a_{t+1} \geq a_{t-j}$ and for the same reason $a_{t+1} > a_{t-j}$, which was the greatest peak so far, therefore a_{t+1} is also a peak.
- If $a_{t+1} < a_t$, then, by contradiction, if $a_{t+1} \neq a_t - 1$ then the firing at a_t does not influence the slope at a_{t+1}, and firing this latter after a_t contradicts the minimality of the avalanche according the lexicographic order, because column a_{t+1} was already unstable at time t. Therefore, a_{t+1} is a col. □

Interestingly, avalanches are local processes because they cannot fire a column too far (neither on the left nor on the right) from the last fired column, as it is proved in the following lemma.

Lemma 3. *Let a be the avalanche of a configuration $s \in$ **gSM**, $q > 0$ is a peak of a implies that $s_q = p$ and there exists another peak q' satisfying $q - q' \leq p$.*

Proof. Let t be such that $q = a_t$. By definition of peak, at time t column q could only have received units of slope from columns on its left, that is, by Lemma 1 it received at most 1 unit of slope from column $q - p$. Since it was stable on configuration s, it has necessarily received this unique unit from column $q-p$ and became unstable thanks to it, which straightforwardly proves both claims. □

Note that the converse implication is false. Figure 2 illustrates the results of this section.

Fig. 2. For $p = 4$, the arrow pictures the proceedings of an avalanche, which is a concatenation of peaks and cols (Lemma 2) where two consecutive peaks are at distance at most p (Lemma 3).

5 AP is in NC^1 in dimension one

We consider that the input configuration is represented as a sequence of slopes, since it is possible to efficiently transform a representation into another in parallel (for a configuration of size n, it requires constant time on n parallel processors). We consider the parameter p as a fixed constant, as it is part of the model definition

Remark 1. *In this paper, we consider the parameter p as a fixed constant which is part of the model definition. Indeed, if p would have been part of the input, which would therefore have size $(|s| + 2) \log p$, then comparing the height of a column to p (in order to know if the rule can be applied at this column) would not take a constant time anymore. This implies many low level considerations we want to avoid and inflate complexity.*

We recall that $\mathsf{NC}= \bigcup_{k\in\mathbb{N}} \mathsf{PT/WK}(\log^k n, n^k)$, where $\mathsf{PT/WK}(f(n), g(n))$ (Parallel Time / WorK) is the class of decision problems solvable by a uniform family of Boolean circuits with depth upper-bounded by $f(n)$ and size (number of gates) upper-bounded by $g(n)$, which is more conveniently seen for our purpose as solvable in time $\mathcal{O}(f(n))$ on $\mathcal{O}(g(n))$ parallel PRAM processors. We recall that $\mathsf{NC}^1 = \mathsf{PT/WK}(\log n, \mathbb{R}[n])$ where $\mathbb{R}[n]$ denotes the set of polynomial functions.

As a consequence of Lemmas 2 and 3, the avalanche process is local. Moreover, if we cut the configuration into two parts, we can compute both parts of the avalanche independently, provided a small amount of information linking the two parts. This independency will be at the heart of our construction in order to compute the avalanche efficiently in parallel. Let us have a closer look at how to encode this "midway information", which we call *status* (a notion named *trace* has been defined in [12], which shares some of those ideas).

For a column $i > p$ of a configuration s, the *status* at i of the avalanche a for s is the boolean p-tuple $(b_0, \ldots, b_{p-1})$ such that $b_j = 1$ if column $i - p + j$ is fired within a, and 0 otherwise. For example, consider the avalanche of Fig. 2, its status at column 8 (the column where the avalanche starts has index 1) is $(0, 1, 0, 1)$.

We claim that given a column i, the incomplete configuration $s \cap [\![i, |s|)$ and the status at i of the avalanche a for s, we can compute the avalanche on the part of s that we have, that is, $a \cap [\![i, |s|)$.

Note that in the proof of Theorem 1 we use only simple instances of Lemma 4, but we still present it in a general form.

Lemma 4. *Given*

- *a part* $s \cap [\![i, j)$ *with* $i + p < j$,
- *the status at* i *of the avalanche* a *for* s,

one can compute

- *the avalanche on* $a \cap [\![i, j - p]\!]$,
- *the status of* a *at* $j - p + 1$,

in time $\mathcal{O}(j - i)$ *on one processor.*

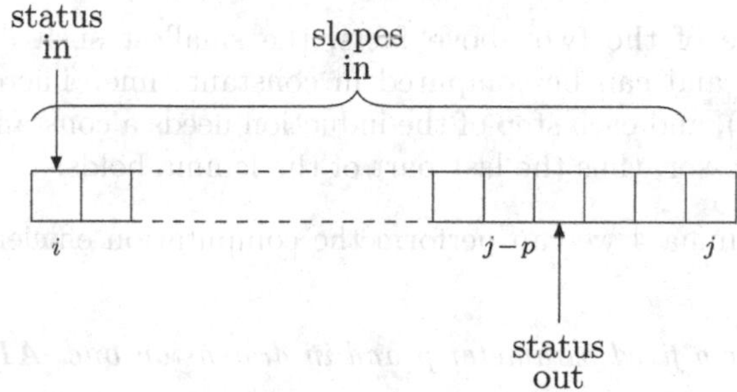

Proof. We claim that given the status of the avalanche a at a column k, we can find the smallest (leftmost) peak after column k, let us denote it by $q = \min\{q \mid q \geq k \text{ and } q \text{ is a peak}\}$, and the part of a between k and q, *i.e.*, $a \cap [\![k, q]\!]$. This will be done in constant time thanks to Lemma 3: $q - k < p$ so we have to check a constant number of columns. The result then follows an induction on the peaks within $[\![i, j)$: from the status at k (initialized for $k = i$), we find the next peak q and compute $a \cap [\![k, q]\!]$, append it to the previously computed $a \cap [\![i, k]\!]$, which also allows to construct the status at $q + 1$ in constant time. And this process is repeated at most a linear number of times:

- either the avalanche stops at some time,
- or the greatest peak encountered is between $j - p$ and $j - 1$,

and in both cases we can compute the intended objects by appending the previously computed parts of the avalanche (Lemma 2, recall that the status at $j - p + 1$ tells wether columns between $j - p + 1 - p$ and $j - p$ are fired or not).

Knowing the status of a at k, let us explain how to compute the smallest peak after column k, denoted q, and $a \cap [\![k, q]\!]$. Let $(b_0, \ldots, b_{p-1})$ be the status of a at k. From Lemma 3 the peak q has a value of slope equal to p in s and is at distance smaller than p from k. We will now prove that it is very easy to find q in constant time: q is the smallest column ℓ such that $0 \leq \ell - k < p$, and $s_\ell = p$ and $b_{\ell-k} = 1$.

- Such an ℓ is a peak: since $b_{\ell-k} = 1$, column $\ell - p$ is fired. When it is fired, it gives one unit of slope to column ℓ which can be fired since its slope is initially equal to p and becomes $p+1$. It cannot be a col, which would mean that there is another peak q'', greater, which is fired before ℓ, but from Lemmas 2 and 3 this contradicts the minimality of the avalanche because when q'' is fired the column ℓ is also firable ($\ell - p$ has already been fired since it is at distance strictly greater than p of q'').
- The smallest peak greater or equal to k satisfies those three conditions: the two first conditions are straightforward from Lemma 3. The last condition can be proved by contradiction: suppose there is a peak q'' such that $b_{q''-k} = 0$, *i.e.*, column $q'' - p$ is not fired in the avalanche, then q'' still needs to receive some units of slope to become unstable, which can only come from its left neighbor $q'' + 1$ thus this latter has to be fired before it, a contradiction.

As a consequence of the two above facts, the smallest such ℓ is indeed the intended peak q, and can be computed in constant time. There are $\mathcal{O}(j - i)$ peaks within $[\![i, j)$, and each step of the induction needs a constant computation time on one processor, thus the last part of the lemma holds. □

Thanks to Lemma 4 we can perform the computation efficiently in parallel as follows.

Theorem 1. *For a fixed parameter p and in dimension one,* ***AP*** *is in* NC^1.

Proof. An input of **AP** is a configuration $s \in$ **gSM** and a column $k \in (|s|, |s|+p]\!]$. Let $k = |s| + \kappa$ with $\kappa \in (0, p]\!]$.

The proof works in two stages: first, we compute for every position i the function that associates to each status at i, the corresponding status at $i+1$, which we call "the function status at $i \to$ status at $i+1$" (since status are elements of $\{0,1\}^p$, the size of these functions is a constant). This can be done in constant time on $|s|$ parallel PRAM using Lemma 4; and in a second stage we compute in parallel the function status at $p+1 \to$ status at $|s|+1$ using $log|s|$ steps, by pairwise composing the functions as illustrated in Fig. 3.

One of the processors can then finish the job in constant time by first computing the status $\dot{b}$ at $p+1$, which can easily be done in constant time using only $(s_1, \ldots, s_{p+1})$ since either s_1 is a peak or the avalanche stops, then either s_{p+1} is a peak or the avalanche stops, and finally the cols within s_1 and s_{p+1} are straightforwardly found thanks to Lemma 2. Then, it computes the status $\ddot{b} = \mu(\dot{b})$ at $|s|+1$, and answers *yes* if and only if $\ddot{b}_{\kappa-1} = 1$, because columns on the right of $|s|$ cannot be fired but can only receive grains from their left neighbor at distance p, so does column $k = |s| + \kappa$.

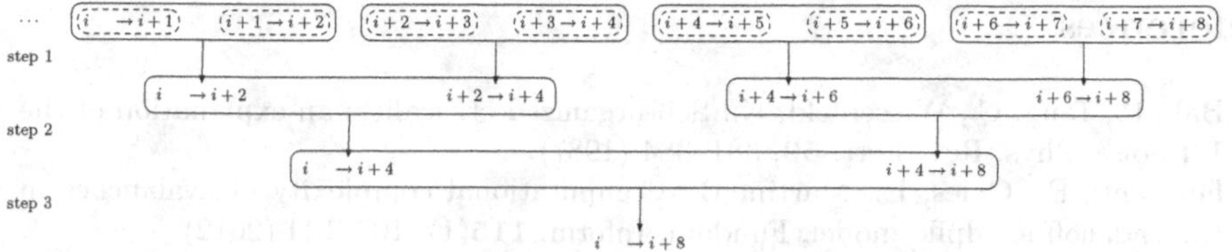

Fig. 3. Illustration of the parallel computation, each symbol $x \rightarrow y$ represents the function status at $x \rightarrow$ status at y. Dashed on the top are the functions computed during the first stage. Then, in $log|s|$ steps (each of them uses a polynomial number of parallel processors and a constant amount of time) we compose the circled functions in order to compute the function pointed out with an arrow. This composition is straightforwardly performed in constant time with the two processors: one of them transmits its function to the other one (a function of constant size is transmitted in constant time), and the latter composes two functions of constant size... in constant time. We perform those computations such that the resulting function μ has type: status at $p+1 \rightarrow$ status at $|s|+1$.

The complete procedure uses a logarithmic amount of time on a polynomial number of parallel processors (the input has size $\Theta(|s|)$), *i.e.*, the decision problem **AP** is in the complexity class NC^1. □

6 Conclusion and Open Problem

In this paper we proved that **AP** is in NC^1 in dimension 1 solving an open question of [2]. Going in the direction of [3], one might ask what is the complexity of **AP** when the constraint on monotonicity is relaxed. Clearly, by the results of [3], the problem is in P, but is it complete?

Another possible generalisation concerns symmetric sandpiles (see [4,5,10], for example). In this case, the lattice structure of the phase space is lost and therefore we cannot exploit it in the solving algorithms. This would probably direct the investigations towards non-deterministic computation and shift complexity results from P-completeness to NP-completeness.

It also remains to classify the computational complexity of avalanches in two dimensions when the parameter p equals 1 (that is, in the classical model introduced by Bak *et al.* [1]). As it is exposed in [6], this question interestingly emphasizes the links between NC, P-completeness, and information crossing.

Acknowledgments. This work was partially supported by IXXI (Complex System Institute, Lyon), ANR projects Subtile, Dynamite and QuasiCool (ANR-12-JS02-011-01), Modmad Federation of U. St-Etienne, the French National Research Agency project EMC (ANR-09-BLAN-0164), FONDECYT Grant 3140527, and Núcleo Milenio Información y Coordinación en Redes (ACGO).

References

1. Bak, P., Tang, C., Wiesenfeld, K.: Self-organized criticality: an explanation of the 1/f noise. Phys. Rev. Lett. **59**, 381–384 (1987)
2. Formenti, E., Goles, E., Martin, B.: Computational complexity of avalanches in the kadanoff sandpile model. Fundam. Inform. **115**(1), 107–124 (2012)
3. Formenti, E., Masson, B.: On computing fixed points for generalized sand piles. Int. J. on Unconventional Comput. **2**(1), 13–25 (2005)
4. Formenti, E., Masson, B., Pisokas, T.: Advances in symmetric sandpiles. Fundam. Inform. **76**(1–2), 91–112 (2007)
5. Formenti, E., Van Pham, T., Phan, H.D., Tran, T.H.: Fixed point forms of the parallel symmetric sandpile model. Theor. Comput. Sci. **322**(2), 383–407 (2014)
6. Gajardo, A., Goles, E.: Crossing information in two-dimensional sandpiles. Theor. Comput. Sci. **369**(1–3), 463–469 (2006)
7. Goles, E., Margenstern, M.: Sand pile as a universal computer. Int. J. Mod. Phys. C **7**(2), 113–122 (1996)
8. Goles, E., Morvan, M., Phan, H.D.: The structure of a linear chip firing game and related models. Theor. Comput. Sci. **270**(1–2), 827–841 (2002)
9. Laredo, J.L.J., Bouvry, P., Guinand, F., Dorronsoro, B., Fernandes, C.: The sandpile scheduler. Cluster Comput. **17**(2), 191–204 (2014)
10. Perrot, K., Phan, H.D., Van Pham, T.: On the set of fixed points of the parallel symmetric sand pile model. Full Pap. AUTOMATA **2011**, 17–28 (2011)
11. Perrot, K., Rémila, E.: Avalanche structure in the kadanoff sand pile model. In: Dediu, A.-H., Inenaga, S., Martín-Vide, C. (eds.) LATA 2011. LNCS, vol. 6638, pp. 427–439. Springer, Heidelberg (2011)
12. Perrot, K., Rémila, E.: Transduction on kadanoff sand pile model avalanches, application to wave pattern emergence. In: Murlak, F., Sankowski, P. (eds.) MFCS 2011. LNCS, vol. 6907, pp. 508–519. Springer, Heidelberg (2011)

5-State Rotation-Symmetric Number-Conserving Cellular Automata are not Strongly Universal

Katsunobu Imai[1] (✉), Hisamichi Ishizaka[1], and Victor Poupet[2]

[1] Graduate School of Engineering, Hiroshima University, Higashi-Hiroshima 739-8527, Japan
imai@iec.hiroshima-u.ac.jp

[2] LIRMM, Université de Montpellier 2, 161 Rue Ada, 34392 Montpellier, France
victor.poupet@lirmm.fr

Abstract. We study two-dimensional rotation-symmetric number-conserving cellular automata working on the von Neumann neighborhood (RNCA). It is known that such automata with 4 states or less are trivial, so we investigate the possible rules with 5 states. We give a full characterization of these automata and show that they cannot be strongly Turing universal. However, we give example of constructions that allow to embed some boolean circuit elements in a 5-states RNCA.

1 Introduction

Cellular automata (CA) are widely studied deterministic, discrete and massively parallel dynamical systems. They were introduced by J. von Neumann and S. Ulam in the 1940s (published posthumously in 1966) to study self replicating systems [10].

Von Neumann developped a 29-states CA working on the "4 closest cells" neighborhood (that would later be known as the "von Neumann neighborhood") capable of replicating patterns, and used it to describe the notion of computational universality. In 1968, E. Codd improved von Neumann's construction by devising an 8-states universal rotation-symmetric CA working on the same neighborhood [3] and proving that 2-states von Neumann neighborhood CA could not be strongly universal. In 1970, E. Banks proved the existence of a 4-states strongly universal rotation-symmetric CA on von Neumann's neighborhood and a 2-states weakly universal one [1]. This search for small universal automata was finally completed in 1987 when T. Serizawa published a 3-states strongly universal CA on the von Neumann neighborhood [7].

Since their introduction, cellular automata have been broadly used as a model for biological, chemical and physical processes. In 1969, K. Zuse was the first to propose the theory that physics is computation and that the universe could be seen as a cellular automaton [11]. The notion of number conservation appeared as a result of attempts to implement physical conservation laws (energy, mass, particles, etc.) in cellular automata. It was first defined by K. Nagel and M. Schreckenberg to model road traffic flow [6] and has since become an important subject of research in the

T. Isokawa et al. (Eds.): AUTOMATA 2014, LNCS 8996, pp. 31–43, 2015.
DOI: 10.1007/978-3-319-18812-6_3

cellular automata community as a natural example of global property enforced by local conditions.

In the early 2000s, H. Fuks and N. Boccara [2], B. Durand et al. [4] and A. Moreira [5] independently proved that number-conservation was a decidable property by giving explicit characterizations of local transition rules of number-conserving cellular automata (NCCA).

Imai et al. proved the existence of a weakly universal 29-states von Neumann neighborhood rotation-symmetric NCCA and this result was later improved by N. Tanimoto and K. Imai who managed to reduce the number of required states to 14 by using an exact characterization of von Neumann neighborhood NCCA [8]. From the same characterization, N. Tanimoto et al. proved that von Neumann neighborhood rotation-symmetric NCCA with 4 states or less are all trivial [9].

In this article, we investigate the computational power of 5-states von Neumann neighborhood rotation-symmetric NCCA. We obtain a precise description of the possible transition rules of such automata and prove that none of them can be strongly universal as their evolution from a finite initial configuration must be ultimately periodic. However, we show that they are capable of some computation by exhibiting patterns that simulate the behavior of some boolean circuit elements.

2 Definitions

In this article, we will only consider deterministic 2-dimensional cellular automata working on the von Neumann neighborhood.

Definition 1 (Cellular Automaton). *A 2-dimensional von Neumann neighborhood cellular automaton (CA) is a triple $\mathcal{A} = (Q, f, q_0)$ where*

- *Q is a finite set. The elements of Q are called* states*;*
- *$f : Q^5 \to Q$ is a function called the* local transition function *of $\mathcal{A}$;*
- *$q_0 \in Q$ is called the* quiescent state *and $f(q_0, q_0, q_0, q_0, q_0) = q_0$.*

A 2-dimensional configuration *over Q is a mapping $\mathfrak{C} : \mathbb{Z}^2 \to Q$. The elements of $\mathbb{Z}^2$ are called* cells *and for a cell $c \in \mathbb{Z}^2$, we say that $\mathfrak{C}(c)$ is the* state *of c in the configuration $\mathfrak{C}$.*

The set of all configurations over Q is denoted by

$$\mathrm{Conf}(Q) = \{c, c : \mathbb{Z}^2 \to Q\}$$

From the local transition function f, we define a global transition function $F : \mathrm{Conf}(Q) \to \mathrm{Conf}(Q)$ obtained by replacing the state of each cell by the result of f applied to the cell's state and the states of its 4 closest neighbors[1]*: $\forall \mathfrak{C} \in \mathrm{Conf}(Q)$,*

$$F(\mathfrak{C}) = \begin{cases} \mathbb{Z}^2 \to Q \\ (x, y) \mapsto f(\mathfrak{C}(x, y), \mathfrak{C}(x, y+1), \mathfrak{C}(x+1, y), \mathfrak{C}(x, y-1), \mathfrak{C}(x-1, y)) \end{cases}$$

[1] This is the von Neumann neighborhood.

As is commonly done in dynamical systems theory, we will use the same notation for the cellular automaton and its global transition function. The image of a configuration $\mathfrak{C}$ by the global transition function of an automaton $\mathcal{A}$ will therefore be denoted $\mathcal{A}(\mathfrak{C})$.

Definition 2 (Finite Configurations). *Given a cellular automaton* $\mathcal{A} = (Q, f, q_0)$*, we say that a configuration* $\mathfrak{C} \in \mathrm{Conf}(Q)$ *is* finite *if only a finite number of cells are in a state other than* q_0 *in* $\mathfrak{C}$.

The rectangular bound *of a finite configuration* $\mathfrak{C}$ *is the smallest rectangle containing all the non-quiescent cells of* $\mathfrak{C}$*. We call* width *and* height *of the configuration* $\mathfrak{C}$ *the width and height of its rectangular bound.*

From the locality of the transition rule of the automaton and the fact that $f(q_0, q_0, q_0, q_0, q_0) = q_0$ it is clear that the image by a CA of a finite configuration $\mathfrak{C}$ of dimensions $(w \times h)$ is also finite and of dimensions $(w' \times h')$ with $w' \leq w+2$ and $h' \leq h+2$.

Definition 3 (Rotation-Symmetry). *A von Neumann neighborhood cellular automaton* $\mathcal{A} = (Q, f, q_0)$ *is said to be* rotation-symmetric *if its local transition function* f *is invariant by rotation of a quarter cycle:*

$$\forall c, u, r, d, l \in Q, \quad f(c, u, r, d, l) = f(c, r, d, l, u)$$

If the set of states of the automaton is a subset of $\mathbb{Z}$, it is possible to quantify the variations of state values between a configuration and its image. The notion of number-conservation is inspired from physical conservation laws and states that the total sum of all states on a configuration is conserved by the global transition function.

Definition 4 (Number Conservation). *A* number-conserving cellular automaton *(NCCA) is a cellular automaton* $\mathcal{A} = (Q, f, q_0)$ *such that* $Q \subset \mathbb{Z}$ *and for any finite configuration* $\mathfrak{C} \in \mathrm{Conf}(Q)$,

$$\sum_{c \in \mathbb{Z}^2} \mathcal{A}(\mathfrak{C})(c) - \mathfrak{C}(c) = 0$$

There are other commonly used definitions of number-conservation, some of which apply to infinite configurations as well, but most of these definitions are known to be equivalent [4].

In this article, we will be studying von Neumann neighborhood rotation-symmetric number-conserving cellular automata. These will be denoted RNCA from now on.

Definition 5 (Trivial Automaton). *A cellular automaton* $\mathcal{A} = (Q, f, q_0)$ *is said to be* trivial *if for every configuration* $\mathfrak{C} \in \mathrm{Conf}(Q)$, $\mathcal{A}(\mathfrak{C}) = \mathfrak{C}$.

Definition 6 (Strong Turing Universality). *A cellular automaton* $\mathcal{A}$ *is said to be strongly Turing-universal if it can simulate any deterministic Turing machine from a finite initial configuration.*

3 Characterization of 5-States RNCA

In this section, we consider 5-states RNCA. We use the characterization by Tanimoto et al. [8] to show that all RNCA with less than 5 states are trivial and describe precisely the possible local transition functions of 5-states RNCA.

Theorem 1 (Tanimoto et al. [8]). *A rotation-symmetric von Neumann neighborhood CA $\mathcal{A} = (Q, f, q_0)$ with $Q \subset \mathbb{Z}$ is number-conserving if and only if $\exists g, h : Q^2 \to \mathbb{Z}$, $\forall c, u, r, d, l \in Q$,*

$$\begin{aligned} f(c,u,r,d,l) &= c + g(c,u) + g(c,r) + g(c,d) + g(c,l) \\ &\quad + h(u,r) + h(r,d) + h(d,l) + h(l,u) \\ g(c,u) &= -\,g(u,c), \qquad h(u,r) = -h(r,u) \end{aligned}$$

The function g represents direct transfers of value to the central cell from its neighbors (along the horizontal and vertical directions). The function h corresponds to indirect (diagonal) transfer between the neighbors of the central cell. The functions g and h are called *flow functions* of the automaton $\mathcal{A}$.

Remark: If $\mathcal{A} = (Q, f, q_0)$ is a RNCA, the function g is uniquely defined by f since for all states $x, y \in Q$,

$$f(x,y,y,y,y) = x + 4g(x,y) + 4h(y,y) = x + 4g(x,y)$$

As for the function h, for all states $x, y, z, t \in Q$ the value of $h(x,y) + h(y,z) + h(z,t) + h(t,x)$ is uniquely defined but there are multiple functions matching this condition as discussed in Subsect. 3.2.

3.1 Direct Flow

Lemma 1. *For a RNCA $\mathcal{A} = (Q, f, q_0)$ with flow functions g and h, if $g \equiv 0$ then $\mathcal{A}$ is trivial.*

Proof. We show that if the automaton is not trivial, it must have infinitely many states. According to Theorem 1, if $g \equiv 0$, the local transition function of the automaton is

$$f(c,u,r,d,l) = c + h(u,r) + h(r,d) + h(d,l) + h(l,u)$$

If $\mathcal{A}$ is not trivial, there exist states $c, u, r, d, l \in Q$ and an integer $\delta \neq 0$ such that

$$f(c,u,r,d,l) = c + \delta$$

so $h(u,r) + h(r,d) + h(d,l) + h(l,u) = \delta$ and for any state $q \in Q$,

$$f(q,u,r,d,l) = q + h(u,r) + h(r,d) + h(d,l) + h(l,u) = q + \delta$$

This means that for any $q \in Q$, $(q + \delta)$ is also a state of $\mathcal{A}$ which is not possible if Q is finite. □

Lemma 2. *Let $\mathcal{A} = (Q, f, q_0)$ be a RNCA with flow functions g and h. For any two states $a, b \in Q$ if we denote $g(a, b) = \alpha$, then*

$$\{a, a+\alpha, a+2\alpha, a+3\alpha, a+4\alpha, b, b-\alpha, b-2\alpha, b-3\alpha, b-4\alpha\} \subseteq Q$$

Proof. We know that

$$\begin{aligned} g(a,b) &= -g(b,a) = \alpha, & g(a,a) &= g(b,b) = 0,\\ h(a,b) &= -h(b,a), & h(a,a) &= h(b,b) = 0 \end{aligned}$$

By Theorem 1, we have

$$\begin{aligned} f(a,a,a,a,b) &= a + 3g(a,a) + g(a,b) + h(a,b) + h(b,a) + 2h(a,a)\\ &= a + g(a,b) = a + \alpha \end{aligned}$$

Similarly, we get

$$\begin{aligned} f(a,a,a,b,b) &= a+2\alpha, & f(a,a,b,b,b) &= a+3\alpha, & f(a,b,b,b,b) &= a+4\alpha,\\ f(b,b,b,b,a) &= b-\alpha, & f(b,b,b,a,a) &= b-2\alpha, & f(b,b,a,a,a) &= b-3\alpha,\\ f(b,a,a,a,a) &= b-4\alpha \end{aligned}$$

□

As a consequence of Lemmas 1 and 2, if a RNCA $\mathcal{A} = (Q, f, q_0)$ with flow functions g and h is not trivial, there exist two states $a, b \in Q$ such that $g(a, b) = \alpha > 0$ and the set of states of the automaton contains 5 elements in arithmetic progression from a of difference α. Since the 5 first elements of the arithmetic progression from b of difference $-\alpha$ are also in Q, the only way for the CA to have only 5 states is that

$$b = a + 4\alpha$$

$$\text{and} \quad \begin{cases} g(a,b) = \alpha \\ g(b,a) = -\alpha \\ g(x,y) = 0 \quad \text{otherwise} \end{cases}$$

3.2 Indirect Flow

Let us now consider the possibilities for h. The function h is slightly more complex than g because it is only properly characterized on cycles: the exact value of $h(a, b)$ for two states has no meaning in terms of CA dynamics, the real constraints are on the sums $h(a, b) + h(b, c) + h(c, d) + h(d, a)$ for states a, b, c, d.

Definition 7. *Given a finite set $Q \subseteq \mathbb{Z}$ and a function $h : Q^2 \to \mathbb{Z}$ such that for all $a, b \in Q$, $h(a, b) = -h(b, a)$, we define the* cyclic extension *$\widetilde{h}$ of h as*

$$\widetilde{h} : \begin{cases} Q^* \to \mathbb{Z} \\ (q_1, q_2, \ldots, q_n) \mapsto h(q_1, q_2) + h(q_2, q_3) + \ldots + h(q_{n-1}, q_n) + h(q_n, q_1) \end{cases}$$

Note that although $\widetilde{h}$ is entirely defined by h, different functions can have the same cyclic extension. For instance if $h'(x,y) = y - x + h(x,y)$ then $\widetilde{h} = \widetilde{h'}$. However, in Theorem 1 only the cyclic extension of h is actually used to define the behavior of the automaton.

The function $\widetilde{h}$ is entirely defined by its values on triples:
$\forall q_1, q_2, \ldots, q_n \in Q$,

$$\begin{aligned}\widetilde{h}(q_1, q_2, \ldots, q_n) &= h(q_1, q_2) + \ldots + h(q_n, q_1)\\ &= h(q_1, q_2) + h(q_2, q_3) + h(q_3, q_1)\\ &\quad + h(q_1, q_3) + h(q_3, q_4) + h(q_4, q_1)\\ &\quad + \ldots\\ &\quad + h(q_1, q_{n-1}) + h(q_{n-1}, q_n) + h(q_n, 1)\\ &= \widetilde{h}(q_1, q_2, q_3) + \widetilde{h}(q_1, q_3, q_4) + \ldots + \widetilde{h}(q_1, q_{n-1}, q_n)\end{aligned}$$

Moreover, it is easy to check from the definition that $\widetilde{h}$ is

- null on pairs: $\widetilde{h}(a, b) = 0$;
- invariant by repetition of a state: $\widetilde{h}(a, a, q_1, q_2, \ldots, q_n) = \widetilde{h}(a, q_1, q_2, \ldots, q_n)$;
- invariant by rotation: $\widetilde{h}(q_1, q_2, \ldots, q_n) = \widetilde{h}(q_2, q_3, \ldots, q_n, q_1)$;
- anti-symmetric: $\widetilde{h}(q_1, q_2, \ldots, q_n) = -\widetilde{h}(q_n, q_{n-1}, \ldots, q_1)$.

Let us now consider a 5-states non trivial RNCA $\mathcal{A} = (Q, f, q_0)$ with flow functions g and h. We have already shown that the states of the automaton are $Q = \{a + i\alpha \mid 0 \leq i \leq 4\}$. Without loss of generality we can renormalize the states to $Q = \{0, 1, 2, 3, 4\}$ (substracting a constant to all states and dividing by a common factor does not affect the number conservation of the CA). We also know that $g(0, 4) = 1$, $g(4, 0) = -1$ and for all other $x, y \in Q$, $g(x, y) = 0$.

First, let us consider $x, y, z \in Q \setminus \{0\}$. From Theorem 1, we have

$$\begin{aligned}f(4, x, x, y, z) &= 4 + 2g(4, x) + g(4, y) + g(4, z) + \widetilde{h}(x, x, y, z)\\ &= 4 + \widetilde{h}(x, y, z)\end{aligned}$$

This means that $(4 + \widetilde{h}(x, y, z)) \in Q$ and since 4 is the largest element of Q, we have $\widetilde{h}(x, y, z) \leq 0$. Because x, y and z could be any state other than 0, the same reasoning gives $\widetilde{h}(z, y, x) = -\widetilde{h}(x, y, z) \leq 0$ which implies $\widetilde{h}(x, y, z) = 0$.

Similarly, for states $x, y, z \in Q \setminus \{4\}$, by considering $f(0, x, x, y, z)$ we get $\widetilde{h}(x, y, z) = 0$.

So the only possible non-zero triples of $\widetilde{h}$ are triples containing both 0 and 4. Because $\widetilde{h}(0, 0, 4) = \widetilde{h}(0, 4) = 0$, and $\widetilde{h}(4, 4, 0) = \widetilde{h}(4, 0) = 0$, the only possible non-zero triples of $\widetilde{h}$ are those including 0, 4 and a third different state.

Moreover, for $x, y \in Q \setminus \{0, 4\}$, we have

$$\begin{aligned}\widetilde{h}(0, 4, x, y) &= h(0, 4) + h(4, x) + h(x, y) + h(y, 0)\\ &= h(0, 4) + h(4, x) + h(x, 0) + h(0, x) + h(x, y) + h(y, 0)\\ &= \widetilde{h}(0, 4, x) + \widetilde{h}(0, x, y)\\ &= \widetilde{h}(0, 4, x)\end{aligned}$$

but also

$$\begin{aligned}\widetilde{h}(0,4,x,y) &= \widetilde{h}(4,x,y,0)\\ &= h(4,x) + h(x,y) + h(y,0) + h(0,4)\\ &= h(4,x) + h(x,y) + h(y,4) + h(4,y) + h(y,0) + h(0,4)\\ &= \widetilde{h}(4,x,y) + \widetilde{h}(4,y,0)\\ &= \widetilde{h}(4,y,0) = \widetilde{h}(0,4,y)\end{aligned}$$

So for $x, y \in Q \setminus \{0,4\}$, $\widetilde{h}(0,4,x) = \widetilde{h}(0,4,y)$. All that remains to do now is consider what are the possible values for $\widetilde{h}(0,4,1)$. By considering

$$\begin{aligned}f(0,0,0,4,1) &= 0 + g(0,4) + \widetilde{h}(0,0,4,1)\\ &= 1 + \widetilde{h}(0,4,1)\end{aligned}$$

we get that $(1+\widetilde{h}(0,4,1)) \in Q$ so $\widetilde{h}(0,4,1) \geq -1$. Similarly, by considering $f(4,0,4,4,1)$ we get $\widetilde{h}(0,4,1) \leq 1$.

The value of $\widetilde{h}(0,4,1)$ fully defines $\widetilde{h}$, as we know that the function is zero-valued on all triples not containing 0 and 4 and all values on triples containing 0 and 4 can be obtained from $\widetilde{h}(0,4,1)$ by cycle, symmetry and replacing 1 with any other state in $Q \setminus \{0,4\}$. A possible function h that would correspond to such an $\widetilde{h}$ would be defined by

$$\begin{aligned}h(0,4) &= \widetilde{h}(0,4,1)\\ h(4,0) &= -\widetilde{h}(0,4,1)\\ h(x,y) &= 0 \quad \text{otherwise}\end{aligned}$$

We have therefore proved the following result

Lemma 3. *If $\mathcal{A}$ is a 5-states non-trivial RNCA, there exists a constant $\beta \in \{-1,0,1\}$ such that $\mathcal{A}$ is equivalent (up to state renaming) to an RNCA with states $Q = \{0,1,2,3,4\}$ and flow functions g and h such that:*

$$\begin{aligned}g(0,4) &= 1 & h(0,4) &= \beta\\ g(4,0) &= -1 & h(4,0) &= -\beta\\ g(x,y) &= 0 \quad \textit{otherwise} & h(x,y) &= 0 \quad \textit{otherwise}\end{aligned}$$

Remark: Choosing $\beta = 0$ corresponds to $h \equiv 0$, which leads to a very simple CA for which states 1, 2 and 3 are permanent (a cell in one of these states can never change) and the state of a cell in state 0 (resp. 4) increases (resp. decreases) by the number of its neighbors in state 4 (resp. 0).

Choosing $\beta = 1$ or $\beta = -1$ leads to two different RNCA that are mirror images of each other.

4 The Power of 5-States RNCA

In this section we use the characterization of 5-states RNCA from Lemma 3 to investigate the computational power of such automata. We show that although they cannot be strongly Turing universal, they can simulate some logical circuit elements, indicating that they can perform some sorts of computations.

4.1 Strong Universality

Theorem 2. *The evolution of a 5-states RNCA $\mathcal{A}$ from a finite configuration $\mathfrak{C}$ is ultimately periodic:*

$$\exists i, j \in \mathbb{N}, \quad i < j, \quad \mathcal{A}^i(\mathfrak{C}) = \mathcal{A}^j(\mathfrak{C})$$

Proof. Consider a non-trivial 5-states RNCA $\mathcal{A}$. From Lemma 3 we can assume that $\mathcal{A} = (Q, f, q_0)$ with $Q = \{0, 1, 2, 3, 4\}$ and consider that its flow functions g and h satisfy the descriptions of the lemma. We show that starting from a finite configuration $\mathfrak{C}_0$, non-quiescent states cannot appear arbitrarily far in any direction.

There are two cases to consider, depending on the choice of the quiescent state q_0. First if $q_0 \in Q \setminus \{0, 4\}$, we show that non-quiescent states cannot appear outside of the bounding rectangle of the starting configuration $\mathfrak{C}_0$ (see Fig. 1).

By induction, if at time t all cells outside of the rectangular bounds of $\mathfrak{C}_0$ are quiescent, then each of these cells has at least 3 neighbors in state q_0. Since $q_0 \neq 0$ and $q_0 \neq 4$, for all $x \in Q$, $g(q_0, x) = \widetilde{h}(q_0, q_0, q_0, x) = 0$, so $f(q_0, q_0, q_0, q_0, x) = q_0$ and all cells outside of the rectangular bound of $\mathfrak{C}_0$ remain in state q_0 at time $(t + 1)$.

The second case is when $q_0 \in \{0, 4\}$. Assume that $q_0 = 0$ and let N_0 be the total sum of all the states in $\mathfrak{C}_0$ (the argument for $q_0 = 4$ is similar but we

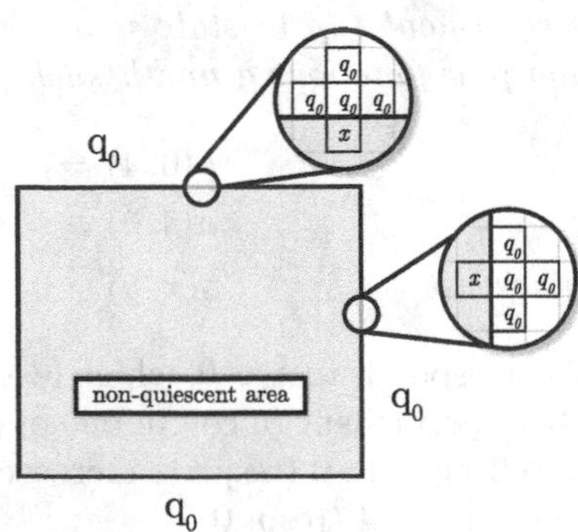

Fig. 1. If $q_0 \in Q \setminus \{0, 4\}$, cells outside of the rectangular bounds of the initial configuration (represented in blue) remain in state q_0 at all times (Color figure online).

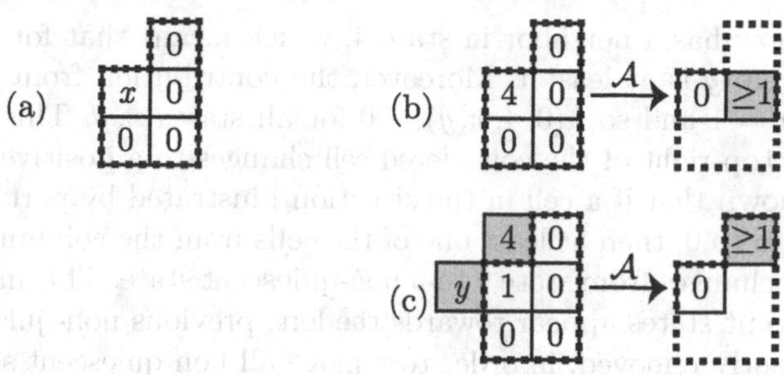

Fig. 2. Case study. If a cell is in the situation (a) where x is a non-quiescent state, in order to change to state 0 one of the 3 cells on the right must change from state 0 to a non-quiescent state.

consider the sum of $(q_0 - q)$ for all states q in $\mathfrak{C}_0$). Since $\mathcal{A}$ is number conserving, the total sum of all states in subsequent configurations of the automaton remains equal to N_0. Moreover, because all non-quiescent states are positive, the total number of non-quiescent states on any configuration generated from $\mathfrak{C}_0$ cannot exceed N_0.

If quiescent states appear arbitrarily far in one direction in the evolution of $\mathcal{A}$ from $\mathfrak{C}_0$, some cells must go from a non-quiescent state back to the quiescent state 0 in order to keep the total number of non-quiescent states bounded. We will now assume that the direction in which the non-quiescent states appear arbitrarily far is left (it is enough to consider one direction since the automaton is rotation-symmetric).

Assume that $h(0,4) \geq 0$ and consider the situation illustrated by part (a) of Fig. 2: a cell in a non-quiescent state x with 4 cells in state 0 around it, 3 on its right side and one under (for the case $h(0,4) \leq 0$ we would consider the symmetric situation with a quiescent cell on top of the cell in state x instead of under it). Let us see how such a cell can change to state 0. There are two possibilities, represented by parts (b) and (c) in Fig. 2. Either $x = 4$ and we can use the function g to lower the state of the cell to 0 or the contribution of g on the cell is 0 and only $\widetilde{h}$ can lower the state of the cell, in which case only state 1 can be lowered to 0.

(b) If $x = 4$, then the cell on the right of the cell in state 4 will necessarily change to a positive state. For this cell, the contribution from g will be positive (at least 1 from the central cell) and the contribution from h will be 0 since $\widetilde{h}(0,4,0,y) = 0$ for all states y.

(c) If $x = 1$, then in order to change the state to 0, the contribution from $\widetilde{h}$ must be -1 since $g(1,y) = 0$ for all states y. We have previously chosen to consider the case $h(0,4) \geq 0$. If $h(0,4) = 0$, then the contribution from h is 0 and the state of the cell cannot change to 0. However if $h(0,4) = 1$, then the contribution from $\widetilde{h}$ can be -1 only if the top neighbor is in state 4 and the left neighbor is in a state $y \in Q \setminus \{0,4\}$ (as illustrated by Fig. 2). In that case, $\widetilde{h}(4,0,0,y) = -1$ and the cell changes to state 0. However, the cell on the top-right now has a neighbor in state 4, which means that for this cell the contribution from g is at least 1. Moreover, the contribution from $\widetilde{h}$ is at least 0, since $h(0,4) = 1$ and so $\widetilde{h}(0,4,x,y) \geq 0$ for all states x, y. This means that the cell on the top-right of the considered cell changes to a positive state.

We have shown that if a cell in the situation illustrated by part (a) of Fig. 2 changes its state to 0, then at least one of the cells from the column right of the considered cell changes from state 0 to a non-quiescent state. This means that as new non-quiescent states appear towards the left, previous non-quiescent states cannot be properly removed: in order to remove all non-quiescent states from a given column, it is necessary to create new ones on the column at its right, so as the non-quiescent states move towards the left, new ones appear towards the right. Eventually, the total number of non-quiescent states will be greater than N_0 which contradicts number-conservation.

So we know that the evolution $(\mathcal{A}^i(\mathfrak{C}_0))_{i\in\mathbb{N}}$ of a 5-states RNCA $\mathcal{A}$ from a finite configuration $\mathfrak{C}_0$ can only have non-quiescent states inside of a bounded area. Because there are only finitely many such bounded configurations, eventually the automaton must re-enter a previous configuration. □

Corollary 1. *There are no 5-states strongly Turing universal RNCA.*

Proof. The evolution of a 5-states RNCA from a finite starting configuration is ultimately periodic (Theorem 2) and therefore decidable. If such CA could simulate a Turing machine then the halting problem and all other behavioral problems on Turing machines would be decidable. □

4.2 Simulation of Logical Circuits

Although the evolution of a 5-states RNCA from a finite configuration is ultimately periodic, some non-trivial behaviors can still be observed. In particular, it is possible to simulate some key elements of boolean circuits. In this section, we consider the 5-states RNCA obtained by choosing $\beta = 1$ in the characterization from Lemma 3.

Figures 3, 4 and 5 illustrate how to create a simple wire along which a signal can travel. The wire is made of two layers of state 2 (red), and the signal is represented by two cells in state 4 (yellow) that are "pushed" forward by a cell in state 1 (blue). As the signal traverses the wire, the top layer of red states is changed into blue and green states. These wires can therefore be traversed only once, which is enough for simple boolean circuit simulation but not for being used as a control circuit for a universal machine.

The wires can be split in two to duplicate a signal (Fig. 4). By changing the second row of red cell into green states, the signal can be accelerated to move by one cell at each time step (Fig. 5) which can be a convenient way to synchronize signals.

As for logical gates, Figs. 6 and 7 illustrate how to implement an `AND` and a $\overline{A}$ `AND B` gate. It is known that the $\overline{A}$ `AND B` gate alone is sufficient to simulate a `NOT` and an `OR` gate so these elements would be sufficient for boolean operations [1].

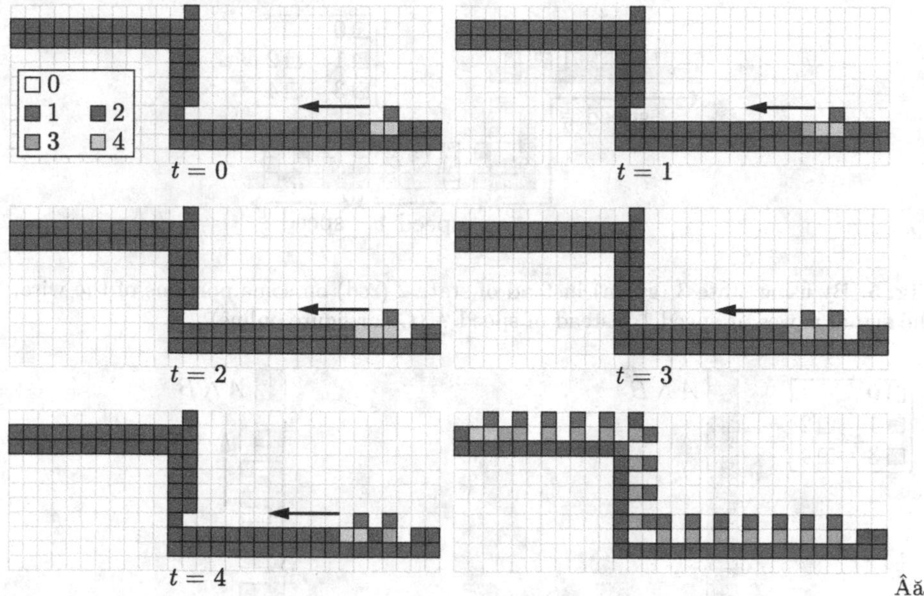

Fig. 3. A signal moving through a simple wire (Color figure online).

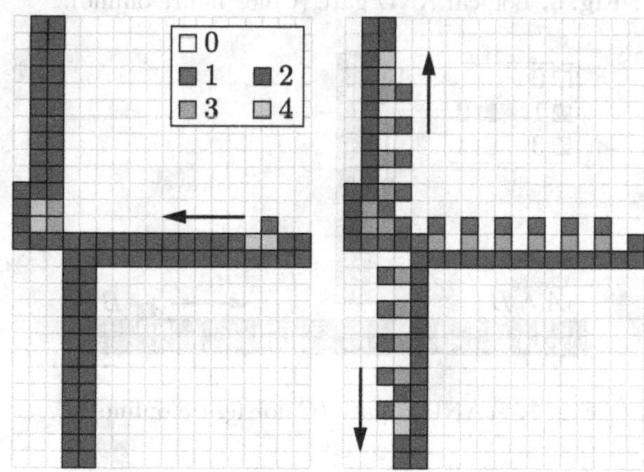

Fig. 4. A branching wire (Color figure online).

Note that the boolean value for 0 is simply represented by the absence of a signal. Therefore, careful synchronisation is required when implementing multiple input logical gates as the possible input signals must arrive at the same time (but this can be done either by using the variable speed wires from Fig. 5 or by artificially increasing the length of a wire with a detour).

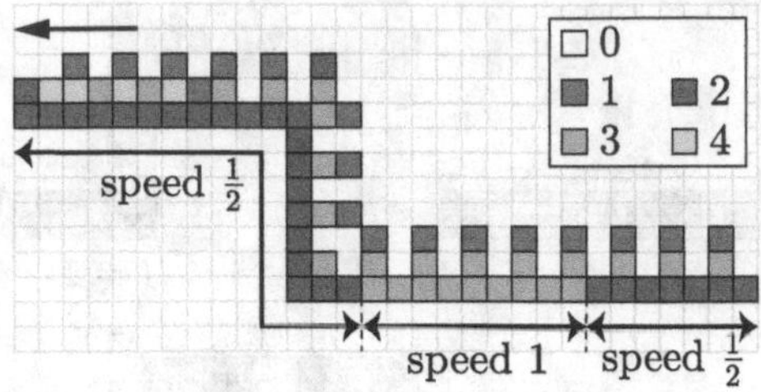

Fig. 5. By using state 3 (green) instead of state 2 (red) on some portions of the wire, the signal moves at speed 1 instead of speed $\frac{1}{2}$ (Color figure online).

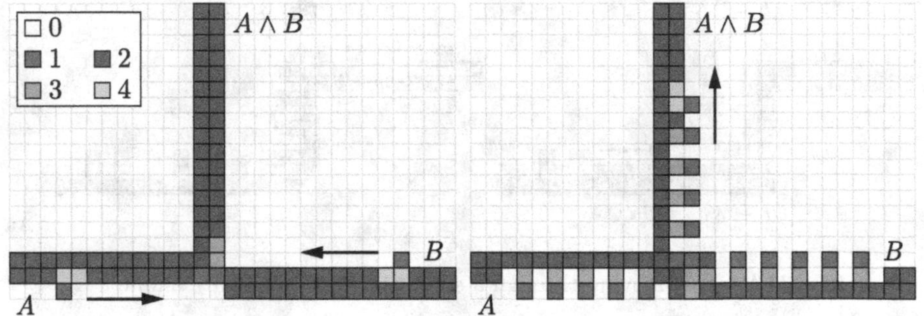

Fig. 6. Logical AND gate (Color figure online).

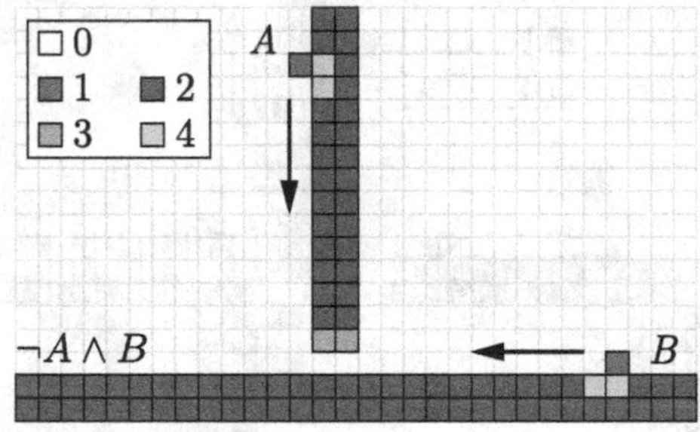

Fig. 7. $\overline{A}$ AND B gate (Color figure online).

However, until now we have been unable to devise a wire crossing pattern which is required for a full simulation of boolean circuits. Because of the destructive nature of signal propagation along a wire, wire crossing might prove impossible to implement.

References

1. Banks, E.R.: Universality in cellular automata. In: SWAT (FOCS), pp. 194–215. IEEE Computer Society (1970)

2. Boccara, N., Fukś, H.: Number-conserving cellular automaton rules. Fundam. Inform. **52**(1–3), 1–13 (2002)
3. Codd, E.F.: Cellular Automata. ACM Monograph Series. Academic Press, New York (1968)
4. Durand, B., Formenti, E., Róka, Z.: Number-conserving cellular automata i: decidability. Theor. Comput. Sci. **1–3**(299), 523–535 (2003)
5. Moreira, A.: Universality and decidability of number-conserving cellular automata. Theoret. Comput. Sci. **292**(3), 711–721 (2003). Algorithms in Quantum Information Prcoessing
6. Nagel, K., Schreckenberg, M.: A cellular automaton model for freeway traffic. J. Phys. I **2**(12), 2221–2229 (1992)
7. Serizawa, T.: Three-state neumann neighbor cellular automata capable of constructing self-reproducing machines. Syst. Comput. Japan **18**(4), 33–40 (1987)
8. Tanimoto, N., Imai, K.: A characterization of von neumann neighbor number-conserving cellular automata. J. Cell. Automata **4**(1), 39–54 (2009)
9. Tanimoto, N., Imai, K., Iwamoto, C., Morita, K.: On the non-existance of rotation-symmetric von neumann neighbor number-conserving cellular automata of which the state number is less than four. IEICE Trans. **92–D**(2), 255–257 (2009)
10. von Neumann, J.: Theory of Self-Reproducing Automata. University of Illinois Press, Urbana (1966)
11. Zuse, K.: Rechnender Raum. Friedrich Vieweg and Sohn, Braunschweig (1969)

A Universal Cellular Automaton Without Sensitive Subsystems

Jarkko Kari[(✉)]

Department of Mathematics and Statistics, University of Turku, FI-20014 Turku, Finland

jkari@utu.fi

Abstract. We construct a one-dimensional reversible cellular automaton that is computationally universal in a rather strong sense while being highly non-sensitive to initial conditions as a dynamical system. The cellular automaton has no sensitive subsystems. The construction is based on a simulation of a reversible Turing machine, where a bouncing signal activates the Turing machine to make single steps whenever the signal passes over the machine.

Keywords: Reversible cellular automata · Reversible turing machine · Universality · Edge of chaos · Sensitivity

1 Introduction

Cellular automata (CA) are discrete dynamical systems and models of massively parallel computation, and thus a convenient platform to study the relationship between computation and dynamics. It is clear that too simple dynamics (e.g., periodic systems) cannot support computation, while [7] suggests that too chaotic systems cannot do it either. To study this phenomenon precisely one needs to choose good definitions for "computational universality" and "chaos". For both concepts, a multitude of choices exist. For universality of discrete time symbolic dynamical systems (such as cellular automata), Delvenne et al. propose a robust definition that does not depend on details of encoding inputs and conditions of acceptance [3]. A central aspect of dynamical complexity, on the other hand, is sensitivity to initial conditions. The most widely used definition of chaos by Devaney [4] requires sensitivity, but also transitivity and denseness of periodic points.

In [6] we proved that there are cellular automata that are Devaney-chaotic and universal, answering a question posed in [3]. So the upper boundary of Langton's "edge of chaos", the proper amount of sensitivity that can support computational universality, is not below Devaney-chaos. It remains an interesting question whether increasing sensitivity indeed eventually prevents computation: it would be nice to know, for example, whether an expansive cellular automaton can be universal in the sense of [3].

Research supported by the Academy of Finland Grant 131558.

T. Isokawa et al. (Eds.): AUTOMATA 2014, LNCS 8996, pp. 44–55, 2015.
DOI: 10.1007/978-3-319-18812-6_4

In this paper we study the lower boundary of the "edge of chaos". It is trivial to construct a non-sensitive but universal cellular automaton: simply add to any universal CA a new spreading state. The new state is a blocking word that makes the system non-sensitive, but universality remains in configurations that do not contain the spreading state. However, this construction is cheating since the original (possibly sensitive) CA exists as a subsystem. In this paper we construct a cellular automaton that is universal (even in the strongest sense in [3]), and does not have any subsystems that are sensitive to initial conditions. The automaton that we construct is reversible, as is the chaotic one that we presented in [6].

The paper is organized as follows. In Sect. 2 we recall basic aspects of cellular automata and reversible Turing machines, and define the concepts of universality and sensitivity that we use. In Sect. 3 we describe our reversible cellular automaton, and in Sect. 4 we prove that it has the claimed properties of universality and non-existence of sensitive subsystems.

2 Definitions

2.1 Cellular Automata and Sensitivity to Initial Conditions

For a finite set S, the *alphabet*, we denote by S^* the set of finite words over S, and by $S^{\mathbb{Z}}$ the set of bi-infinite words over S. Elements of $x \in S^{\mathbb{Z}}$ are called *configurations* and their indices $i \in \mathbb{Z}$ are *cells*. When writing down configurations we mark the place between cells -1 and 0 by a dot, that is, a configuration $x \in S^{\mathbb{Z}}$ may be written as

$$\ldots x_{-2}x_{-1} \cdot x_0x_1x_2 \ldots$$

For finite $E \subseteq \mathbb{Z}$, elements of S^E are *finite patterns* with domain E. We denote by $x_E \in S^E$ the restriction of configuration x on E and call it the pattern in x on domain E. In particular, for $i \leq j$ the pattern $x_{[i,j]} = x_ix_{i+1} \ldots x_j$ is viewed as a finite word of length $j - i + 1$.

The set $S^{\mathbb{Z}}$ is equipped with the usual product topology, which makes it a compact space. Each finite pattern $p \in S^E$ determines a *cylinder* $\{x \in S^{\mathbb{Z}} \mid x_E = p\}$ that contains all configurations with pattern p on domain E. Cylinders are clopen (closed and open) and they form a base of the topology. Clopen sets are precisely the finite unions of cylinders. The shift function $\sigma : S^{\mathbb{Z}} \longrightarrow S^{\mathbb{Z}}$ is the automorphism defined by $\sigma(x)_i = x_{i+1}$ for all $x \in S^{\mathbb{Z}}$ and $i \in \mathbb{Z}$.

A *cellular automaton* (CA) is a function $F : S^{\mathbb{Z}} \longrightarrow S^{\mathbb{Z}}$ that is continuous and commutes with the shift σ. Equivalently, F is determined by a *local rule* $f : S^{2r+1} \longrightarrow S$ of some *radius* r as follows:

$$\forall i \in \mathbb{Z} : F(x)_i = f(x_{[i-r,i+r]}).$$

A bijective CA $F : S^{\mathbb{Z}} \longrightarrow S^{\mathbb{Z}}$ is *reversible*: the inverse function F^{-1} is automatically a CA as well.

The pair $(S^{\mathbb{Z}}, F)$ is a *dynamical system*: a compact space $S^{\mathbb{Z}}$ with a continuous transformation $F\colon S^{\mathbb{Z}} \longrightarrow S^{\mathbb{Z}}$. A topologically closed $X \subseteq S^{\mathbb{Z}}$ is said to be F-*invariant* if $F(X) \subseteq X$, and we say that (X, F) is then a *subsystem* of $(S^{\mathbb{Z}}, F)$. If a topologically closed $X \subseteq S^{\mathbb{Z}}$ is also shift-invariant then X is a *subshift* of the full shift $S^{\mathbb{Z}}$.

Consider an arbitrary subsystem (X, F) of $(S^{\mathbb{Z}}, F)$. The system is

- *sensitive to initial conditions* (or simply *sensitive*) if there exists a finite *observation window* $W \subseteq \mathbb{Z}$ such that

$$\forall_{\text{finite}} E \subseteq \mathbb{Z}, \forall x \in X: \exists y \in X, \exists n \in \mathbb{N}: y_E = x_E \text{and} F^n(y)_W \neq F^n(x)_W.$$

  In other words, any configuration x can be modified at arbitrarily distant cells in such a way that eventually the change will be observed inside window W.
- *transitive* if for all cylinders $U, V \subseteq S^{\mathbb{Z}}$

$$U \cap X \neq \emptyset, V \cap X \neq \emptyset \Longrightarrow \exists n \in \mathbb{N}: F^n(U) \cap V \cap X \neq \emptyset.$$

Following [4], the system (X, F) is *Devaney-chaotic* if it is sensitive, transitive and the periodic points are dense. It is known that sensitivity is a weak condition in the sense that it is implied by transitivity and denseness of periodic points [1]. In this paper we construct a CA that is not sensitive and does not have any sensitive subsystems, and hence has no Devaney-chaotic subsystems.

2.2 Universality of Cellular Automata

Computational universality refers to a system's ability to simulate arbitrary effective processes. This idea needs to be precisely formalized before it can be mathematically treated. It is reasonable to require that the dynamics of the system "solves" some Σ_1^0-complete decision problem, meaning that the halting problem of Turing machines can be many-one reduced to instances of the problem. Delvenne et al. in [3] introduced the following natural decision problem to consider for a cellular automaton $F: S^{\mathbb{Z}} \longrightarrow S^{\mathbb{Z}}$ (or more generally, on any discrete time symbolic dynamical system):

(TRACE) "Given a clopen partitioning $C_1, C_2, \ldots C_k$ of $S^{\mathbb{Z}}$ and a regular language $L \subseteq \{1, 2, \ldots, k\}^*$, does there exist $x \in S^{\mathbb{Z}}$ and $n \in \mathbb{N}$ such that $\chi(x)\chi(F(x)) \ldots \chi(F^n(x)) \in L$?"

The observation function χ is defined by $\chi(y) = i$ iff $y \in C_i$.

So the problem asks if a finite segment of the *trace* of some orbit with respect to the clopen partitioning is in a given regular language. The CA F is *universal* if the problem TRACE is Σ_1^0-complete.

We actually consider the more restricted halting problem of dynamical systems, also defined in [3]:

(Reach) "Given non-empty clopen sets $C_1, C_2 \subseteq S^{\mathbb{Z}}$, does there exist $n \in \mathbb{N}$ such that $F^n(C_1) \cap C_2 \neq \emptyset$?"

It is clear that if the problem Reach is Σ_1^0-complete, so is Trace. Our universal CA will be universal in the strong sense that Reach is Σ_1^0-complete. Note that in a transitive system the problem Reach is trivial, so a Devaney-chaotic CA can be universal only in the weaker sense given by Trace.

2.3 Reversible Turing Machines

A *Turing machine* (TM) is a triplet $M = (Q, A, T)$ where Q is a finite set of *states*, A is a finite *tape alphabet*, and

$$T \subseteq (Q \times \{-1, +1\} \times Q) \cup (Q \times A \times Q \times A)$$

is a set of *instructions*. Elements of $Q \times \{-1, +1\} \times Q$ and $Q \times A \times Q \times A$ are called *move instructions* and *write instructions*, respectively. A *configuration* of M is a triplet $(q, i, t) \in Q \times \mathbb{Z} \times A^{\mathbb{Z}}$ where q is the current state, i is the position of the machine on the tape, and t is the content of the tape.

- A move instruction $(q, \delta, q') \in T$ from state q to state q' allows the machine to convert configuration (q, i, t) into $(q', i + \delta, t)$, for all $i \in \mathbb{Z}$ and all $t \in A^{\mathbb{Z}}$.
- A write instruction $(q, a, q', a') \in T$ from q to q' allows to change any (q, i, t) into (q', i, t'), provided $t(i) = a$, $t'(i) = a'$ and $t(j) = t'(j)$ for all $j \neq i$.

A single step transformation of a configuration c into c' is denoted by $c \vdash c'$. As usual, $\vdash^*$ is the reflexive and transitive closure of the relation $\vdash$.

The Turing machine is *deterministic* if for each configuration there is at most one instruction applicable, so that $\vdash$ is a partial function. This property has an easy to check characterization in terms of the instruction set T:

$$\begin{aligned}
(q, \delta_1, q_1), (q, \delta_2, q_2) \in T \quad &\Longrightarrow \quad \delta_1 = \delta_2 \text{ and } q_1 = q_2 \\
(q, a, q_1, a_1'), (q, a, q_2, a_2') \in T \quad &\Longrightarrow \quad q_1 = q_2 \text{ and } a_1' = a_2' \\
(q, \delta, q') \in T \quad &\Longrightarrow \quad \forall a, a', q'' : (q, a, q'', a') \notin T.
\end{aligned}$$

Each instruction has an inverse, defined as follows:

- The inverse of a move instruction (q, δ, q') is $(q', -\delta, q)$, where we use the notation $-(-1) = +1$ and $-(+1) = -1$.
- The inverse of a write instruction (q, a, q', a') is (q', a', q, a).

It is clear that the inverse always undoes the effect of the forward instruction, and vice versa. We denote by T^{-1} the set of inverses of instructions in T, and the TM $M^{-1} = (Q, A, T^{-1})$ is the inverse TM of $M = (Q, A, T)$. If M^{-1} is deterministic then M is *reversible*. In this work we only use deterministic and reversible Turing machines (DRTM).

Deterministic reversible Turing machines are known to be able to simulate arbitrary Turing machines [2]. A construction of a single tape universal DRTM

$M = (Q, A, T)$ is given in [8]. This machine has specified initial and final states $i, f \in Q$ and a blank tape symbol $B \in A$, and there are no instructions in T into state i or from state f. To each word $w \in (A \setminus \{B\})^*$ that does not contain the symbol B we associate the initial tape content $\iota_w = {}^\infty B \,.\, wB^\infty$ where w is written on the otherwise blank tape starting at position 0. The universality result of [8] states that the standard halting problem of Turing machines

(TMHALT) "For given $w \in (A \setminus \{B\})^*$, does $(i, 0, \iota_w) \vdash^* (f, j, t)$ for some $j \in \mathbb{Z}$ and $t \in A^{\mathbb{Z}}$?"

is Σ_1^0-complete.

In this work we consider universality in the sense of Delvenne et al., and for that purpose we need a DRTM universality variant where the tape content outside the input word w is not known to be initially blank, and where the final state appears in position 0 of the tape upon acceptance. So we associate to any Turing machine with specified initial state q_0 and final state q_f the following decision problem that is an adaptation of REACH from Sect. 2.2:

(TMREACH) "For given $w \in A^*$, do there exist tape contents $t, t' \in A^{\mathbb{Z}}$ with $t_{[0,|w|-1]} = w$ such that $(q_0, 0, t) \vdash^* (q_f, 0, t')$? "

Lemma 1. *There exists a DRTM U with specified initial and final states such that* TMREACH *is Σ_1^0-complete. There is no instruction in U into the initial state q_0.*

Proof. Let $M = (Q, A, T)$ be the universal DRTM from [8] with initial and final states i and f, and a blank tape symbol B. So there are no instructions in T into state i or from f, and TMHALT is Σ_1^0-complete. Moreover, we may assume that M is forced to execute a write instruction at odd time steps. This is established by splitting each state $q \in Q$ into two states $q^{(1)}$ and $q^{(2)}$, replacing any original instruction from state q into state p by an analogous instruction from state $q^{(2)}$ into state $p^{(1)}$, and by adding for all $q \in Q$ and all $a \in A$ the tape check instruction $(q^{(1)}, a, q^{(2)}, a)$.

We next construct a DRTM U with Σ_1^0-complete TMREACH. The new state set consists of Q and 18 additional states. The tape alphabet is $A \cup A' \cup \{[,]\}$ where $A' = \{a' \mid a \in A\}$ is a disjoint copy of alphabet A. All instructions in T are also instructions of U and, in addition, there are several instructions to be executed before and after simulating M. The instructions are shown in Fig. 1. In the figure, vertices represent states and edges are instructions. A move instruction (q, δ, q') is represented by a directed edge from q to q' with label L or R, corresponding to cases $\delta = -1$ and $\delta = +1$, respectively. A write instruction (q, a, q', a') is given as a directed edge from q to q' with label a/a'. The subgraph corresponding to instructions of M is indicated as an oval with label M. It is straightforward to verify that the given TM is deterministic and reversible. Note how the marked versions a' of letters $a \in A$ are needed to guarantee reversibility.

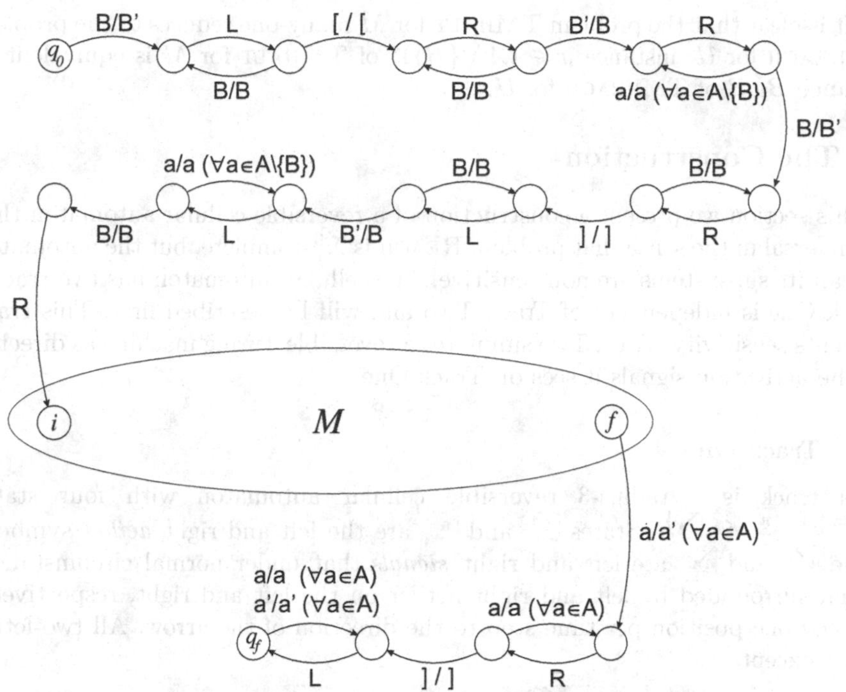

Fig. 1. A deterministic, reversible Turing machine with Σ_1^0-complete decision problem TMREACH.

Considering the first 14 states, it is easy to see that state i will be reached from initial configuration $(q_0, 0, t)$ if and only if the content t of the tape is

$$x[B^n \;.\; BwBB^m]y$$

for some $w \in (A \setminus \{B\})^*$, some $n, m \geq 0$, and arbitrary left- and right-infinite words x and y. In this case, when entering state i the machine is in position 1 of the tape (hence reading the first letter of w) and the tape content is t as in the beginning.

From state i only instructions of M can be executed until (if ever) state f is reached. Note that M automatically stops if it accesses a boundary symbol [or]. This is due to the property of M that it executes a write instruction at odd time steps and hence can only continue on cells that contain an element of A. It is then clear that state f is reached if and only if M reaches state f on input ι_w, and n and m are sufficiently large so that the accepting computation by M fits between the boundary symbols.

Last four states of U guarantee that the final state q_f will be seen in every tape position between the boundary symbols, and in particular then, in position 0 as required. (Note that this last part is not actually necessary since the DRTM M constructed in [8] has the property that the Turing machine halts at cell 0.)

It is clear that the problem TMHALT for M many-one reduces to the problem TMREACH for U: instance $w \in (A \setminus \{B\})^*$ of TMHALT for M is equivalent to instance BwB of TMREACH for U. □

3 The Construction

In this section we present a construction of a reversible cellular automaton that is universal in the sense that problem REACH is Σ_1^0-complete, but the automaton and all its subsystems are non-sensitive. The cellular automaton has two tracks. Track One is independent of Track Two and will be described first. This track prevents sensitivity. Track Two simulates a reversible Turing machine as directed by the activation signals it sees on Track One.

3.1 Track One

This track is a radius-3 reversible cellular automaton with four states $S_1 = \{$L, R, ↙, ↘$\}$. States L and R are the left and right *aether* symbols, while ↙ and ↘ are left and right *signals* that under normal circumstances (when surrounded by left and right aether on the left and right, respectively) proceed one position per time step to the direction of the arrow. All two-letter words except

L L   R R   L ↙   L ↘   ↙ R   ↘ R

are *walls*. Walls remain stationary: a cell that is part of a wall never changes its state, and therefore also remains part of the wall forever. A radius-3 local rule allows a cell to determine all wall cells within distance 2. Segments between walls are of four possible forms

L*   R*   *L ↙ R*   *L ↘ R*

where, as usual, * indicates an arbitrarily long repetition.

The dynamics of an arrow that is not part of a wall is as follows.

- If the arrow is next to a wall then it stays put:

  ▦↙ ⟶ ▦↙   ▦↘ ⟶ ▦↘   ↙▦ ⟶ ↙▦   ↘▦ ⟶ ↘▦

  Here, and in the following, ▦ indicates a cell that belongs to a wall.
- Otherwise, if there is a wall at distance two in front of the arrow then the arrow flips its direction:

  L ↘ R ▦ ⟶ L ↙ R ▦   and   ▦ L ↙ R ⟶ ▦ L ↘ R

- Otherwise (i.e., the two cells in front of the arrow and the first cell behind it are not wall cells) the arrow moves one position:

  L ↘ R R ⟶ L L ↘ R   and   L L ↙ R ⟶ L ↙ R R

Figure 2 shows a sample space-time diagram of Track One. It is easy to see that the CA is reversible. Walls are never created or destroyed. All configurationsare

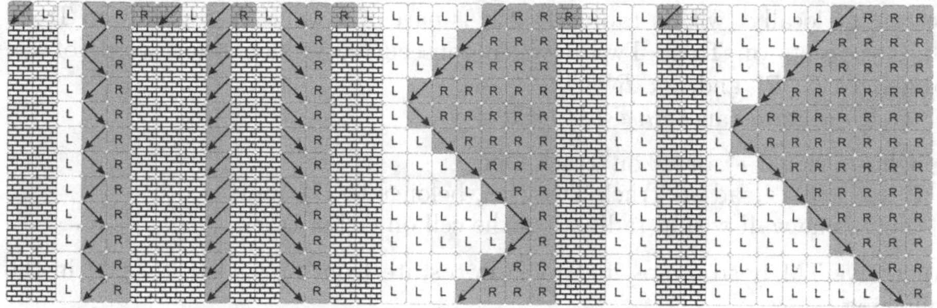

Fig. 2. A sample space-time diagram of Track One. Time increases down. From the second time step onward, symbol ▤ is used to indicate cells that are part of a wall.

made of segments separated by walls. Each segment is either unchanged forever, or contains a single arrow that bounces between the walls.

3.2 Track Two

Track Two simulates the universal DRTM U provided by Lemma 1. The standard technique of identifying a computation zone using left and right markers is used to prevent several TM heads interfering with each other. Whenever the TM head bumps into the end of its zone (or sees a wall on Track One), the simulation is reversed and the machine starts retracing its computation backwards in time. The construction is similar to the one used in the proof of Theorem 12 in [5]. A new aspect is that the TM makes a step only when passed over by an active signal on Track One.

More precisely, let $U = (Q, A, T)$ be a DRTM with initial and final states q_0 and q_f whose TMREACH-problem is Σ_1^0-complete. There is no instruction in T into state q_0.

Track Two uses a radius-3 local rule. The state set is $S_2 = L \cup C \cup R$ where

$$L = A \times \{\rightarrow\},$$
$$C = A \times Q \times \{\uparrow, \downarrow\},$$
$$R = A \times \{\leftarrow\}.$$

A state $(a, q, \downarrow) \in C$ represents a TM tape cell that contains symbol a and is scanned by the TM in state q running forward in time, while $(a, q, \uparrow) \in C$ is the same situation except that the TM is running backward in time. States $(a, \rightarrow) \in L$ and $(a, \leftarrow) \in R$ are tape positions with symbol a that are to the left and to the right of the TM head, respectively. (So the arrow points to the direction where the TM head is to be found.)

We define *walls* on Track Two analogously to Track One. All length two words except ones that belong to LL, LC, CR or RR are walls on Track Two. We consider walls of both tracks, so a cell is a wall cell if it is part of a wall on either track. Any cell that is part of a wall does not change its Track Two content in any way, so it remains in the wall forever. It is clear that a cell can determine locally (within radius-1) if it is part of a wall. Analogously to Track One, segments on Track Two between consecutive walls contain words of the languages L^*, R^* and L^*CR^*.

Cell i contains an *active TM head* if

1 it has a signal ↙ or ↘ on Track One,
2 It has a TM head on Track Two (i.e., belongs to C), and
3 there is no wall within radius-1 of the cell on either track.

An active TM head swaps its Track Two state from $(a, q, \downarrow)$ to $(a, q, \uparrow)$ in the following cases:

- There is no instruction (q, δ, q') or (q, a, q', a') in T that U could execute, or
- There is in T a move instruction (q, δ, q') but the new position $i + \delta$ is next to a wall (on either track), where i is the current position of the active TM head.

Analogously, state $(a, q, \uparrow)$ becomes $(a, q, \downarrow)$ in symmetric cases using the inverse instruction set T^{-1} in place of T. In other words, the machine simply reverses time if there is no applicable instruction or if the machine would move to a position next to a wall.

Otherwise, an active TM head executes on Track Two the unique applicable instruction in T or T^{-1}, in the cases of state $(a, q, \downarrow)$ or $(a, q, \uparrow)$, respectively. Note that in the case of a move instruction this involves updating the neighboring cell also. In no other cases is Track Two state changed.

Note that the TM head "bounces" from walls in an analogous manner as the signals on Track One: The head never moves next to a wall, and instead changes the direction of time and starts tracing its steps backwards. It is clear that this construction guarantees reversibility.

The two tracks together constitute the CA $F : S^{\mathbb{Z}} \longrightarrow S^{\mathbb{Z}}$ with state set $S = S_1 \times S_2$. We denote by $\pi_1 : S^{\mathbb{Z}} \longrightarrow S_1^{\mathbb{Z}}$ and $\pi_2 : S^{\mathbb{Z}} \longrightarrow S_2^{\mathbb{Z}}$ the projections of configurations on the tracks. Based on the discussions above, the CA F has the following properties:

- F is reversible and has radius-3 local rule,
- Track One operates independently of Track Two, that is, there is a CA $F_1 : S_1^{\mathbb{Z}} \longrightarrow S_1^{\mathbb{Z}}$ such that $\pi_1 \circ F = F_1 \circ \pi_1$,
- Track Two is changed only at positions having an activation signal within radius-1 on Track One.

4 Main Properties of the CA

In this section we show that the reversible CA constructed in Sect. 3 has the required properties.

Theorem 1. *The reversible CA* $F : S^{\mathbb{Z}} \longrightarrow S^{\mathbb{Z}}$

(a) is universal in the sense that the decision problem REACH *is* Σ_1^0*-complete, and*
(b) has no sensitive subsystems.

The proofs of (a) and (b) are presented in Sects. 4.1–4.2.

4.1 Universality

We prove that REACH is Σ_1^0-complete for CA F by many-one reducing TMREACH for TM U. Let $w = a_0a_1 \ldots a_{n-1}$ be an arbitrary instance of TMREACH for U. An equivalent instance of REACH for F is the pair

$$C_1 = \{x \in S^{\mathbb{Z}} \mid \pi_2(x)_{[0,n-1]} = (a_0, q_0, \downarrow)(a_1, \leftarrow)(a_2, \leftarrow) \ldots (a_{n-1}, \leftarrow)\},$$
$$C_2 = \{y \in S^{\mathbb{Z}} \mid \pi_2(y)_0 = (a, q_f, \downarrow) \text{ for some } a \in A\ \}$$

of effectively formed clopen sets $C_1, C_2 \subseteq S^{\mathbb{Z}}$.

($\Longrightarrow$) If w is a positive instance of TMREACH then there exist $t, t' \in A^{\mathbb{Z}}$ such that $t_{[0,n-1]} = w$ and $(q_0, 0, t) \vdash^* (q_f, 0, t')$ by U. Machine U can read only a finite number of tape positions before reaching the accepting configuration so for some $m \in \mathbb{N}$, all intermediate configurations (q, i, t'') have $|i| < m$. Consider the configuration $x \in S^{\mathbb{Z}}$ with

$$\pi_1(x) = \ldots ▦▦\boxed{\text{L}}^m \,.\, \boxed{\searrow}\boxed{\text{R}}^m ▦▦ \ldots$$
$$\pi_2(x) = \ldots (t_{-1}, \rightarrow) \,.\, (t_0, q_0, \downarrow)(t_1, \leftarrow) \ldots$$

where all ▦ are, for example, equal to $\boxed{\swarrow}$ to cause walls on Track One. We have $x \in C_1$. From initial configuration x, the CA has the following behavior: on Track One a single signal bounces between positions $-(m-1)$ and $m-1$. Each time the signal crosses the TM head on Track Two, one step of U is simulated. This happens repeatedly as long as the TM head remains in the interval $[-(m-1), m-1]$. We then eventually have $F^i(x) \in C_2$, so the instance C_1, C_2 is positive for REACH.

($\Longleftarrow$) Conversely, suppose C_1, C_2 is a positive instance of REACH for U. There is then $x \in C_1$ such that $F^i(x) \in C_2$ for some $i \in \mathbb{N}$. Let $t \in A^{\mathbb{Z}}$ be the tape content expressed in x, that is, $\pi_2(x)_j = (t[j], \ldots)$ for all j. The only way to change the Track Two state $(t[0], q_0, \downarrow)$ into some $(a, q_f, \downarrow)$ in cell 0 is by repeatedly simulating U on Track Two. Note that the simulation cannot change the time direction before reaching state q_f, since otherwise U^{-1} would be simulated, retracing the computation back to the initial state q_0. As there are no instructions in U^{-1} from state q_0, the time direction would be swapped again, leading to a periodic behavior that never leads to state q_f. We conclude that $(q_0, 0, t) \vdash^* (q_f, 0, t')$ by U. As $t_{[0,|w|-1]} = w$, word w is a positive instance of TMREACH.

4.2 Sensitive Subsystems Do Not Exist

Let us prove next that CA F has no sensitive subsystems. Recall that a subsystem is any topologically closed $X \subseteq S^{\mathbb{Z}}$ that satisfies $F(X) \subseteq X$. Note that we do not require the subsystem to be a subshift, as it does not need to be shift-invariant. The proof is based on properties of Track One: the only fact about Track Two that we need is that the content of Track Two is only changed in the vicinity of a signal on Track One.

For the sake of argument, suppose there is a subsystem X on which F is sensitive to initial conditions. There is then a finite observation window W such that for any $x \in X$ and any finite $E \subseteq \mathbb{Z}$ there exists $y \in X$ such that $x_E = y_E$ but $F^n(x)_W \neq F^n(y)_W$ for some $n \geq 0$. Notice that this directly implies that

- for all $x \in X$, the first track $\pi_1(x)$ does not have wall states both to the right and to the left of window W.

This is because the walls are blocking words: future states between the walls are not influenced by any states outside the walls.

Let us consider the following two cases:

(1) There is a finite window W such that all Track One walls of all $x \in X$ are inside W. We can choose this W to be also an observation window for the definition of sensitivity.
(2) For arbitrarily large k, there are $x \in X$ with a Track One wall in some position i satisfying $|i| > k$.

Case (1): Let $x \in X$ have the maximum number of Track One arrows outside W, among all $x \in X$. This number is 0,1 or 2 since the segments outside W do not contain a wall. Let $E = [a, b]$ be a finite segment that contains the radius-3 neighborhood of W and all the positions where x has arrows on Track One. (We include the radius-3 neighborhood because the local rule of F uses radius 3.) There are then uniform aethers in $\pi_1(x)$ to the left and to the right of E.

If $y \in X$ and $y_E = x_E$ then necessarily $\pi_1(y) = \pi_1(x)$. Since Track One operates independently of the content of Track Two, for all $n \geq 0$ we have $\pi_1(F^n(y)) = \pi_1(F^n(x))$. Both boundaries of E are crossed by a Track One signal at most once, and in such a case the signal moves out from E. Consequently, only three cells on each boundary can be updated differently in x and y, and it follows that $F^n(y)_W = F^n(x)_W$ for all $n \in \mathbb{N}$. This contradicts sensitivity (and means that x is an equicontinuity point).

Case (2): Let $x \in X$ be such that $\pi_1(x)$ has a wall in position i to the right of W but no wall in any position to the left of W. (The other case is symmetric.) Note that property ($\bullet$) excludes the possibility of walls on both sides of W. As in case (1) we assume that x has the maximal number of Track One arrows to the left of W. Let $E = [a, b]$ be a finite segment that contains the radius-3 neighborhood of the sensitivity window W, position i and the possible position left of W where x has an arrow on Track One. If $y \in X$ satisfies $y_E = x_E$ then $\pi_1(y)$ cannot contain a wall in any position $< a$ by property ($\bullet$). We then have that $\pi_1(y)$ and $\pi_1(x)$ are identical at all cells $\leq b$. As there is a wall in cell i, we clearly have also for all $n \in \mathbb{N}$ that $\pi_1(F^n(y))_{(-\infty,i]} = \pi_1(F^n(x))_{(-\infty,i]}$. As in case (1), a signal crosses the left boundary of E at most once (moving out of E), so at most three leftmost cells of E can be affected by the states to the left of E. The wall at position i prevents any influence on W by states on the right of E. We see that $F^n(y)_W = F^n(x)_W$ for all $n \in \mathbb{N}$. □

References

1. Banks, J., Brooks, J., Cairns, G., Davis, G., Stacey, P.: On devaney's definition of chaos. Am. Math. Mon. **99**(4), 332–334 (1992)
2. Bennett, C.H.: Logical reversibility of computation. IBM J. Res. Dev. **17**(6), 525–532 (1973)
3. Delvenne, J.C., Kurka, P., Blondel, V.D.: Decidability and universality in symbolic dynamical systems. Fundam. Inform. **74**(4), 463–490 (2006)
4. Devaney, R.: An introduction to chaotic dynamical systems. Global analysis, pure and applied, Benjamin/Cummings (1986)
5. Kari, J., Ollinger, N.: Periodicity and immortality in reversible computing. In: Ochmański, E., Tyszkiewicz, J. (eds.) MFCS 2008. LNCS, vol. 5162, pp. 419–430. Springer, Heidelberg (2008)
6. Kari, J., Salo, V., Törmä, I.: Trace complexity of chaotic reversible cellular automata. In: Yamashita, S., Minato, S. (eds.) RC 2014. LNCS, vol. 8507, pp. 54–66. Springer, Heidelberg (2014)
7. Langton, C.G.: Computation at the edge of chaos: Phase transitions and emergent computation. Phys. D **42**(1–3), 12–37 (1990)
8. Morita, K., Shirasaki, A., Gono, Y.: A 1-tape 2-symbol reversible turing machine. Trans. IEICE Japan **E72**, 223–228 (1989)

Real-Time Reversible One-Way Cellular Automata

Martin Kutrib, Andreas Malcher(✉), and Matthias Wendlandt

Institut Für Informatik, Universität Giessen,
Arndtstr. 2, 35392 Giessen, Germany
{kutrib,malcher,matthias.wendlandt}@informatik.uni-giessen.de

Abstract. Real-time one-way cellular automata (OCA) are investigated towards their ability to perform reversible computations with regard to formal language recognition. It turns out that the standard model with fixed boundary conditions is quite weak in terms of reversible information processing, since it is shown that in this case exactly the regular languages can be accepted reversibly. We then study a modest extension which allows that information may flow circularly from the leftmost cell into the rightmost cell. It is shown that this extension does not increase the computational power in the general case, but does increase it for reversible computations. On the other hand, the model is less powerful than real-time reversible two-way cellular automata. Additionally, we obtain that the corresponding language class is closed under Boolean operations, and we prove the undecidability of several decidability questions. Finally, it is shown that the reversibility of an arbitrary real-time circular one-way cellular automaton is undecidable as well.

Keywords: Reversibility · One-way cellular automata · Language recognition · Closure properties · Decidability

1 Introduction

Computational devices that are able to perform reversible computations have gained a lot of interest in the last years. The main property of reversible computations is that every configuration has a unique successor configuration as well as a unique predecessor configuration. Thus, in reversible computations no information is lost which is an appealing property from a physical point of view, because it has been observed that a loss of information results in heat dissipation [15]. Bennett [3] was the first who studied reversibility in computational devices, namely, in Turing machines. His fundamental result is that every Turing machine can be transformed into an equivalent reversible Turing machine. Thus, every recursively enumerable language can be processed in such a way that no information is lost. Less powerful classes with regard to the Chomsky hierarchy are the regular languages, which are accepted, for example, by deterministic finite automata (DFA), and the deterministic context-free languages,

T. Isokawa et al. (Eds.): AUTOMATA 2014, LNCS 8996, pp. 56–69, 2015.
DOI: 10.1007/978-3-319-18812-6_5

which are accepted, for example, by deterministic pushdown automata (DPDA). Reversible DFA are introduced in [2] and it is known [19] that there are regular languages for which no reversible DFA exists. This means that there are computations performed by DFA in which a loss of information cannot be avoided. Similar results are obtained for reversible DPDA in [13]. Recently, reversibility is also studied for multi-head finite automata. Morita shows in [18] that every multi-head finite automaton can be transformed into an equivalent reversible multi-head finite automaton under the condition of two-way motion of the multiple heads. In case of one-way motion, it is shown in [14] that the reversible variant is less powerful.

For cellular automata, injectivity of the global transition function is equivalent to the reversibility of the automaton. It is shown in [1] that global reversibility is decidable for one-dimensional cellular automata, whereas the problem is undecidable for higher dimensions [7]. For a detailed discussion we refer to the survey given in [17]. Additional information about some aspects of cellular automata may be found in [8]. All these results concern unbounded configurations. Moreover, in order to obtain a reversible device the neighborhood as well as the time complexity may be increased. In [5] it is shown that the neighborhood of a reverse CA is at most $n - 1$ when the given reversible CA has n states. In connection with the ability to accept formal languages under real-time conditions, reversibility has been studied in [11,12] for real-time two-way cellular automata and real-time two-way iterative arrays with fixed boundary conditions. Cellular language acceptors are working on finite configurations with fixed boundary conditions (see, for example, [10]) and, thus, these devices cannot be reversible in the classical sense. Their number of different configurations is bounded. So, the system will run into loops that are reversible only if the initial configuration is reached again. In contrast to the traditional notion of reversibility, cellular language acceptors are considered that are reversible on the core of computation, that is, from initial configuration to the configuration given by the time complexity. This point of view is rather different from the traditional notion of reversibility since only configurations are considered that are reachable from initial configurations. At first glance, such a setting should simplify matters. But quite the contrary, we prove that real-time reversibility is undecidable.

In this paper, we continue the research on real-time reversibility and investigate one-way cellular automata (OCA). For the definition of reversible OCA, we first observe that information flow is from right to left in a forward computation and from left to right in a backward computation. Then, the following problem may occur: intuitively, every information which has passed the leftmost cell cannot be reconstructed since the leftmost cell always gets the border symbol from the left in the backward computation. Thus, such computations will be in general irreversible. We will show that this intuition is in fact right by proving that any real-time reversible OCA accepts a regular language. To obtain a more powerful model, we will allow that information may additionally flow circularly from the leftmost cell into the rightmost cell. It is shown that the language class accepted by real-time OCA with this extension, called circular OCA (COCA) is equivalent to the class accepted by classical real-time OCA.

Thus, the computational power of the general models is not increased, but it turns out that reversible COCA are more powerful than reversible OCA. First, we can prove that the computational power of reversible COCA lies properly in between reversible OCA and reversible two-way CA. Second, by a suitable simulation of reversible linearly bounded Turing machines by real-time COCA we obtain that emptiness and finiteness are undecidable for reversible real-time COCA. This implies the undecidability of inclusion and equivalence as well. Moreover, the problem of whether a given COCA is real-time reversible is also undecidable. These results are in line with the results for real-time two-way CA and real-time iterative arrays. Furthermore, we obtain also that the language class accepted by real-time COCA is closed under Boolean operations.

2 Preliminaries and Definitions

We denote the set of non-negative integers by $\mathbb{N}$. The reversal of a word w is denoted by w^R. For the length of w we write $|w|$. We write $\subseteq$ for set inclusion, and $\subset$ for strict set inclusion. In order to avoid technical overloading in writing, two languages L and L' are considered to be equal, if they differ at most by the empty word. Throughout the article two devices are said to be *equivalent* if and only if they accept the same language.

A one-way cellular automaton is a linear array of identical deterministic finite state machines, called cells, that are identified by natural numbers. In case of fixed boundary condition, each but the rightmost cell is connected to its nearest neighbor to the right. Cell 0 is in a distinguished permanent boundary state, and the rightmost cell is connected to cell 0. In case of circular boundary condition, the boundary state is not necessarily permanent [20] (see Fig. 1). The state transition depends on the current state of a cell itself and the current state of its neighbor. The state changes take place simultaneously at discrete time steps. The input mode for cellular automata is called parallel. One can suppose that all cells fetch their input symbol during a pre-initial step.

Definition 1. *A* (circular) one-way cellular automaton *((C)OCA) is a system* $\langle S, F, A, \#, \delta \rangle$, *where* S *is the finite, nonempty set of* cell states, $F \subseteq S$ *is the set of* accepting states, $A \subseteq S$ *is the nonempty set of* input symbols, $\# \in S \setminus A$ *is the distinguished* boundary state, *and* $\delta : S \times S \to S$ *is the* local transition function.

A configuration *of a (circular) one-way cellular automaton* $\langle S, F, A, \#, \delta \rangle$ *at time* $t \geq 0$ *is a mapping* $c_t : \{0, 1, 2, \ldots, n\} \to S$, *for* $n \geq 1$, *that assigns a state to each cell. The operation starts at time 0 in a so-called* initial configuration, *which is defined by the given input* $w = a_1 a_2 \cdots a_n \in A^+$. *We set* $c_0(i) = a_i$, *for* $1 \leq i \leq n$ *and* $c_0(0) = \#$. *Successor configurations are computed according to the global transition function* Δ. *Let* c_t, $t \geq 0$, *be a configuration with* $n \geq 1$, *then the successor* c_{t+1} *of a* one-way cellular automaton with fixed boundary condition *(OCA) is*

$$c_{t+1} = \Delta(c_t) \iff \begin{cases} c_{t+1}(0) = \# \\ c_{t+1}(i) = \delta(c_t(i), c_t(i+1)), i \in \{1, 2, \ldots, n-1\} \\ c_{t+1}(n) = \delta(c_t(n), c_t(0)) \end{cases} .$$

The successor c_{t+1} *of a* one-way cellular automaton *with circular boundary condition (COCA) is*

$$c_{t+1} = \Delta(c_t) \iff \begin{cases} c_{t+1}(i) = \delta(c_t(i), c_t(i+1)), i \in \{0, 1, \dots, n-1\} \\ c_{t+1}(n) = \delta(c_t(n), c_t(0)) \end{cases} .$$

In order to distinguish between the boundary conditions, we write circular one-way cellular automaton for arrays with circular boundary conditions.

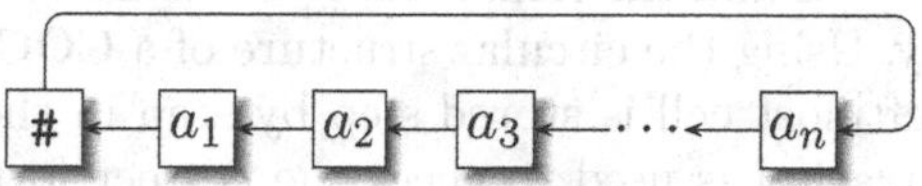

Fig. 1. A (circular) one-way cellular automaton.

An input w is accepted by a (circular) one-way cellular automaton if at some time step during its course of computation the leftmost cell receiving an input symbol, that is, cell 1, enters an accepting state. The *language accepted by* M is denoted by $L(M)$. Let $t : \mathbb{N} \to \mathbb{N}$, $t(n) \geq n$, be a mapping. If all $w \in L(M)$ are accepted with at most $t(|w|)$ time steps, then M is said to be of time complexity t.

Observe that time complexities do not have to meet any further conditions. This general treatment is made possible by the way of acceptance. An input w is accepted if cell 1 enters an accepting state at some time $i \leq t(|w|)$. Subsequent states of the cell are not relevant. However, in the sequel we are particularly interested in fast devices operating in *real-time*, that is, obeying the time complexity $t(n) = n$. In general, the family of languages accepted by some device X with time complexity t is denoted by $\mathscr{L}_t(\text{X})$, where $\mathscr{L}_{rt}(\text{X})$ is written for real time.

Now we turn to cellular automata that are reversible on the core of computation, that is, from initial configuration to the configuration given by the time complexity. Consequently, we call them t-time reversible if the time complexity t is obeyed. One can imagine that the devices are switched off or reset after the computation. In this way only configurations are considered that are reachable from initial configurations. However, since the predecessor of such a configuration is unique, there cannot be an unreachable configuration as predecessor of a reachable one. Basically, reversibility is meant with respect to the possibility of stepping the computation back and forth. So, there must exist a reverse local transition function. Due to the domain S^2 and the range S, obviously, the local transition function cannot be injective in general. However, for reverse computation steps we may utilize the information which is available for the cells. In particular, the flow of information is reversed as well, and each cell receives the state of its *left* neighbor (the left neighbor of cell 0 is cell n).

For some mapping $t : \mathbb{N} \to \mathbb{N}$ let $M = \langle S, F, A, \#, \delta \rangle$ be a t-time ((C)OCA). Then M is said to be t *reversible* (REV-(C)OCA), if there exists a reverse local transition function $\delta_R : S \times S \to S$ so that $\Delta_R(\Delta(c_i)) = c_i$, for all configurations c_i

of M, $0 \leq i \leq t(n) - 1$. The global transition functions Δ and Δ_R are induced by δ and δ_R, respectively. For distinctness, we denote $\langle S, F, A, \#, \delta_R \rangle$ by M_R.

In order to clarify the notation we give an example.

Example 2. Language $L = \{ a^n b^m \mid m \geq n \geq 1 \}$ is accepted by a real-time REV-COCA. For the construction we consider that each cell is divided into four tracks. Track 1 is used to store the original input permanently. Tracks 2 and 3 are used to shift input blocks of b's to the left. Here, every cell initially carrying an a (a-cell) uses both tracks, first track 3 and then track 2, to shift the input with speed 1/2. The #-cell and the remaining b-cells shift b's with speed 1 to the left using track 3 only. Using the circular structure of a COCA, any information shifted beyond the leftmost cell is stored step by step in the rightmost part of the COCA. Finally, track 4 is used to check the correct format and that there have been more b's than a's in the input. The latter check can be performed by every a-cell testing at the right time whether it is carrying a b on track 3. Only in this case an accepting state is entered.

Let us now argue why the automaton constructed accepts L. Assume that the input is $a^n b^n$. Since a-cells shift with speed 1/2 and b-cells shift with speed 1, the first b at cell $n+1$ enters track 3 of the first a at cell 1 at time $2n-1$. More generally, the ith b at cell $n+i$ enters track 3 of the ith a at cell i at time $2n-i$. Thus, it is possible for the signal started on track 4 of cell $2n$ at time 1 which reaches cell i at time $2n-i+1$ to check whether every cell i carries a b on its track 3 at time $2n-i$. If the input is $a^n b^m$ with $n \leq m$, the behavior is identical and an accepting state is entered if $n \geq 1$. If the input is $a^n b^m$ with $n > m$, then there is no b on track 3 of cell 1 at time $m+n$ and the input is not accepted. If the input is not of the form $a^+ b^+$, this can be detected by the check on track 4 and the entering of an accepting state is avoided. Nevertheless, the shifting and checking is continued.

To show that the automaton constructed is reversible we first note that the shifting of b's is reversible, since every b is shifted at every time step and the speed of shifting is uniquely determined by the original input stored on track 1. By the circular structure of the automaton, also no information is lost. Moreover, the actions on track 1 are reversible since its contents are never changing. The check of the correct format on track 4 can be done reversibly by simulating a deterministic finite automaton. Details are given in the proof of Theorem 4. For the remaining check we send a signal with maximum speed to the left started in the rightmost cell and enter an accepting state every time when the check on track 3 is successful. This can clearly be done reversibly.

Finally, we have to make sure that the original input is restored when going from time 1 to time 0. This can be ensured by a suitable interpretation of the input symbols. We identify symbol b with a state whose tracks 1 and 3 carry symbol b while tracks 2 and 4 are empty. In this way, the input symbol b can be used in later calculations and the need to restore them in the backward initial step is not occurring. On the other hand, we have to differentiate between an input symbol b and a state with b on its first track and empty track 3 which may occur when a blank is shifted into the cell. To this end, the latter states

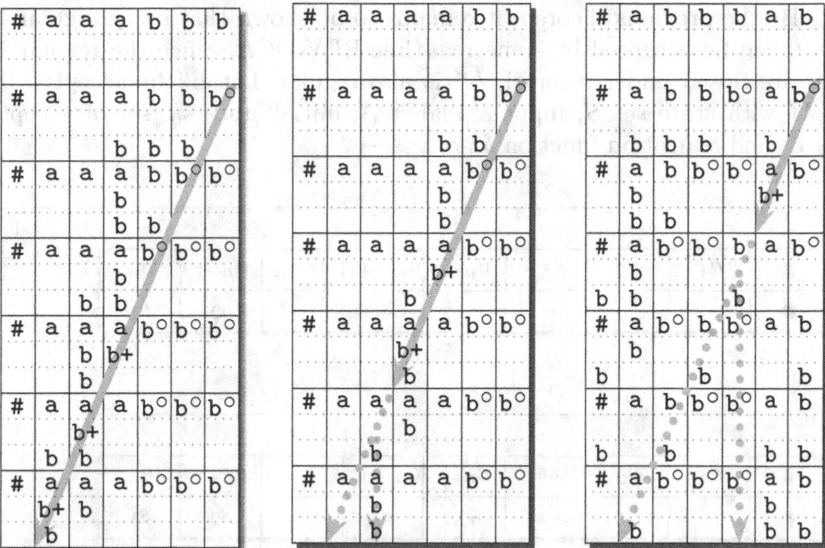

Fig. 2. Three example computations. A + denotes an accepting state, and a ∘ marks a cell into which a blank has been shifted on the third track. A solid arrow denotes the final check on the fourth track. If an error is encountered, the arrow is changed to a dotted arrow. Additionally, the time step is kept by storing a permanent information in the cell in which the error is encountered. This is depicted by the vertical dotted arrow. This construction is reversible since it occurs at most once.

are marked with ∘. Altogether, we obtain that L can be accepted by a real-time REV-COCA. Some example calculations to illustrate the construction are given in Fig. 2. □

3 Computational Capacity of Reversible (C)OCA

The classical definition of one-way cellular automata is the non-circular variant. However, for reversible real-time computations the slight generalization to circular cellular automata has a big impact. So, first we elaborate on this point.

Theorem 3. *Any language accepted by a real-time REV-OCA is regular.*

So, the condition to be reversible drastically reduces the computational capacity of OCA to that of deterministic finite automata, that is, a single cell. On the other hand, the next result says that every regular language can be accepted by a reversible real-time OCA. This is in contrast to the fact that there are regular languages that are not accepted by reversible DFA [2,19].

Theorem 4. *The family of regular languages and the family $\mathscr{L}_{rt}$(REV-OCA) are equal.*

Proof. By the previous theorem it remains to be shown that every regular language L can be accepted by some real-time REV-OCA. Since the regular languages are closed under reversal, L^R is also regular. Let L^R be accepted by a DFA M with state set S, input alphabet A, initial state s_0, set of accepting states F, and transition function $\delta : S \times A \to S$.

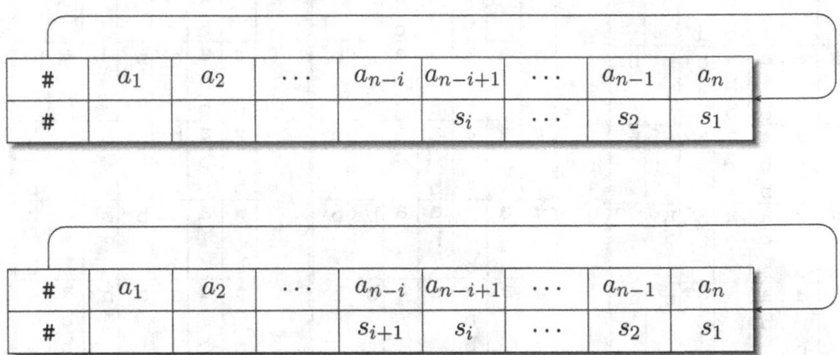

Fig. 3. Subsequent configurations of the REV-OCA M' in the proof of Theorem 4.

The idea for the simulation of L by a REV-OCA M' is first to divide its state set into two tracks. Track 1 is used to store the input permanently, while track 2 is used to send a signal from the rightmost cell with maximum speed to the left. The signal simulates the DFA M in such a way, that the state history is stored permanently on track 2. More precisely, let the input of M' be $a_1 a_2 \cdots a_n$. At time step 1, the rightmost cell n initiates the signal by calculating and storing $s_1 = \delta(s_0, a_n)$ on track 2. In general, for $0 \leq i \leq n-1$, the signal reaches cell $n-i$ at time $i+1$ and calculates and stores state $s_{i+1} = \delta(s_i, a_{n-i})$ on track 2 (see Fig. 3). The accepting states of M' are defined as those states having an accepting state of M on track 2. Clearly, M' accepts L. Trivially, the permanent storing of the input on track 1 is reversible. Moreover, since on track 2 the state history of M is stored, also the signal is reversible. □

The previous results justify a slight generalization of reversible OCA. Moreover, the next result shows that for real-time computations the slight generalization to circular devices does not increase the computational capacity.

Theorem 5. *The language families $\mathscr{L}_{rt}(OCA)$ and $\mathscr{L}_{rt}(COCA)$ are equal.*

Proof. By definition, every OCA is a special case of a COCA. On the other hand, let M be a real-time COCA and $w \in L(M)$ be some accepted input. The states passed through by cell 1 up to time $|w|$ depend only on the states of cell 1 and 2 at time $|w|-1$, the states of cells 1 to 3 at time $|w|-2$, and so on until the states of cells 1 to $|w|$ at time 1, and the states of cells 1 to $|w|$ and 0 at time 0. Therefore, information sent by cell 1 to its left neighbor and further via cell $|w|$ towards cell 1 again can reach cell 1 not before time $|w|+1$. Thus, it cannot affect the overall computation result for real-time computations. □

Since real-time OCA and real-time COCA characterize the same family of languages and the computational capacity of reversible OCA reduces to that of deterministic finite automata, we now turn to investigate the computational capacity of reversible real-time COCA. An immediate corollary is that the latter are strictly more powerful than the former, since Example 2 provides a non-regular language belonging to $\mathscr{L}_{rt}$(REV-COCA). So we have:

Lemma 6. *The family $\mathscr{L}_{rt}$(REV-COCA) properly includes $\mathscr{L}_{rt}$(REV-OCA).*

Next we turn to compare real-time reversible REV-COCA with real-time reversible *two-way* cellular automata (REV-CA). Basically, REV-CA are defined as REV-OCA with the exception that now the flow of information is two-way, that is, each cell is connected to its both nearest neighbors and the transition function δ maps $S \times S \times S$ to S.

Theorem 7. *The family $\mathscr{L}_{rt}$(REV-CA) properly includes $\mathscr{L}_{rt}$(REV-COCA).*

Proof. The inclusion follows for structural reasons. For the properness we use a unary witness language. It is well known that the language $L = \{ a^{2^n} \mid n \geq 0 \}$ is not accepted by any real-time OCA (see, for example, [9,10]).

On the other hand, in [4] it is shown that L is accepted by some CA in real time. The basic idea is depicted in Fig. 4. Initially a signal with speed 1/3 is sent to the right. Additionally, a signal with speed 1 that bounces between the slow signal and the leftmost cell is initiated. Now it is immediately verified that the fast signal is in the leftmost cell exactly at time steps 2^i, $i \geq 1$. Finally it suffices to send a signal from the rightmost cell to the left that accepts if and only if it arrives at the leftmost cell together with the fast signal. These three signals can be implemented in a reversible CA. □

So, we have the following three level hierarchy:

$$\text{REG} = \mathscr{L}_{rt}(\text{REV-OCA}) \subset \mathscr{L}_{rt}(\text{REV-COCA}) \subset \mathscr{L}_{rt}(\text{REV-CA})$$

4 Closure Properties

This section is devoted to the closures of $\mathscr{L}_{rt}$(REV-COCA) under Boolean operations. A family of languages is said to be *effectively* closed under some operation if the result of the operation can be constructed from the given language(s).

Theorem 8. *The language family $\mathscr{L}_{rt}$(REV-COCA) is effectively closed under the Boolean operations complementation, union, and intersection.*

Proof. The effective closure under union and intersection can be proved the same way as for reversible real-time two-way CA [11]. The construction there is based on the well-known two-track technique and a suitable interpretation of accepting states. Both techniques do not require two-way communication and apply to REV-OCA as well.

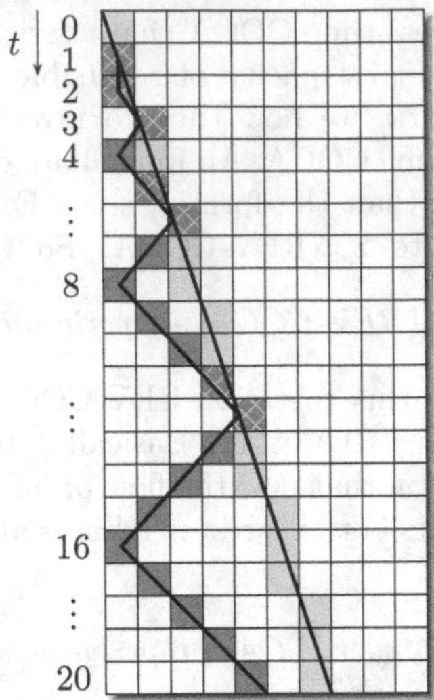

Fig. 4. Signals in a two-way cellular automaton accepting $\{ a^{2^n} \mid n \geq 0 \}$.

The principal idea for the construction showing the closure under complementation is to interchange accepting and non-accepting states. To enable this we have to make sure that the given REV-COCA accepts exactly at time step n on an input of length n and never before. This can be achieved by adding a copy S' of the state set S and by modifying the local transition function such that a state in S' is entered when an accepting state in S would have been entered. The transitions on S' are defined analogously to those of S. In this way, a cell remembers that it has entered an accepting state at some time step. Additionally, in the first time step a signal is started in the rightmost cell which moves with maximum speed to the left and makes any cell in some state from S' accepting. In this way acceptance in cell 1 at time n is ensured and accepting and non-accepting states can be interchanged. To guarantee the reversibility, we must be able to restore the time step in which cell 1 enters a state from S' for the first time. To this end, a signal Z is started in the next time step in cell 0 initially marked with #. This signal is shifted to the right part of the input by the circular structure of the automaton. Since only one such signal is started, we obtain the reversibility of the construction. A schematic example computation can be found in Fig. 5. □

5 Decidability Questions

To show undecidability results for real-time REV-COCA we reduce the problems for deterministic one-tape one-head Turing machines whose space is limited by the length of the input, so-called linear bounded automata. It is well known that, for example, emptiness, finiteness, equivalence, regularity, and context-freeness is undecidable for such devices (see, for example, [6]).

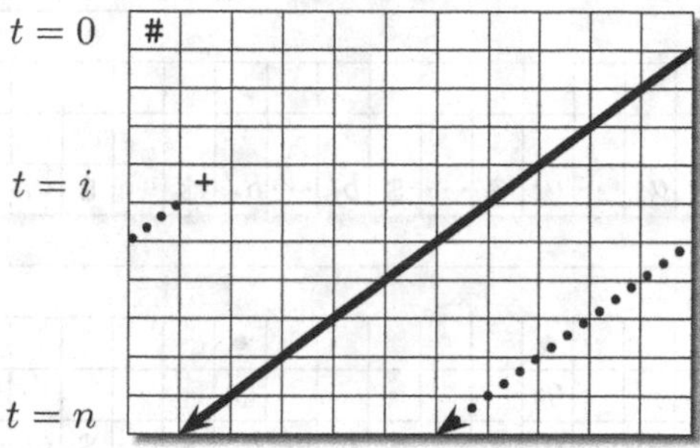

Fig. 5. Schematic construction of the signals used in the proof of closure under complementation. Cell 1 enters a state of S' at time step i for the first time. Signal Z is started at time step $i+1$ in cell 0 and is depicted by a dotted arrow. The solid arrow is the signal which arrives at real time in cell 1.

Theorem 9. *Emptiness is undecidable for real-time REV-COCA.*

Proof. Let T be an arbitrary deterministic linear bounded automaton. In [16] it has been shown that there is an equivalent reversible linear bounded automaton T'. Since T' works on limited space, we may assume that it is always halting. Moreover, by maintaining a counter as mentioned in [16], the backward computations of T' can be made always halting in the initial configuration. Next, T' can be modified to T'' without affecting the reversibility so that it starts with the head on the rightmost tape square and halts (in forward computations) and accepts only if the head is on the leftmost tape square.

Let Q denote the state set, q_0 the initial state, and I the input alphabet of T''. From T'' a new *reversible* linear bounded automaton $\hat{T}$ is constructed as follows. In a first phase, $\hat{T}$ simulates T'' from an initial configuration to a halting configuration. For a second phase a copy Q_b of the state set is used. After halting, $\hat{T}$ enters the copy of its current state. Now the states from Q_b are used to simulate the backward computation of T'' until the initial configuration (with the copy of the initial state) is reached and the backward computation halts.

Next we construct a REV-COCA $M = \langle S, F, A, \#, \delta \rangle$ that, to some extent, simulates $\hat{T}$ as follows. The input alphabet A is $I \cup \{\$\}$, where $ is a new symbol. Basically, M uses three tracks. The input is provided on the third track, while the first and second one are initially empty.

The purpose of the third track is to simulate the tape of $\hat{T}$. The second track is used to store the current state of $\hat{T}$, and the first track is used to mark cells. Initially, every cell with an input symbol from I whose right neighbor carries either $ or # marks itself on the first track. In addition, it writes the initial state of $\hat{T}$ on its second track. See Fig. 6 for an example of the initial and first configuration.

Next, the simulation of $\hat{T}$ starts, where the simulation of one step of $\hat{T}$ takes two steps of M. To this end, the content of the third track is circularly shifted to the left at every other time step. Figure 7 shows how the transitions of $\hat{T}$ are simulated.

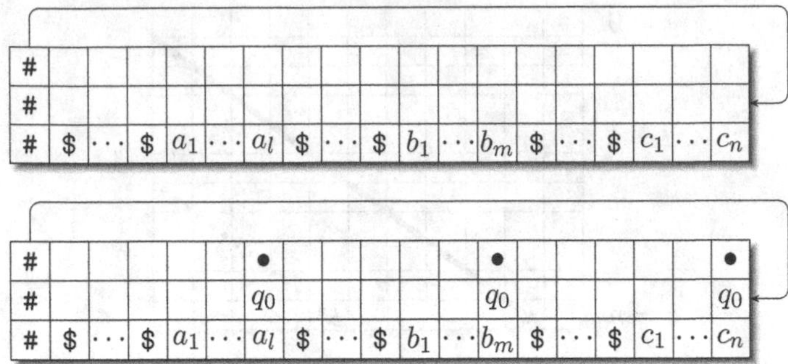

Fig. 6. Initial (top) and first (bottom) configuration of the REV-COCA M in the proof of Theorem 9.

When the simulation of $\hat{T}$ halts, that is, apart from the copy of its initial state, $\hat{T}$ is in its initial configuration again, the marked cells delete their mark and the state on their second track. The effect is that the original input is restored though cyclically shifted. Therefore, the whole simulation process repeats. Clearly, M is reversible since $\hat{T}$ is.

It remains to be explained how an input is accepted. To this end, M is extended by another, initially empty track that does not affect the behavior on the other tracks. In the first time step the rightmost cell initiates a signal on that track that moves to the left and simulates a deterministic finite automaton A. On its way the state history is stored so that the whole process is again reversible. Automaton A checks the structure of the input that has to be of the form $\$^+I^+\$^+$. Moreover, A enters an accepting state if and only if the structure is correct, and exactly at the moment it arrives in a cell the forward simulation of $\hat{T}$ halts accepting. The accepting states of M are now defined to be those states with an accepting state of A on the additional track.

Assume that $\hat{T}$ and, thus, the given linear bounded automaton T accepts an input. Then there exist appropriated numbers of \$ to the left and to the right of the input so that M accepts as well. On the other hand, if $\hat{T}$ does not accept any input, also M does not accept any input. So, if emptiness would be decidable for real-time REV-COCA it would be decidable for linear bounded automata, a contradiction. □

The reduction in the proof of the previous theorem shows even more:

Theorem 10. *(In)finiteness is undecidable for real-time REV-COCA.*

Proof. If the real-time REV-COCA in the proof of Theorem 9 accepts, the numbers of \$ to the left and to the right of the input over I is not unique. The simulation of $\hat{T}$ can go through further rounds. By adjusting the number of \$ appropriately, we can find further inputs accepted by M without changing the input over I. Therefore, $L(M)$ is finite if and only if $L(T)$ is empty. This implies that neither finiteness nor infiniteness is decidable. □

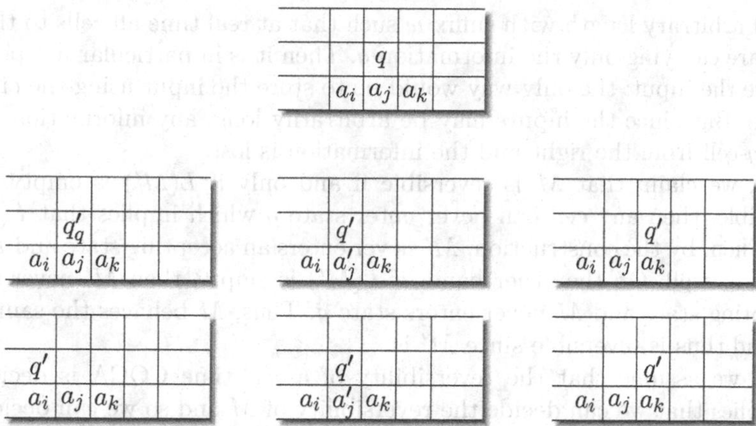

Fig. 7. Simulation of transitions of the linear bounded automaton. The initial situation is depicted at the top row. The two subconfigurations of the left column show the simulation of a left move, that is, (q, a_j) is mapped to (q', left). Here the intermediate state q'_q is used to indicate the following left move of the state. The two subconfigurations of the center column show the simulation of a stay/write move, that is, (q, a_j) is mapped to (q', a'_j), and the two subconfigurations of the right column show the simulation of a right move, that is, (q, a_j) is mapped to (q', right). The part of the state controlling the shift at *every other* step is omitted.

Theorem 11. *Equivalence and, thus, inclusion are undecidable for real-time REV-COCA.*

Proof. A COCA that simply does nothing is trivially reversible and accepts the empty language if the set of accepting states is empty. So, if equivalence would be decidable, emptiness would be decidable as well.

Two COCA M_1 and M_2 are equivalent if and only if $L(M_1) \subseteq L(M_2)$ and $L(M_2) \subseteq L(M_2)$. So, the decidability of inclusion would imply the decidability of equivalence. □

Theorem 12. *Let M be a real-time COCA. It is undecidable whether or not M is real-time reversible.*

Proof. Let M' be a real-time REV-COCA and F its set of accepting states. We modify M' to a real-time COCA M in such a way that we first add a new state g to the state set. Second, $\{g\}$ is defined to be the set of accepting states of M. Finally, the transition function is modified such that every cell in M enters state g whenever the cell would enter some state from the set F. Additionally, every cell in state g stays for the rest of the computation in this state and propagates state g with maximum speed to the left. We claim that the computation becomes irreversible whenever g is entered at least once. Let cell i enter state g at time step t on input w. Then, the behavior of state g destroys for the remaining time any information stored in cells $1, 2, \ldots, i$. Since the information flow in M is from right to left only, there are infinitely many inputs of arbitrary length with suffix w such that at real time all cells to the left of cell i are carrying only the information g. Then it is in particular not possible to restore the input: the only way would be to store the input using the circular structure. But since the inputs may be arbitrarily long, any information would reach a g-cell from the right and the information is lost.

Next, we claim that M is reversible if and only if $L(M')$ is empty. If M is reversible, then any cell can never enter state g which implies that $L(M)$ is empty. Then, by the construction, M' never enters an accepting state and $L(M')$ is empty as well. On the other hand, if $L(M')$ is empty, then M' never enters an accepting state and M never enters state g. Thus, M behaves the same way as M' and thus is reversible since M' is.

Now, we assume that the reversibility of a real-time COCA is decidable. This implies that we can decide the reversibility of M and so we can decide the emptiness of M'. This is a contradiction to Theorem 9. □

6 Conclusion

Concerning the language recognition capacity of reversible cellular automata we obtained the strict hierarchy

$$\text{REG} = \mathscr{L}_{rt}(\text{REV-OCA}) \subset \mathscr{L}_{rt}(\text{REV-COCA}) \subset \mathscr{L}_{rt}(\text{REV-CA}).$$

Nevertheless, several questions remain unanswered. Exemplarily, we mention the relation between reversible real-time COCA and general real-time OCA. Can every language from $\mathscr{L}_{rt}(\text{OCA})$ reversibly be accepted by some real-time REV-COCA? In order to approach this problem, one can investigate counters. Is there a reversible COCA that passes through k^n different configurations on inputs of length n? The languages $L_k = \{\, a^n b^{k^n} \mid n \geq 1 \,\}$ belong to the family $\mathscr{L}_{rt}(\text{OCA})$. Moreover, it is known that all linear context-free languages are accepted by real-time OCA. For example, to accept the mirror language without center marker $\{\, w \mid w \in \{a,b\}^*, w = w^R \,\}$ a real-time OCA has to treat several different positions as centers. Can this computation be done reversibly by a REV-COCA?

The relations between $\mathscr{L}_{rt}(\text{REV-COCA})$ and the family of languages accepted by reversible as well as general iterative arrays, or between the families $\mathscr{L}_{lt}(\text{REV-COCA})$ and $\mathscr{L}_{rt}(\text{REV-CA})$ are also promising fields for further investigations.

References

1. Amoroso, S., Patt, Y.N.: Decision procedures for surjectivity and injectivity of parallel maps for tesselation structures. J. Comput. System Sci. **6**, 448–464 (1972)
2. Angluin, D.: Inference of reversible languages. J. ACM **29**, 741–765 (1982)
3. Bennett, C.H.: Logical reversibility of computation. IBM J. Res. Dev. **17**, 525–532 (1973)

4. Choffrut, C., Čulik II, K.: On real-time cellular automata and trellis automata. Acta Inform. **21**, 393–407 (1984)
5. Czeizler, E., Kari, J.: A tight linear bound on the neighborhood of inverse cellular automata. In: Caires, L., Italiano, G.F., Monteiro, L., Palamidessi, C., Yung, M. (eds.) ICALP 2005. LNCS, vol. 3580, pp. 410–420. Springer, Heidelberg (2005)
6. Hopcroft, J.E., Ullman, J.D.: Introduction to Automata Theory, Languages, and Computation. Addison-Wesley, Cambridge (1979)
7. Kari, J.: Reversibility and surjectivity problems of cellular automata. J. Comput. System Sci. **48**, 149–182 (1994)
8. Kari, J.: Theory of cellular automata: a survey. Theoret. Comput. Sci. **334**, 3–33 (2005)
9. Kutrib, M.: Cellular automata - a computational point of view. In: Bel-Enguix, G., Jiménez-López, M.D., Martín-Vide, C. (eds.) New Developments in Formal Languages and Applications. Studies in Computational Intelligence, vol. 113, pp. 183–227. Springer, Heidelberg (2008)
10. Kutrib, M.: Cellular automata and language theory. In: Meyers, R.A. (ed.) Encyclopedia of Complexity and System Science, pp. 800–823. Springer, New York (2009)
11. Kutrib, M., Malcher, A.: Fast reversible language recognition using cellular automata. Inform. Comput. **206**, 1142–1151 (2008)
12. Kutrib, M., Malcher, A.: Real-time reversible iterative arrays. Theoret. Comput. Sci. **411**, 812–822 (2010)
13. Kutrib, M., Malcher, A.: Reversible pushdown automata. J. Comput. System Sci. **78**, 1814–1827 (2012)
14. Kutrib, M., Malcher, A.: One-way reversible multi-head finite automata. In: Glück, R., Yokoyama, T. (eds.) RC 2012. LNCS, vol. 7581, pp. 14–28. Springer, Heidelberg (2013)
15. Landauer, R.: Irreversibility and heat generation in the computing process. IBM J. Res. Dev. **5**, 183–191 (1961)
16. Lange, K.J., McKenzie, P., Tapp, A.: Reversible space equals deterministic space. J. Comput. System Sci. **60**, 354–367 (2000)
17. Morita, K.: Reversible computing and cellular automata - a survey. Theoret. Comput. Sci. **395**, 101–131 (2008)
18. Morita, K.: Two-way reversible multi-head finite automata. Fund. Inform. **110**, 241–254 (2011)
19. Pin, J.-C.: On reversible automata. In: Simon, I. (ed.) LATIN 1992. LNCS, vol. 583, pp. 401–416. Springer, Heidelberg (1992)
20. Umeo, H., Morita, K., Sugata, K.: Deterministic one-way simulation of two-way real-time cellular automata and its related problems. Inform. Process. Lett. **14**, 158–161 (1982)

Cycle Equivalence of Finite Dynamical Systems Containing Symmetries

Matthew Macauley[1] and Henning S. Mortveit[2(✉)]

[1] Department of Mathematical Sciences, Clemson University, Clemson, USA
macaule@clemson.edu

[2] Department of Mathematics and Network Dynamics and Simulation Science Laboratory, Virginia Tech, Blacksburg, USA
henning.mortveit@vt.edu

Abstract. Two dynamical systems are cycle equivalent if they are topologically conjugate when restricted to their periodic points. In this paper, we extend our earlier results on cycle equivalence of asynchronous finite dynamical systems (FDSs) where the dependency graph may have a non-trivial automorphism group. We give conditions for when two update sequences π, π' give cycle equivalent maps $F_\pi, F_{\pi'}$, and we give improved upper bounds for the number of distinct cycle equivalence classes that can be generated by varying the update sequence. This paper contains a brief review of necessary background results and illustrating examples, and concludes with open questions and a conjecture.

Keywords: Acyclic orientations · Finite dynamical systems · Automata networks · Sequential dynamical systems · Graph dynamical systems · Cycle equivalence · Toric poset

1 Introduction

When studying finite dynamical systems (FDSs) of the form

$$F = (F_1, F_2, \ldots, F_n)\colon K^n \longrightarrow K^n\,, \tag{1.1}$$

it is typically unrealistic to determine the entire phase space explicitly. Even a moderately small value for n and binary state space $K = \{0, 1\}$ leads to a number of states that, at best, is challenging to handle computationally. Based on this, reasoning about the dynamics of (1.1) in terms of the map structure itself can often give more insight as outlined in the following.

To the map in (1.1) one may associate its *dependency graph*. Assuming states are given as $x = (x_1, \ldots, x_n)$, the dependency graph has vertex set $\{1, 2, \ldots, n\}$, and there is a directed edge from vertex j to vertex i if $F_i\colon K^n \longrightarrow K^n$ depends non-trivially on x_j. Here, non-trivially means that there is some $x \in K^n$ such that $F(x) \neq F(x')$ where x and x' only differ in the jth coordinate. In general, this graph is directed and it may contain loops.

T. Isokawa et al. (Eds.): AUTOMATA 2014, LNCS 8996, pp. 70–82, 2015.
DOI: 10.1007/978-3-319-18812-6_6

The map F in (1.1) may also have a specific structure or may have been constructed in a specific manner. One example of this is where F has resulted through composition of maps that may only modify one of the states x_v. Specifically, we may have maps of the form $F_v \colon K^n \longrightarrow K^n$ where

$$F_v(x_1,\dots,x_n) = (x_1,\dots,x_{v-1},f_v(x_1,\dots,x_n),x_{v+1},\dots,x_n) \tag{1.2}$$

and where F is given as

$$F = F_n \circ F_{n-1} \circ \cdots \circ F_1 \,.$$

In this case the map F has been constructed by sequentially (or asynchronously) applying the maps F_i in the sequence $(1,2,\dots,n)$. In general one may consider other composition sequences such as a permutation π of the vertex set. We would like to know how the sequence π influences the dynamics of F, and we would also like to compare the dynamics resulting from two different update sequences. We will write F_π instead of F whenever we have a map assembled through composition of maps of the form F_i in (1.2) using the sequence $\pi = \pi_1\pi_2\cdots\pi_n$.

As we illustrate in the background section, many aspects of the dynamics can be analyzed directly in terms of the dependency graph or the update sequence. These are examples of structure-to-function results. Rather than using brute-force, exhaustive computations, we derive insight about the dynamics using the structural properties of the map F in (1.1).

In this paper, we demonstrate how the dependency graph allows us to reason about the long-term dynamics of the class of maps of the form F_π as defined above. These are sometimes called asynchronous automata networks [6], sequential dynamical systems [11], or asynchronous cellular automata.

Throughout, X is an undirected, loop-free graph with vertex set $V = \mathrm{v}[X]$ (usually $\{1,\dots,n\}$) and edge set $E = \mathrm{e}[X]$. For a vertex v of degree $d(v)$, we let $n[v]$ denote its 1-neighborhood, which has size $d(v)+1$. The set of permutations of V is denoted S_X. An element of S_X represents a total ordering of the vertices, which we write as $\pi = \pi_1\pi_2\cdots\pi_n$.

Each vertex v takes on a *vertex state* $x_v \in K$ where K is some finite set. The *global state* is denoted by $x = (x_v) \in K^V$, and the *v-local state* is $x[v] = (x_v) \in K^{n[v]}$. We will omit the qualifiers vertex, global and v-local when specifying states if no ambiguity can arise.

Additionally, each vertex v is assigned a *vertex function* $f_v \colon K^{n[v]} \longrightarrow K$ and an X-local function $F_v \colon K^V \longrightarrow K^V$ given by

$$F_v(x_1,\dots,x_n) = (x_1,\dots,x_{v-1},f_v(x[v]),x_{v+1}\dots,x_n) \,. \tag{1.3}$$

Here, the vertex function f_v updates the state x_v from time t to time $t+1$ locally. The reason for introducing X-local functions is that they can be composed.

A vertex function f_v is *symmetric* if any permutation of the input vector does not change the function. Common examples of symmetric functions include logical AND, OR, XOR, and their negations. A slightly weaker condition is being *outer symmetric*, which means that f_v is symmetric in the arguments corresponding to the states of the $d(v)$ neighbors of v in X. A sequence $(g_i)_{i=1}^n$ of symmetric functions, where $g_k\colon K^i \longrightarrow K$, *induces* a sequence of vertex functions $(f_v)_v$ on X by setting $f_v = g_{d(v)+1}$. Outer symmetric functions also can induce vertex functions, though slighly more care is needed in the notation.

Let $(F_v)_{v\in V}$ be a sequence of X-local functions and $\pi \in S_X$. The asynchronous finite dynamical system map $F_\pi\colon K^n \longrightarrow K^n$ is given by

$$F_\pi = F_{\pi(n)} \circ F_{\pi(n-1)} \circ \cdots \circ F_{\pi(1)} \,.$$

In other words, the map F_π is constructed by applying the vertex functions f_v in the sequence given by π. The map F_π is sometimes called a sequential dynamical system or an asynchronous automata network. If the vertex functions are induced we also say that the map F_π is induced.

A sequence of local functions $(F_v)_{v\in V}$ defines a (directed) dependency graph. However, for the questions we want to address, it is advantageous to use the undirected, simple, loop-free graph X. From the dependency graph, one may always construct the graph X by omitting loops and converting every directed edge into an undirected edge while eliminating multiple edges.

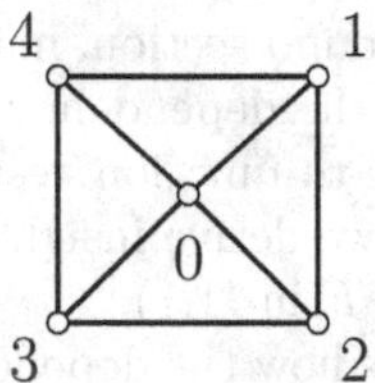

Fig. 1. The graph Wheel_4 from Example 1.

Example 1. Let $X' = \mathrm{Circ}_4$, the circle graph on 4 vertices, and let $X = \mathrm{Wheel}_4 = X' \oplus 0$ be the graph obtained form X' as the vertex join of X' and 0, as shown in Fig. 1. In this case $n[1] = (0, 1, 2, 4)$ whereas $n[0] = (0, 1, 2, 3, 4)$. We assign each vertex a state in $K = \mathbb{F}_2 = \{0, 1\}$ and let the vertex functions be induced by the logical NOR functions

$$\mathrm{nor}_m\colon K^m \longrightarrow K\,, \qquad \mathrm{nor}_m(x_1, \ldots, x_m) = \prod_{i=1}^{m} (1 + x_i)\,.$$

In other words, nor_m returns 1 if and only if all its arguments are 0. As an example, the X-local function $F_1\colon K^5 \longrightarrow K^5$ is here defined by

$$F_1(x_0, x_1, x_2, x_3, x_4) = (x_0, \mathrm{nor}_4(x[1]), x_2, x_3, x_4)\,.$$

If we use the permutation $\pi = (0, 1, 2, 3, 4)$ we get the composed map

$$F_\pi = F_4 \circ F_3 \circ F_2 \circ F_1 \circ F_0\,,$$

which in particular means that $F_\pi(0, 0, 0, 0, 0) = (1, 0, 0, 0, 0)$. If we instead use the sequence $\pi' = (1, 0, 2, 3, 4)$, we get $F_{\pi'}(0, 0, 0, 0, 0) = (0, 1, 0, 1, 0)$, illustrating the fact that the choice of sequence affects the dynamics. For comparison, note that using a parallel update scheme the state $(0, 0, 0, 0, 0)$ maps to the state $(1, 1, 1, 1, 1)$.

2 Equivalence of Maps of the Form F_π

In this section we review the notions of *functional equivalence*, *dynamical equivalence* and *cycle equivalence* along with condensed versions of the key results. These are all needed for our consideration of how symmetries of X govern results on cycle equivalence.

2.1 Functional Equivalence

Functional equivalence is simply equality of functions. Every permutation $\pi = \pi_1\pi_2\cdots\pi_n$ of the vertices of X canonically determines a partial order on X, or equivalently, an acyclic orientation O_π of X (under a slight absuse of notation, we will use both of these terms interchangeably). Specifically, orient edge $\{i, j\}$ as (i, j) if i appears before j in π. This defines a mapping

$$S_X \longrightarrow \mathrm{Acyc}(X), \qquad \pi \longmapsto O_\pi .$$

where $\mathrm{Acyc}(X)$ is the set of acyclic orientations of X. The fibers of this map define an equivalence relation $\sim_\alpha$ on S_X, and it is easily seen that $\pi \sim_\alpha \pi'$ if and only if both are linear extensions of the same $O \in \mathrm{Acyc}(X)$. Since any two linear extensions of the same finite poset differ by a sequence of transposing adjacent incomparable elements, the following result is immediate.

Proposition 1. *Let $(F_v)_{v\in V}$ be a sequence of X-local functions and $\pi, \pi' \in S_X$. If $O_\pi = O_{\pi'}$ then $F_\pi = F_{\pi'}$.*

Thus, $\alpha(X) := |\mathrm{Acyc}(X)|$ is an upper bound for the number of distinct maps F_π, where $\pi \in S_X$. For certain classes functions, such as when each vertex function is a nor-function, this bound is known to be sharp [1].

It is well-known that the quantity $\alpha(X)$ satisfies the deletion-contraction recurrence

$$\alpha(X) = \alpha(X\backslash e) + \alpha(X/e),$$

for any edge e of X. Here, $X\backslash e$ is the graph X with the edge e deleted, X/e is the graph X with e contracted. As such, $\alpha(X) = T_X(2, 0)$, where T_X is the *Tutte polynomial* of X (see [14]).

Example 2. We continue Example 1 using the graph $X = \mathrm{Wheel}_4$. The two update sequences $\pi = (0, 2, 4, 1, 3)$ and $\pi' = (0, 4, 2, 3, 1)$ give identical maps F_π and $F_{\pi'}$ since $O_\pi = O_{\pi'}$. Both acyclic orientations orient the edges of X as $(0, 1)$, $(0, 2)$, $(0, 3)$, $(0, 4)$, $(4, 1)$, $(2, 1)$, $(2, 3)$, and $(4, 3)$.

Using the deletion/contraction recursion above, one obtains $\alpha(X) = 78$. In other words, for this graph and a fixed sequence $(F_v)_v$ of X-local functions, there are at most 78 distinct composed maps of the form F_π. If all vertex functions are nor-functions, this bound is sharp, and the 78 corresponding compositions are indeed distinct.

2.2 Dynamical Equivalence

Two finite dynamical systems $\phi, \psi\colon K^n \longrightarrow K^n$ are *dynamically equivalent* (or topologically conjugate in the discrete topology) if there is a bijection $h\colon K^n \longrightarrow K^n$ such that

$$\psi \circ h = h \circ \phi\,. \tag{2.1}$$

This is equivalent to saying that the phase spaces $\Gamma(\phi)$ and $\Gamma(\psi)$ are isomorphic as directed graphs.

The automorphism group of X, denoted by $\mathrm{Aut}(X)$, acts on $\mathrm{Acyc}(X)$ by

$$O \overset{\gamma}{\longmapsto} \gamma O\,, \qquad (\gamma O)(\{v,w\}) = \gamma\big(O(\{\gamma^{-1}(v), \gamma^{-1}(w)\})\big)\,, \tag{2.2}$$

where $\gamma(v,w) = (\gamma(v), \gamma(w))$. Let $\bar{\alpha}(X)$ denote the number of orbits under this action. In [11], the bijection

$$\mathrm{Fix}(\gamma) \longrightarrow \mathrm{Acyc}(\langle\gamma\rangle \setminus X) \tag{2.3}$$

is established. Here $\langle\gamma\rangle \setminus X$ is the *orbit graph* of X and the cyclic group $\langle\gamma\rangle$. This is the multi-graph whose vertices (resp. edges) are the orbits of the action of $\langle\gamma\rangle$ on V (resp. E). An edge (orbit) connects the vertex orbits corresponding to any of its edges. Note that the orbit graph may have loops and parallel edges. The orbit graph $\langle(13)(24)\rangle \setminus \mathrm{Wheel}_4$ is illustrated in Fig. 2.

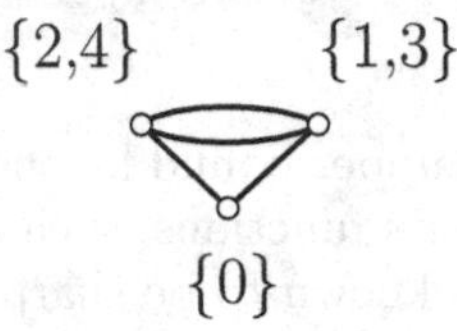

Fig. 2. The orbit graph $\langle(13)(24)\rangle \setminus \mathrm{Wheel}_4$.

Combining (2.3) with Burnside's Lemma, one obtains

$$\bar{\alpha}(X) = \frac{1}{|\mathrm{Aut}(X)|} \sum_{\gamma \in \mathrm{Aut}(X)} |\mathrm{Fix}(\gamma)| = \frac{1}{|\mathrm{Aut}(X)|} \sum_{\gamma \in \mathrm{Aut}(X)} \alpha(\langle\gamma\rangle \setminus X)\,. \tag{2.4}$$

The computation of $\bar{\alpha}(X)$ is simplified by the fact that the orbit graph often contains loops and therefore has no acyclic orientations.

Any $\sigma \in S_X$ defines a canonical mapping $\mathbb{R}^n \to \mathbb{R}^n$ by permuting the coordinates:

$$\sigma\colon (x_1, \ldots, x_n) \longmapsto (x_{\sigma^{-1}(1)}, \ldots, x_{\sigma^{-1}(n)})\,.$$

A sequence of vertex functions $(f_v)_{v\in V}$ is $\mathrm{Aut}(X)$-*invariant* if either of the following two equivalent conditions hold:

- $f_v = f_{\gamma(v)}$ for all $\gamma \in \mathrm{Aut}(X)$;
- $\gamma \circ F_v \circ \gamma^{-1} = F_{\gamma(v)}$ for every v and all $\gamma \in \mathrm{Aut}(X)$.

Note that vertex functions induced by a set of symmetric or outer-symmetric functions $(g_i)_{i=1}^n$ are always $\mathrm{Aut}(X)$-invariant.

Theorem 1. *For any sequence $(f_v)_{v\in V}$ of* $\mathrm{Aut}(X)$*-invariant vertex functions, the maps F_π and $F_{\gamma\pi}$ are dynamically equivalent, and $\bar{\alpha}(X)$ is an upper bound for the number of such maps, up to dynamical equivalence.*

We conjecture that this upper bound is sharp, but so far, this has only been shown for a few graph classes.

Example 3. We continue our running example with $X = \mathrm{Wheel}_4$, whose automorphism group is $\mathrm{Aut}(X) \cong D_4$, the symmetry group of the square:

$$\mathrm{Aut}(X) = \{\mathrm{id},\ (1234),\ (13)(24),\ (1432),\ (14)(23),\ (12)(34),\ (13),\ (24)\}. \quad (2.5)$$

Taking $\gamma = (1234)$ and $\pi = (0, 1, 2, 3, 4)$ we have $\gamma\pi = (0, 2, 3, 4, 1)$. With nor-functions at each vertex, the conditions in Theorem 1 are satisfied and we conclude that two update sequences π and $\pi' = \gamma\pi$ yield dynamically equivalent maps F_π and $F_{\pi'}$.

To determine the upper bound $\bar{\alpha}(X)$, we compute the orbits graphs $\langle\gamma\rangle \setminus X$ for $\gamma \in \mathrm{Aut}(X)$. Note that $\langle\mathrm{id}\rangle \setminus X$ is always isomorphic to X while the orbit graphs corresponding to $\gamma \in \{(1234), (1432), (13)(23), (12)(34)\}$ have loops and therefore no acyclic orientations. The orbit graphs resulting from $\gamma \in \{(13), (24)\}$ are isomorphic to the square with a diagonal which has 18 acyclic orientations. This leaves $\gamma = (13)(24)$, whose orbit graph $\langle\gamma\rangle \setminus X$ is shown in Fig. 2 which has 6 acyclic orientations. Using (2.4), we obtain

$$\bar{\alpha}(X) = \tfrac{1}{8}(78 + 0 + 6 + 0 + 0 + 0 + 18 + 18) = 15\,,$$

which implies that there are at most 15 dynamically distinct maps F_π over X arising from a fixed sequence of $\mathrm{Aut}(X)$-invariant functions.

2.3 Cycle Equivalence

Cycle equivalence is a coarsening of dynamical equivalence. In this case, we only compare the periodic points of the maps. For a discrete dynamical system $F\colon K^n \longrightarrow K^n$, let $\mathrm{Per}(F)$ denote its periodic points and let $\mathrm{Fix}(F)$ denote its fixed points. Two dynamical systems $\phi\colon K_1^n \longrightarrow K_1^n$ and $\psi\colon K_2^n \longrightarrow K_2^n$ are *cycle equivalent* if there is a bijection $h\colon \mathrm{Per}(\phi) \longrightarrow \mathrm{Per}(\psi)$ such that the equation

$$\psi \circ h = h \circ \phi$$

holds when restricted to $\mathrm{Per}(\phi)$. When K is finite, it follows that ϕ and ψ are cycle equivalent if their multi-sets of periodic orbits sizes are the same. It is clear that functional and dynamical equivalence both imply cycle equivalence.

Given an update sequence $\pi = \pi_1\pi_2\cdots\pi_n \in S_X$, define

$$\text{shift}(\pi) = \pi_2\pi_3\cdots\pi_n\pi_1\,, \qquad \text{and} \qquad \text{reverse}(\pi) = \pi_n\pi_{n-1}\cdots\pi_1\,.$$

The following theorem shows how shifts and reversals of the update sequence give rise to cycle equivalent composed maps. One of these requires the functions to be *update sequence independent*, which means that $\text{Per}(F_\pi)$, set-wise, is independent of $\pi \in S_X$. This perhaps peculiar requirement holds for 104 of the 256 elementary cellular automata rules [7]. It is needed because it ensures that F_π and $F_{\text{reverse}(\pi)}$ are inverses when restricted to their periodic points.

Theorem 2 **([9]).** *For any set $(f_v)_{v\in V}$ of vertex functions, the maps F_π and $F_{\text{shift}(\pi)}$ are cycle equivalent. Moreover, if $|K| = 2$ and $(f_i)_{i\in V}$ is update sequence independent, then F_π and $F_{\text{reverse}(\pi)}$ are cycle equivalent.*

It is easy to extend this result from update sequences that are permutations to general words over V.

On the level of acyclic orientations, transforming π into $\text{shift}(\pi)$ corresponds to converting π_1 from a source in O_π to a sink in $O_{\text{shift}(\pi)}$. Such an operation is called a *flip*, and it generates an equivalence relation on $\text{Acyc}(X)$ called *toric equivalence* and denoted by $\sim_\kappa$. The equivalence classes are called *toric posets.* The name is motivated from a bijection between the toric posets over X and the chambers of the toric graphic (hyperplane) arrangement $\mathcal{A}_{\text{tor}}(X)$ in the torus $\mathbb{R}^V/\mathbb{Z}^V$, analogous to the bijection between ordinary posets over X and the chambers of the graphic arrangement $\mathcal{A}(X)$ in $\mathbb{R}^V$ (see [4]). Similarly, transforming π into $\text{reverse}(\pi)$ corresponds to reversing each edge orientation in O_π to obtain $O_{\text{reverse}(\pi)}$ – we call this a *reversal*, and denote the equivalence relation generated by flips and reversals by $\sim_\delta$. We let $\kappa(X)$ and (resp. $\delta(X)$) denote the number of $\sim_\kappa$-equivalence (resp. $\sim_\delta$-equivalence) classes.

Let $P = v_1v_2,\ldots,v_k$ be a path in X and define the function $\nu_P\colon \text{Acyc}(X) \longrightarrow \mathbb{Z}$, where $\nu_P(O_X)$ is the number of edges oriented as (v_i, v_{i+1}) (the "forward edges"), minus the number of edges oriented as (v_{i+1}, v_i) ("backward edges"). If P is a cycle then ν_P is preserved under flips, so ν_P extends to a map $\bar{\nu}_P\colon \text{Acyc}(X)/\sim_\kappa \longrightarrow \mathbb{Z}$ on toric posets over X. Two acyclic orientations are torically equivalent if and only if $\nu_C(\omega) = \nu_C(\omega')$ for all cycles C in X. Moreover, $\omega \sim_\delta \omega''$ if and only if $\nu_C(\omega) = \pm\nu_C(\omega'')$. The δ-equivalence classes can be enumerated from the toric equivalence classes, which satisfy a deletion-contraction recurrence for any cycle edge e of X:

$$\begin{aligned} \kappa(X) &= \kappa(X\setminus e) + \kappa(X/e) = T_X(1,0)\,,\\ \delta(X) &= \lceil \kappa(X)/2 \rceil\,, \end{aligned} \tag{2.6}$$

We can now summarize our results on cycle equivalence for maps of the form F_π.

Theorem 3 **([7,9,10]).** *Let K be a finite set, let $(f_i)_{v\in V}$ be a fixed sequence of vertex functions over X. If $O_\pi \sim_\kappa O_{\pi'}$ then F_π and $F_{\pi'}$ are cycle equivalent. If $|K| = 2$ and $(f_v)_{v\in V}$ is update sequence independent, then F_π and $F_{\pi'}$ are cycle equivalent if $O_\pi \sim_\delta O_{\pi'}$.*

Theorem 3 provides an easy way to test if F_π and $F_{\pi'}$ are cycle equivalent: first choose a cycle basis for X and then evaluate ν for O_π and $O_{\pi'}$. If these are identical then the two maps are cycle equivalent. If $\nu(O_\pi) = \pm\nu(O_{\pi'})$, then the maps are also cycle equivalent, provided the functions are update sequence independent. Of course, since this is a sufficient condition, the two maps may still be cycle equivalent if this condition fails to hold.

Example 4. Returning to our running example with $X = \text{Wheel}_4$, we first see that $\kappa(X) = 14$. To see this, one can either use the deletion/contraction recursion relation (2.6) or resort to Proposition 3 (placed in the next section for the purpose of exposition) using the vertex $v = 0$. As a consequence, there are at most 14 distinct long-term behaviors for any finite dynamical system of the form F_π over X assuming fixed functions $(F_v)_{v\in V}$.

As a consequence of Proposition 3, we note that representative update sequences for these 14 classes can be obtained as follows: first direct each edge $\{0, i\}$ as $(0, i)$ where $1 \leq i \leq 4$ and then orient the remaining edges so that the graph is acyclic. There are 14 such acyclic orientations. The representative update sequences result by choosing precisely one linear extension for each of these 14 acyclic orientations.

3 Main Results

The results presented above for cycle equivalence do not consider the effects of symmetries in the graph X. Here we will complete the analysis through an extension of Theorem 1 from Sect. 2.2. As before, when considering graph symmetries, we need to assume that the vertex functions are $\text{Aut}(X)$-invariant.

For $\gamma \in \text{Aut}(X)$, linear extensions π of O and π' of γO give dynamically equivalent maps F_π and $F_{\pi'}$. In the following, we will show that $\text{Aut}(X)$ acts on $\text{Acyc}(X)/\!\sim_\kappa$ via $\gamma[O] = [\gamma O]$. From this it follows that (*i*) linear extensions of κ-classes on the same $\text{Aut}(X)$-orbit give cycle-equivalent maps, and (*ii*) the number of cycle equivalence classes is bounded above by the number $\bar{\kappa}(X)$ of orbits of the action of $\text{Aut}(X)$ on $\text{Acyc}(X)/\!\sim_\kappa$. The same statement holds for δ-classes and the corresponding number $\bar{\delta}(X)$.

To start, we first observe that if v is a source (resp. sink) in the acyclic orientation O then $\gamma(v)$ is a source (resp. sink) in γO. Assume that v is a source in O and let $c = c_v$ be the length one flip-sequence mapping O^1 to O^2. We have a commutative diagram

$$\begin{array}{ccc} O^1 & \xmapsto{\gamma} & \gamma O^1 \\ {\scriptstyle c_v}\downarrow & & \downarrow{\scriptstyle c_{\gamma(v)}} \\ O^2 & \xmapsto[\gamma]{} & \gamma O^2 \end{array} \tag{3.1}$$

which can be verified by examining what happens to each edge $\{u, w\}$.

Lemma 1. *For* $\sim \in \{\sim_\kappa, \sim_\delta\}$, *the group* $\mathrm{Aut}(X)$ *acts on* $\mathrm{Acyc}(X)/\sim$ *by* $\gamma[O] = [\gamma O]$.

Proof. By vertically concatenating diagrams of the form (3.1), we see that the mapping

$$\mathrm{Aut}(X) \times \mathrm{Acyc}(X)/\sim \longrightarrow \mathrm{Acyc}(X)/\sim, \qquad (\gamma, [O]) \longmapsto [\gamma O]$$

is well-defined. It is a group action because the group $\mathrm{Aut}(X)$ acts on $\mathrm{Acyc}(X)$ by $\gamma O = \gamma \circ O \circ \gamma^{-1}$; see for example [11].

Corollary 1. *Let* $\gamma \in \mathrm{Aut}(X)$. *For any permutation* π *with* $O_\pi \in [O]$ *and* π' *for which* $O_{\pi'} \in \gamma[O]$, *the two maps* F_π *and* $F_{\pi'}$ *are cycle equivalent.*

Since $\mathrm{Aut}(X)$ acts on $\mathrm{Acyc}(X)/\sim_\kappa$ and $\mathrm{Acyc}(X)/\sim_\delta$, we may use Burnside's Lemma to determine $\bar{\kappa}(X)$ and $\bar{\delta}(X)$.

Proposition 2. *Let* X *be a finite, undirected graph. Then*

$$\bar{\kappa}(X) = \frac{1}{|\mathrm{Aut}(X)|} \sum_{\gamma \in \mathrm{Aut}(X)} |\mathrm{Fix}(\gamma)|, \tag{3.2}$$

where $\mathrm{Fix}(\gamma) = \{[O] \mid \gamma[O] = [O]\}$.

In this form it is, however, not easy to determine $|\mathrm{Fix}(\gamma)|$. It would be desirable to develop a result analogous to the orbit graph correspondence that what we have when $\mathrm{Aut}(X)$ acts on $\mathrm{Acyc}(X)$ as in (2.4). The following results provide parts of this [3,8].

Proposition 3. *For any fixed vertex* v *of* X, *the set* $\mathrm{Acyc}_v(X) \subset \mathrm{Acyc}(X)$ *consisting of all acyclic orientations where* v *is the unique source, is a complete set of toric equivalence class representatives.*

For determining $\mathrm{Fix}(\gamma)$, this proposition has an immediate consequence if γ fixes a vertex.

Corollary 2. *Let* $\phi_v\colon \mathrm{Acyc}(X)/\sim_\kappa \longrightarrow \mathrm{Acyc}_v(X)$ *be the map that assigns to* $[O]$ *its unique element in* $\mathrm{Acyc}_v(X)$. *If* $\gamma \in \mathrm{Aut}(X)$ *fixes the vertex* $v \in V$ *then* $[O] \in \mathrm{Fix}(\gamma)$ *if and only if* $\gamma\phi_v([O]) = \phi_v([O])$.

Proof. For any $v \in V$ the automorphic image of an element of $\mathrm{Acyc}_v(X)$ is also an element of $\mathrm{Acyc}_v(X)$. If γ fixes v then it follows that γ fixes $[O]$ if and only if γ fixes $\phi_v([O])$.

It follows that in this case one can derive a result analogous to the orbit graph enumeration in (2.4), however, in this case one must take care to only consider those acyclic orientations where v is the unique source.

The fact that the ν-function is a complete invariant for toric equivalence offers an alternative approach:

Proposition 4. *Let X be a graph, let $v \in \mathrm{v}[X]$ and let $\mathcal{C}$ be a cycle basis for X. Then*

$$\bar{\kappa}(X) = \frac{1}{|\mathrm{Acyc}(X)|} \sum_{\gamma \in \mathrm{Aut}(X)} N(\gamma)$$

where $N(\gamma) = |\{O \in \mathrm{Acyc}_v(X) \mid \nu_{\mathcal{C}}(O) = \nu_{\mathcal{C}}(\gamma O)\}|$.

Proof. This follows from the fact that ν evaluated on any cycle-basis is a complete invariant for toric equivalence [12].

The following examples illustrates how Proposition 4 can be used to determine $\bar{\kappa}(X)$ as well as $\bar{\delta}(X)$. We also include the other graph measures mentioned above.

Example 5. As a specific example, take X to be the double square graph as illustrated in Fig. 3. Here

$$\mathrm{Aut}(X) = \{\mathrm{id}, \tau = (1,6)(2,5)(3,4), \sigma = (1,3)(4,6), \sigma\tau = (1,4)(2,5)(3,6)\}, \tag{3.3}$$

leading to $\alpha(X) = 98$, $\bar{\alpha}(X) = 28$, $\kappa(X) = 9$ and $\delta(X) = 5$. Nine torically non-equivalent elements in $\mathrm{Acyc}_2(X)$ are shown in Fig. 4. The letters in

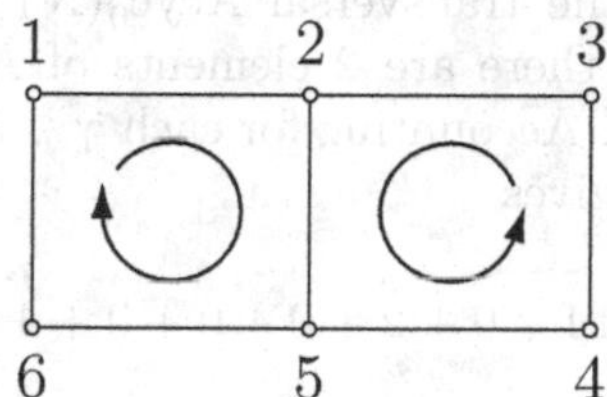

Fig. 3. The graph of Example 5 with orientations for the fundamental cycles of the cycle basis.

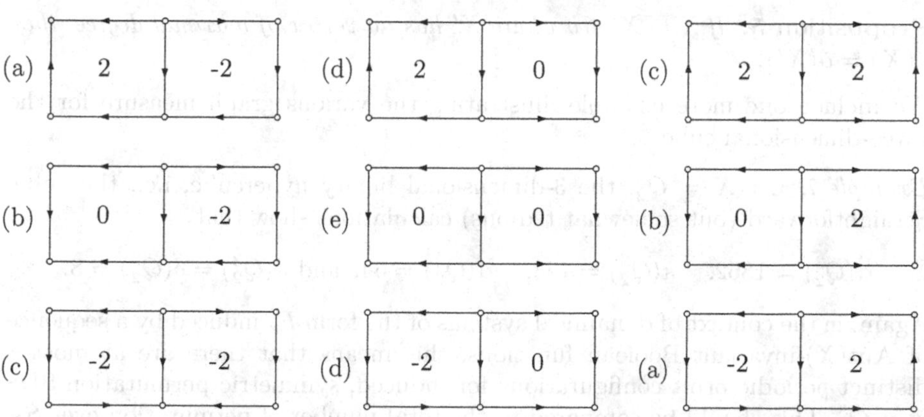

Fig. 4. The transversal $\mathrm{Acyc}_2(X)$ for κ-equivalence of the graph in Example 5.

parentheses on the left show five δ-class representatives. The ν-values are indicated inside each fundamental cycle of the chosen cycle basis.

Let (ν_1, ν_2) denote the value of ν on O. Then $\nu(\tau O) = (-\nu_1, -\nu_2)$, $\nu(\sigma O) = (\nu_2, \nu_1)$, and $\nu(\tau\sigma O) = (-\nu_2, -\nu_1)$. From this we conclude that $N(\mathrm{id}) = 9$, $N(\tau) = 1$, $N(\sigma) = 3$ and $N(\tau\sigma) = 3$. As a result we have $\bar{\kappa}(X) = (9+1+3+3)/4 = 4$.

In the same manner we obtain $\bar{\delta}(X) = 4$. Specifically, we have $|\mathrm{Fix}(\mathrm{id})| = 5$, $|\mathrm{Fix}(\tau)| = 5$, and $|\mathrm{Fix}(\sigma)| = 3$, $|\mathrm{Fix}(\tau\sigma)| = 3$, leading to $\bar{\delta}(X) = (5+5+3+3)/4 = 4$.

Corollary 3. *Let X be the graph in Example 5. Then there are at most four cycle classes for maps of the form* Nor_π *(each vertex function is a* nor*-function) where $\pi \in S_X$.*

This follows directly since nor-functions are symmetric and Boolean. There are $6! = 720$ possible permutation update sequences for this graph. However, for this class of functions, there are at most four distinct long-term behaviors. In our opinion, this is a remarkable result.

Example 6. For the running example with $X = \mathrm{Wheel}_4$ we can use Corollary 2 to take advantage of the fact that this graph is the vertex join of 0 and Circ_4 and that 0 has maximal degree. To determine $\mathrm{Fix}(\gamma)$ in $\mathrm{Acyc}(X)/{\sim_\kappa}$, we can now simply reason about the transversal $\mathrm{Acyc}_0(X)$ and use the orbit graph construction. For example, there are 2 elements of $\mathrm{Acyc}_0(X)$ fixed under the automorphism $\gamma = (13)(24)$. Accounting for each $\gamma \in \mathrm{Aut}(X)$ using the order in which they appear in (2.5) gives

$$\bar{\kappa}(X) = \frac{1}{8}(14+0+2+0+0+0+4+4) = 3$$

which equals $\bar{\kappa}(\mathrm{Circ}_4)$.

The fact that $\bar{\kappa}(\mathrm{Circ}_4 \oplus 0) = \bar{\alpha}(\mathrm{Circ}_4)$ clearly generalizes. We state this without proof:

Proposition 5. *If $X = X' \oplus v$ where X' has no vertex of maximal degree, then $\bar{\kappa}(X) = \bar{\alpha}(X')$.*

We include one more example illustrating the various graph measure for the three-dimensional cube.

Example 7. Let $X = Q_2^3$, the 3-dimensional binary hypercube, i.e., the cube. Straightforward (but somewhat tedious) calculations show that

$$\alpha(Q_2^3) = 1862, \quad \kappa(Q_2^3) = 133, \quad \bar{\alpha}(Q_2^3) = 54, \text{ and } \bar{\kappa}(Q_2^3) = \bar{\delta}(Q_2^3) = 8.$$

Again, in the context of dynamical systems of the form F_π induced by a sequence of $\mathrm{Aut}(X)$-invariant Boolean functions, this means that there are at most 8 distinct periodic orbit configurations for induced, symmetric permutation SDS over Q_2^3. This should be compared to the total number of permutation over S_X which is $8! = 40320$.

4 Summary

In this paper, we extended results on cycle equivalence for finite dynamical systems of the form F_π. The results provide a sufficient condition for determining when F_π and $F_{\pi'}$ are cycle equivalent when taking into account the symmetries of the graph. The restriction that the vertex functions be $\mathrm{Aut}(X)$-invariant functions is not as artificial as it may seem – it includes all symmetric and outer-symmetric functions, which are very common in practice. We also derived a bound for the number cycle-equivalence classes for such maps F_π. As for the measures $\alpha(X)$, $\bar{\alpha}(X)$, $\kappa(X)$ and $\delta(X)$, the conditions and enumerations do not depend on the particular choice of functions – they are graph measures. This means that we can reason about dynamics of maps F_π using only the graph structure. It is another example of mapping structure to dynamics rather than performing brute-force phase space computations.

The structures we have covered above are relevant to other areas beyond asynchronous finite dynamical systems. One example is in the study of Coxeter groups and their Coxeter elements [2]. Let $(W, S = \{s_1, \ldots, s_n\})$ be a Coxeter system with (unlabeled) Coxeter graph X. It is well-known that there is a bijection between $\mathrm{Acyc}(X)$ and the set of Coxeter elements $C(W) = \{c_{\pi(n)} \cdots c_{\pi(1)} \mid \pi \in S_X\}$. Moreover, $O \sim_\kappa O'$ if and only if the corresponding Coxeter elements are conjugate [5,8]. It follows that $\alpha(X) = T_X(2,0)$ and $\kappa(X) = T_X(1,0)$ enumerate the number of Coxeter elements and their conjugacy classes. Moreover, it can be shown that $\bar{\kappa}(X)$ is an upper bound for the number of *spectral class* of Coxeter elements, see for example [13]. We are not aware of any significance for $\bar{\delta}(X)$ in the context of Coxeter groups.

We close with two questions and a conjecture that we invite the reader to explore further:

Question 1. Is it possible to compute $\bar{\delta}(X)$ from $\bar{\kappa}(X)$ in a manner similar to that of $\delta(X) = \lceil \kappa(X)/2 \rceil$? For which graphs are $\bar{\delta}(X)$ and $\bar{\kappa}(X)$ the same?

Question 2. Is there a simpler way to determine $\bar{\kappa}$ than the one in Proposition 4? Is there a result involving $\nu_C(\mathrm{Acyc}_v(X))$ analogous to (2.4) with orbit graphs?

Conjecture 1. The bounds $\bar{\kappa}(X)$ and $\bar{\delta}(X)$ are sharp. In other words, for any graph X, there is a function sequence $(F_v)_{v \in V}$ such the that the number of cycle classes of the maps F_π equals $\bar{\kappa}(X)$ (resp. $\bar{\delta}(X)$).

Acknowledgments. We thank our collaborators and members of the Network Dynamics and Simulation Science Laboratory (NDSSL) for discussions, suggestions and comments. This work has been partially supported by DTRA R&D Grant HDTRA1-09-1-0017, DTRA Grant HDTRA1-11-1-0016, DTRA CNIMS Contract HDTRA1-11-D-0016-0001, DOE Grant DE-SC0003957, and NSF grant DMS-1211691.

References

1. Barrett, C.L., Mortveit, H.S., Reidys, C.M.: Elements of a theory of simulation III: Equivalence of SDS. Appl. Math. Comput. **122**, 325–340 (2001)

2. Björner, A., Brenti, F.: Combinatorics of Coxeter Groups. Springer-Verlag, New York (2005)
3. Chen, B.: Orientations, lattice polytopes, and group arrangements I, chromatic and tension polynomials of graphs. Ann. Comb. **13**(4), 425–452 (2010)
4. Develin, M., Macauley, M., Reiner, V.: Toric partial orders. Trans. Amer. Math. Soc. (2014) (to appear)
5. Eriksson, H., Eriksson, K.: Conjugacy of coxeter elements. Electron. J. Combin. **16**(2), R4 (2009)
6. Goles, E., Martínez., S.: Neural and Automata Networks: Dynamical Behavior and Applications. Mathematics and its Applications, vol. 58. Kluwer Academic, Dordrecht (1990)
7. Macauley, M., McCammond, J., Mortveit, H.S.: Order independence in asynchronous cellular automata. J. Cell. Autom. **3**(1), 37–56 (2008)
8. Macauley, M., Mortveit, H.S.: On enumeration of conjugacy classes of Coxeter elements. Proc. Amer. Math. Soc. **136**(12), 4157–4165 (2008)
9. Macauley, M., Mortveit, H.S.: Cycle equivalence of graph dynamical systems. Nonlinearity **22**, 421–436 (2009)
10. Macauley, M., Mortveit, H.S.: Posets from admissible Coxeter sequences. Electron. J. Combin. **18**(1), #R197 (2011)
11. Mortveit, H.S., Reidys, C.M.: An introduction to sequential dynamical systems. Universitext, Springer, New York (2007)
12. Pretzel, O.: On reorienting graphs by pushing down maximal vertices. Order **3**(2), 135–153 (1986)
13. Shi, J.-Y.: Conjugacy relation on Coxeter elements. Adv. Math. **161**, 1–19 (2001)
14. Tutte, W.T.: A contribution to the theory of chromatic polynomials. Canad. J. Math. **6**, 80–91 (1954)

Generalized FSSP on Hexagonal Tiling: Towards Arbitrary Regular Spaces

Luidnel Maignan[1] and Jean-Baptiste Yunès[2](✉)

[1] LACL, Université Paris-Est-Créteil, Créteil, France
Luidnel.Maignan@u-pec.fr

[2] LIAFA, Université Paris-Diderot, Paris, France
Jean-Baptiste.Yunes@univ-paris-diderot.fr

Abstract. Here we present a solution to the generalized firing squad synchronization problem that works on some class of shapes in the hexagonal tiling of the plane. The solution is obtained from a previous solution which works on grids with either a von Neumann or a Moore neighborhood. Analyzing the construction of this previous solution, we were able to exhibit a parameter that leads us to abstract the solution. First, and for an arbitrary considered neighborhood, we focus our attention on a class of shapes built from this neighborhood, and determine the corresponding parameter value for them. Second, we apply our previous solution with the determined parameter value for the hexagonal neighborhood and show that, indeed, all the considered shapes on the hexagonal tiling synchronizes.

1 Introduction

The Firing Squad Synchronization Problem (FSSP for short) is a very old problem. It has been reported for the first time in 1957 by John Myhill (see [7]). The goal is to design a cellular automaton (CA for short) such that starting from a initial configuration where every cell is inactive except one cell, called the general or the initiator, the dynamics leads to an uniform configuration where all cells are in the same (firing) state that has never been reached before.

There is a lot of solutions to that problem, each focused on some variation of it. One may want to synchronize lines, rectangles (see [2,3]), parallelepipeds (see [14,15,17]), graphs (see [11]), Cayley graphs (see [10]); another may want to be able to start the process at a given special position, at any position (see [8]), start the process at many different places at the same time or not (see [12]), etc. Some others focused their attention on lowering the synchronization time, the set of states (see [1,6,9,13]), or the communication capabilities of cells. Actually, there are probably more than 150 papers on the subject.

But all in all, almost all solutions are recursive as the simple basic idea is to recursively split the space into equals parts, until elementary sub-spaces are obtained that are obvious to synchronize. Most of the solutions split the space into two equals parts (for a more complex scheme see [6]).

This work is partially supported by the French program ANR 12 BS02 007 01.

T. Isokawa et al. (Eds.): AUTOMATA 2014, LNCS 8996, pp. 83–96, 2015.
DOI: 10.1007/978-3-319-18812-6_7

In a previous paper [4], by the use of so-called distance fields we gave a very general scheme that captures the core of many unidimensional solutions. A distance field is an open cellular automaton which ultimately computes on each point of the space its distances to some given set of reference points. We believe that it is a nice way to understand what is behind the scene in many solutions. Although most of them are constructed in an *ad-hoc* way, it seems clear that some distance information, and therefore distance fields, are implicitly used to determine their splitting points.

In [4], we took an explicit approach to build the unidimensional solution. We use distance fields to detect middles as required to split the space into half-spaces, and we compose as many instances of this splitting process as required to split half-spaces into quarter-spaces and so on recursively. Then a reduction to a finite number of states is described that leads to a classical finite cellular automaton. This two-steps approach allows the solution to be correct by construction, the infinities allowing to be abstract, more semantic and clearer. A description with a finite number of states usually leads to less obvious semantics and dynamics of the transition function, especially when minimal synchronization time is aimed.

In [5], we proposed a generalization of this unidimensional solution to handle more different spaces within a single scheme. It was parametrized by some information extracted from the given neighborhood. We showed that it works on the classical and less classical space shapes either with the Moore or the von Neumann neighborhood. We now want to show how all of this can be applied as-is on more general spaces. We tested our construction on various space shapes with an hexagonal neighborhood.

Hexagonal cellular spaces are of special interest because there is no known solution to the generalized FSSP on them up to now. Researchers focused on 1D lines, 2D/3D square grids, some on more general graphs but, to the best of our knowledge, not on hexagonal tilings with arbitrary position of the initiator, or at least not on various shapes on the hexagonal tilings.

In Sect. 2, we give the reader the necessary background on the previous works. The paper is written to ease a global understanding of the key concepts, questions, and answers without having to dig too much in the details of the transition function and the previous results. That section mainly focuses on the parameter of the scheme which allowed to switch from 1D to the various 2D cellular spaces considered in previous works. At that time, some of the values of this parameter were determined in an *ad-hoc* way.

The purpose of Sect. 3 is to extend the work by proposing a procedure to determine the possible values for the parameter. This will also helps to identify a class of synchronizable shapes thus generalizing the set of shapes previously considered.

In Sects. 4 and 5 we proceed with some arguments and experimental results to show and explain how the synchronization is achieved.

In Sect. 7, we finally summarize the paper and discuss interesting future directions of work.

2 Summary of Previous Solutions

As already explained, this work is based on two previous works. The first one [4] gives a very general solution for the 1D FSSP. The second one [5] extends this solution to various 2D space shapes on the Moore and the von Neumann neighborhood.

In this section, we do not give all the details of the internals of the CA as they are not relevant here. Instead, we only introduce the leading concepts of interest for the remaining. The reader is therefore referred to the cited papers for more details.

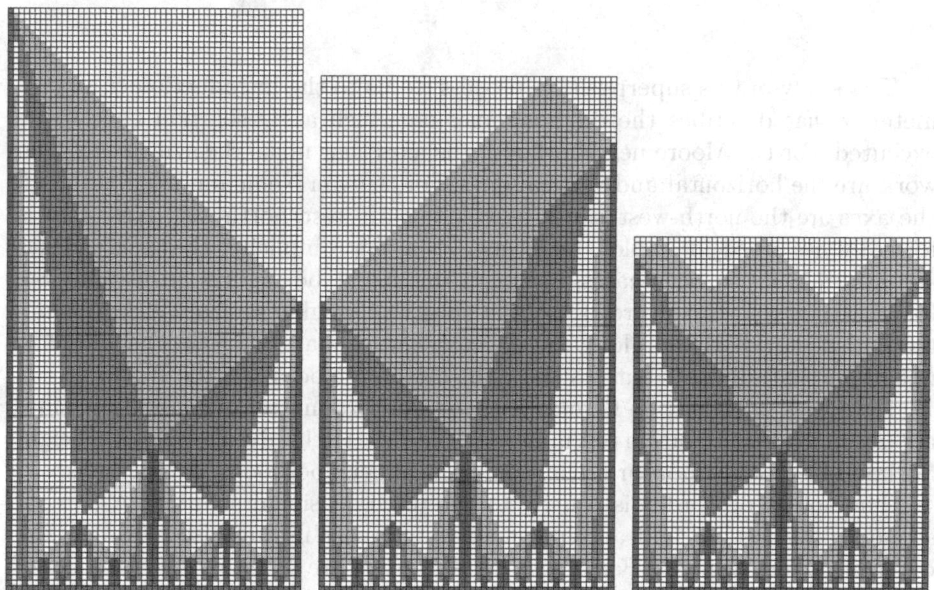

Fig. 1. Evolutions of our 1D algorithm with different sets of generals. The reader must be aware that this does not show the states of the CA but only some "interesting" information extracted from.

Our unidimensional solution was designed from the simple key idea that middles of a space are characterized by their distance to the borders of the space, and that many layers of middles detection have to be stacked to obtain the recursive computation of the synchronization. Figure 1 provides a summarized view of the stack of layers for different sets of initiators, and the space-time diagrams looks a lot like many other optimal time solutions. This is exactly why we claim that our solution captures many classical solutions.

In order to generalize this solution to the case of the classical rectangle, the starting idea was to split this rectangle into four quarter-rectangles and so on recursively. This can be easily achieved by superposing two unidimensional splitting processes: one along the horizontal axis and another one along the vertical axis.

Table 1. Values of parameter ν used for borders

Moore	von Neumann
X-axis	X-axis
$\nu_X^{-1} = \left\{\binom{-1}{-1}, \binom{-1}{0}, \binom{-1}{+1}\right\}$	$\nu_X^{-1} = \left\{\binom{-1}{0}, \binom{0}{+1}\right\}$
$\nu_X^{+1} = \left\{\binom{+1}{-1}, \binom{+1}{0}, \binom{+1}{+1}\right\}$	$\nu_X^{+1} = \left\{\binom{+1}{0}, \binom{0}{-1}\right\}$
Y-axis	Y-axis
$\nu_Y^{-1} = \left\{\binom{-1}{-1}, \binom{0}{-1}, \binom{+1}{-1}\right\}$	$\nu_Y^{-1} = \left\{\binom{-1}{0}, \binom{0}{-1}\right\}$
$\nu_Y^{+1} = \left\{\binom{-1}{+1}, \binom{0}{+1}, \binom{+1}{+1}\right\}$	$\nu_Y^{+1} = \left\{\binom{+1}{0}, \binom{0}{+1}\right\}$

The study of this superposition process led us to the introduction of a parameter ν that describes the different axes on which a 1D solution have to be executed. For the Moore neighborhood, the axes that make the synchronization work are the horizontal and vertical ones. For the von Neumann neighborhood, the axes are the north-west/south-east and south-west/north-east axes. This is formally described in Table 1 in terms of ν's. For simplicity, the axes indexes are $D = \{X, Y\}$ in both cases, although this might be slightly misleading. So, for example, ν_X^{-1} can be read as "the subset of neighbors that all contribute to the left-neighborhood along the X axis" and similarly ν_Y^{+1} as "the subset of neighbors that all contribute to the right-neighborhood along the Y axis".

Here "left", "right", "-1" and "$+1$" are purely a matter of convention, since the unidimensional solution is symmetric. The ν's map the given topological neighborhood into many appropriate unidimensional neighborhoods, one per axis.

The notion of border is centric to the unidimensional solution. As a consequence we need to find an equivalent counterpart in our cases. Borders are determined for each axis. For any axis $d \in D$, they are determined by the use of the following predicate excerpted from the solution described in [5]:

$$\text{border}_{t+1}^{0,d}(c) = \text{input}_{t+1}(c) \wedge \exists i \in \text{I};\ \forall \delta \in \nu_d^i;\ c + \delta \notin \text{S} \tag{1}$$

This equation defines the borders of the space S along the axis d and at time $t+1$ as the cells c that are activated ($\text{input}_{t+1}(c)$) and have no neighbors in at least one direction $i \in I = \{-1, +1\}$ along the axis, *i.e.* no neighbors "on the left", or no neighbors "on the right".

With these definitions of axes and borders, we showed that the solution synchronizes what we called *rectangles* and *diamonds* for any location of the initiator. These spaces are illustrated in Fig. 2. For a given neighborhood, the rectangle has border cells for one or the other axis all along the boundary of the space while the diamond only have isolated border cells according to Eq. (1).

In [5], the values of the ν's for the Moore and von Neumann neighborhoods were obtained in two distinct ways. Now we will show that a common procedure allows to consider more complex shapes, and in particular hexagonal spaces.

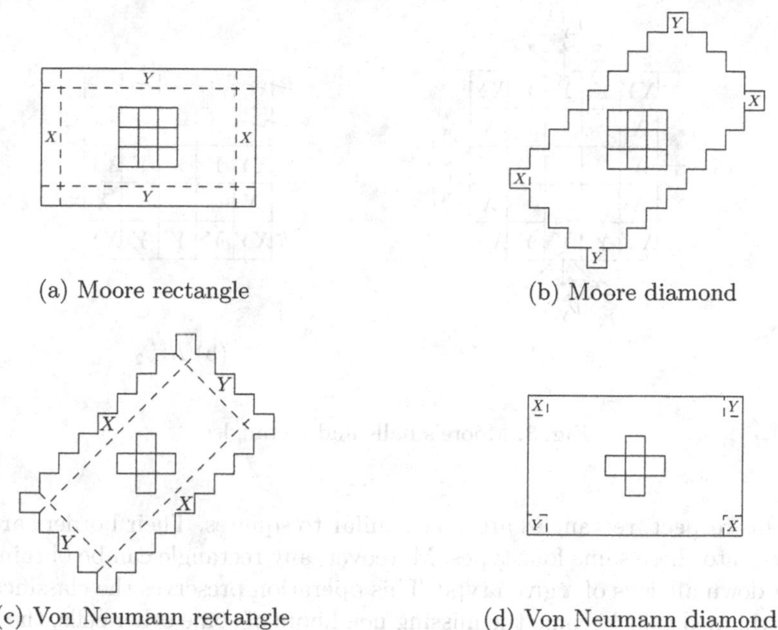

(a) Moore rectangle (b) Moore diamond

(c) Von Neumann rectangle (d) Von Neumann diamond

Fig. 2. Synchronized shapes and their respective borders

3 Determination of the Axes, Borders and Shapes

In the literature, people are usually interested in the synchronization of classical rectangles like Fig. 2a and d. It can be argued that the most natural neighborhood to consider first on a rectangle is the Moore neighborhood as the Moore rectangle exactly corresponds to what one probably think at first about a classical rectangle is (Fig. 2a). So let us describe our general procedure by examining this case first.

3.1 The Moore Case

With the Moore neighborhood a rectangle can easily be considered as a generalization of a square. A square of side length $2r$ is simply a Moore ball B_r^M of radius r. Note that in this paper, all lengths are given in number of hops which corresponds to a distance, and not in terms of numbers of cells which would add many annoying "+1" in the expressions. By observing what characterizes the borders of a Moore's ball, we can obtain the values of the parameter ν and make explicit the relation with the rectangle as illustrated in Fig. 3b.

On a Moore's ball, one can identify four kinds of border cells. These types are characterized by the set of their missing neighbors. These sets can be paired by symmetry and this pairing naturally corresponds to the concept of axis. Here there are two axes X and Y, each of them having two symmetric sets ν_d^{-1}, ν_d^{+1} for $d \in D = \{X, Y\}$.

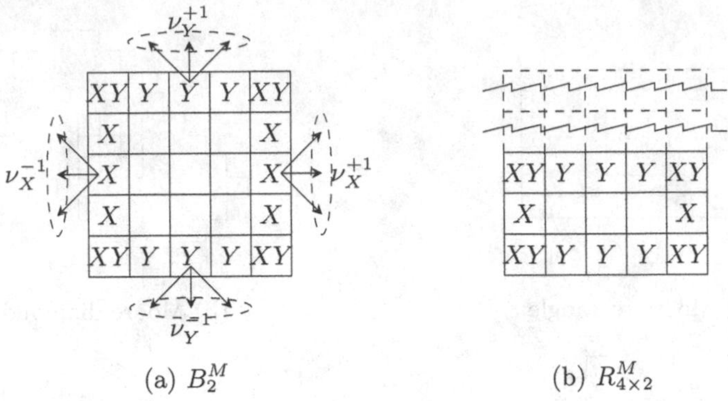

(a) B_2^M (b) $R_{4\times 2}^M$

Fig. 3. Moore's balls and rectangles

In this respect, rectangles are very similar to squares. Their borders are also classified into these same four types. Moreover, any rectangle can be obtained by cutting down all cells of a given type. This operation preserves the classification, as the trimmed cells become the missing neighbors of some other cells, the laters becoming the new border cells of the considered type. This is illustrated in Fig. 3b where a rectangle $R_{4\times 2}^M$ is obtained by two removals of border cells of type ν_Y^{+1} from the ball B_2^M. Let us make two important observations.

First, the borders of squares are parallel by construction and so are the borders of rectangles since the cutting down operation obviously preserves this property.

Second, the sets ν_D^I thus constructed correspond exactly to the values presented in Table 1 and that allowed the synchronization.

Although, these constructions and properties seem to be obvious in the Moore case, things are slightly subtler in the following cases.

3.2 The von Neumann Case

With the von Neumann topology, one can apply exactly the same process: take a ball, identify the sets of missing neighbors, pair them by symmetry, characterize the axes, and cut down some borders. As for the Moore case, the resulting sets of missing neighbors correspond to the values of Table 1. The construction is illustrated in Fig. 4 where a rectangle $R_{3\times 6}^V$ is obtained by three removals of borders of type ν_X^{-1} from a ball B_3^V. However, if instead of removing border of type ν_X^{-1}, we choose to do three removals of border of type ν_X^{+1}, we obtain a different but symmetric instance of a rectangle $R_{3\times 6}^V$. It might seem completely different from the Moore case but it is in fact very similar if we restrict our attention to the lengths: balls B_r^V are rectangles $R_{2r\times 2r}^V$, so cutting down an X (resp. Y) border reduces the length of the shape along the X-axis (resp. Y-axis). Later we will see a more convincing argument about this, but for now it is sufficient to remark that borders on a given axis remains geometrically parallel.

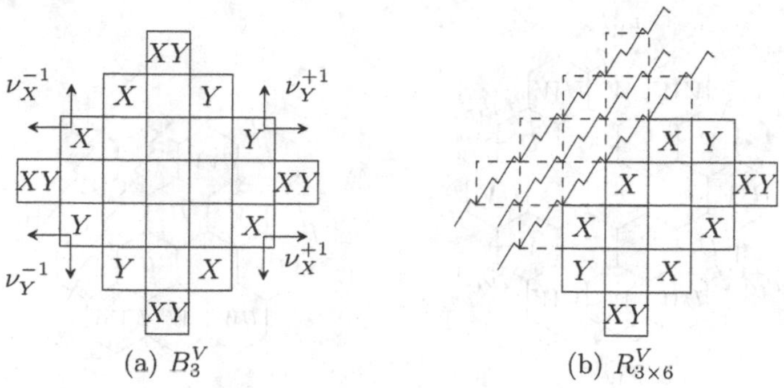

(a) B_3^V (b) $R_{3\times 6}^V$

Fig. 4. Von Neumann balls and rectangles

It is not common to call such shapes "rectangles", this is why we called them von Neumann rectangles. In the literature, the space considered is almost always the "classical" rectangle that we first considered in the Moore case. One can remark that these "classical" rectangles can be considered (see [16] for example) with the von Neumann neighborhood, but the borders are not where one might expect. If one agrees on our process to identify the borders then the border cells of the "classical" rectangle in the case of the von Neumann neighborhood are only the cells at corners. This is why we called this shape the von Neumann diamond, as the axes we identified are (roughly) the diagonals as illustrated in Fig. 2d.

Although this might be surprising, these diamonds have all the good properties to be synchronizable: the borders along a given axis are parallel, and we can remove some borders as described before and preserve the parallelism of the borders. This gives rise to some additional synchronizable shapes, but more is said about this in Sect. 4. As a final note about diamonds, note that the distance between the X borders is the same that the one between the Y borders. In fact, the two axes are totally symmetric in diamonds. Actually, this can be viewed as the reason why a single axis is used in the work presented in [16] which is restricted to von Neumann diamonds.

Similarly the Moore neighborhood can be used on the von Neumann rectangle (this is called a Moore diamond) with the same peculiarities and properties as shown in Fig. 2b.

3.3 The Hexagonal Case

We can now apply the same procedure in the hexagonal case and see what happens. In the hexagonal ball B_r^H of radius r, we can identify six types of borders paired into three axes that we called U, V, and W, as illustrated in Fig. 5a. The values of sets ν_d^{-1}, ν_d^{+1} for $d \in D = \{U, V, W\}$ are shown in Table 2.

Now we cut-down some borders. What is obtained is an object that as three lengths that represents, on each axis, the distance in between parallel borders.

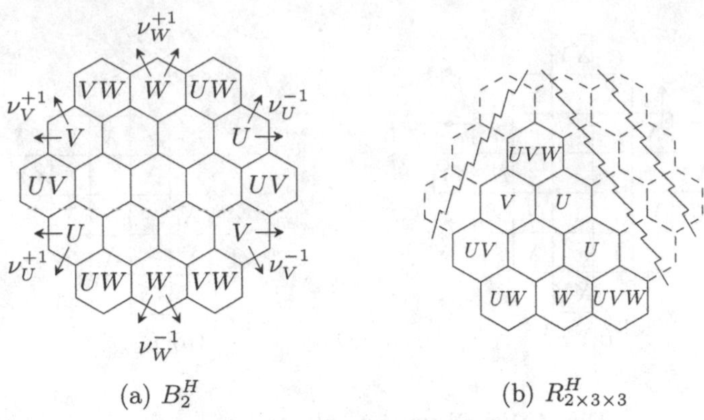

Fig. 5. Hexagonal balls and rectangles

Table 2. Values of parameter ν for the hexagonal case

Hexagonal		
U-axis	V-axis	W-axis
$\nu_U^{-1} = \left\{\binom{+2}{0}, \binom{+1}{+1}\right\}$	$\nu_V^{-1} = \left\{\binom{+2}{0}, \binom{+1}{-1}\right\}$	$\nu_W^{-1} = \left\{\binom{-1}{-1}, \binom{+1}{-1}\right\}$
$\nu_U^{+1} = \left\{\binom{-2}{0}, \binom{-1}{-1}\right\}$	$\nu_V^{+1} = \left\{\binom{-2}{0}, \binom{-1}{+1}\right\}$	$\nu_W^{+1} = \left\{\binom{+1}{+1}, \binom{-1}{+1}\right\}$

By analogy with the previous cases such shapes are called Hexagonal rectangles. This is illustrated in Fig. 5b, where from B_2^H, by removing a border of type ν_V^{+1} and then two borders of type ν_U^{-1} we obtained $R_{2\times3\times3}^H$.

The reader can note some differences with the Moore and von Neumann cases. First in the hexagonal case it possible to remove a border of some type without removing it explicitly. For example, in the figure we removed two U's and one V borders and as a side effect a border of type W also disappeared. Second, our notation $R_{l\times m\times n}^H$ does not represent a single shape as in the Moore case, nor even a class of symmetric shapes as in the von Neumann case, but a class of different shapes (see Fig. 6). But this is really not important for our discussion, as the numbers l, n, m represents the data that really matter for the synchronization, namely the lengths along each axis. Therefore, all shapes in the same class are equivalent for our discussion.

We remind that the important thing is the concept of parallel borders, and this is why we were able to synchronize all those shapes with our algorithm using the right ν's. Now, let us say more about why and how all of this works.

4 Sketch of the Synchronization Process

As we said, the synchronization of the whole space is obtained by superposing independent unidimensional solutions along the identified axis. We therefore

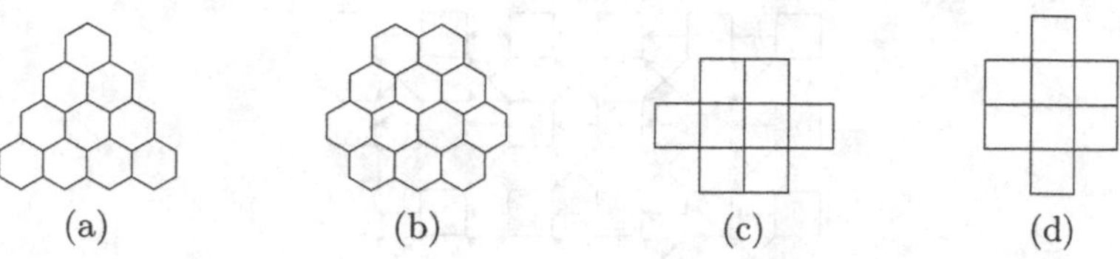

Fig. 6. Two different shapes for $R^H_{3\times3\times3}$ and for $R^V_{3\times3}$

need to explain how the whole is built from the pieces, and then explain what happens along each axis for the whole space.

At the initial configuration, only one cell, the initiator, is active. The first thing to known is that a cell becomes active as soon as one of its neighbors is active, independently of the axes. Once active, a cell participates in all superposed synchronizations, *i.e.* two for the Moore and von Neumann neighborhood, and three for the hexagonal one. For each axis d, the cell uses the corresponding ν_d's to give a real meaning to "left" and "right" in the corresponding unidimensional synchronization. Each instance being independent, it might reach its fire state at a time different from the others. A cell finally fires exactly when *all* the instances have fired. This means that it has to wait for the latest synchronization to effectively fire at the same time.

To have a global meaning for this local behavior, we need to understand how things happen globally for an arbitrary axis, and then see how the independent axes synchronization signals give rise to a coherent compound synchronization signal.

So let us now consider an arbitrary axis d. The first thing to clarify is how the fact that there are many "left" and "right" neighbors (according to the ν_d's) comply with the fact that we execute a single unidimensional synchronization of the axes. This is the reason why we insisted on the parallelism of borders along axes in all considered shapes. This parallelism property means more precisely that for all cells, all unidimensional lines built from them that reach a "left" border using the ν_d^{-1} and that reach a "right" border using the ν_d^{+1} have the same length. Such lines are called *lines along the axis* (see Fig. 7) and their lengths are exactly the ones used in the notation $R_{l\times m}$ and that are given in the figures.

We remind to the reader that our unidimensional solution is based on the notion of distance to the borders, so this parallelism implies that all those lines are equivalent with respect to this notion. When a splitting occurs and new borders are added, we known that the parallelism property still holds for each resulting half-spaces. Indeed the splittings can be described in terms of borders removal, and we showed that this operation preserves the parallelism property. Thanks to this parallelism, the fact that a cell belongs to many lines along a given axis is not a problem. Its goal for all these lines is the same since it has the same distance to the borders for all of them. Also, the unidimensional solution is therefore able to mix distance coming from different "left" neighbors in a

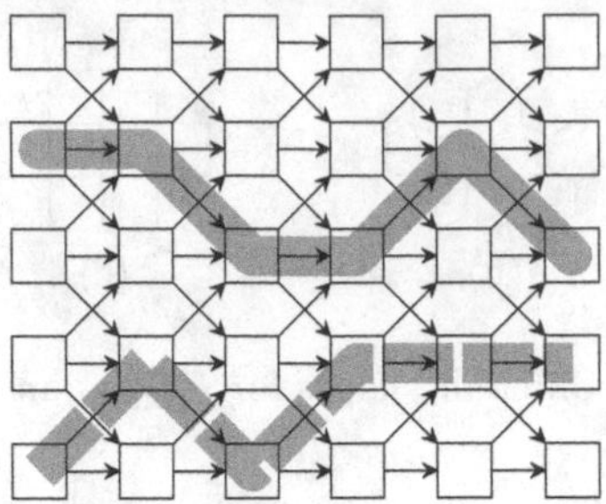

Fig. 7. Two lines along the X axis in the Moore rectangle

single "left" information, and similarly for the right direction. This gives good properties at the global level.

These good properties can be clearly stated in the Moore and von Neumann cases. For any axis, and when we restrict our attention on the activated part of the space, all the lines along the considered axis have exactly the same unidimensional configuration. In particular, when one active cell fires along this axis, all the other active cells fire. So for a given axis either it fires before or after all the cells are active. If it fires after the full activation of the space, its synchronization signal is global. If it fires before the full activation of the space, as illustrated in Fig. 8, then each cell that become active after also fires. The picture is completed by the fact that the last axis to fire necessarily fire after the full activation of the space, and since it is the last to fire, it is the one that determines to complete compound fire.

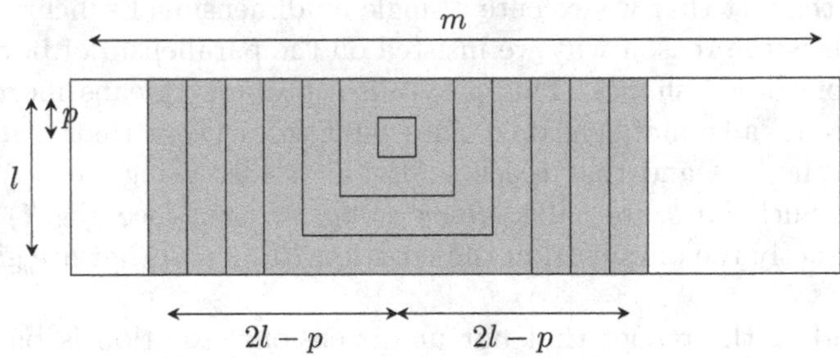

Fig. 8. A Y-axis synchronization on a large rectangle in Moore

For the hexagonal case, it is not the case that all the lines in the active part of the space have the same unidimensional configuration, so a more general argument is needed. The important fact to establish is that when the last axis to fire do so, the axes which were not able to fire globally have already finished to fire all the cells of the space. Instead of digging more into such an argument we provide some executions on the hexagonal case that allows to verify the property in some elementary and understandable cases.

5 Executions of the Algorithm in the Hexagonal Case

In the hexagonal case, we determined that three axes exist. Thus three synchronizations have to be superposed. This represents a lot of information per cell but one can have a good insight of how the synchronization occurs by simply observing how and when the splittings occur.

Figure 9 illustrates the case of a hexagonal ball of radius 15 with the initiator at the center. Looking at the time of apparition, one can see the classical logarithmic behavior of the divide and conquer scheme used: it takes 15 transitions to activate the borders, then 15 more transitions to get the first splittings. The subsequent splittings occur after 8, then 4, and then 2 transitions at which point for each cell its neighborhood is full of borders of all kind. This event triggers the global synchronization signal. One can also note that the hexagon splits into 6 triangles, and that here after each one splits into 4 triangles. In this example, all the axes act symmetrically since the initiator is exactly at the center of the space.

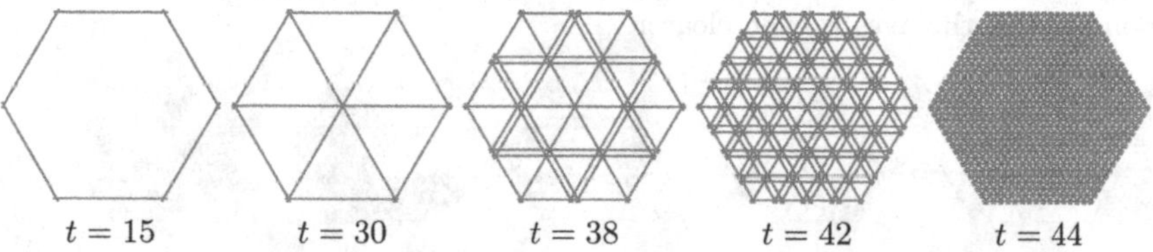

Fig. 9. Splitting of an hexagonal ball of radius 15 with the initiator at the center

In Fig. 10, the independence of the axes and the fact that early splittings end before the final one for each given recursive level can be observed. For time 33 to 39, the axis U starts its splitting, then the axis W, but both of them finished before the axis V finished its first splitting. For the second level of splittings, the same thing can be observed from time 42 to 47, this is harder to observe because the axis U starts its third level of splitting at time 46, making even more explicit the independence of the axes. All in all, V is the last axis to complete the synchronization at all levels, and this determines the global synchronization time that happens at step 54, just after that the whole neighborhood is full of borders of all kind.

In Fig. 11 an even more complex situation is illustrated with splittings occurring during the synchronization of an asymmetric Hexagonal rectangle.

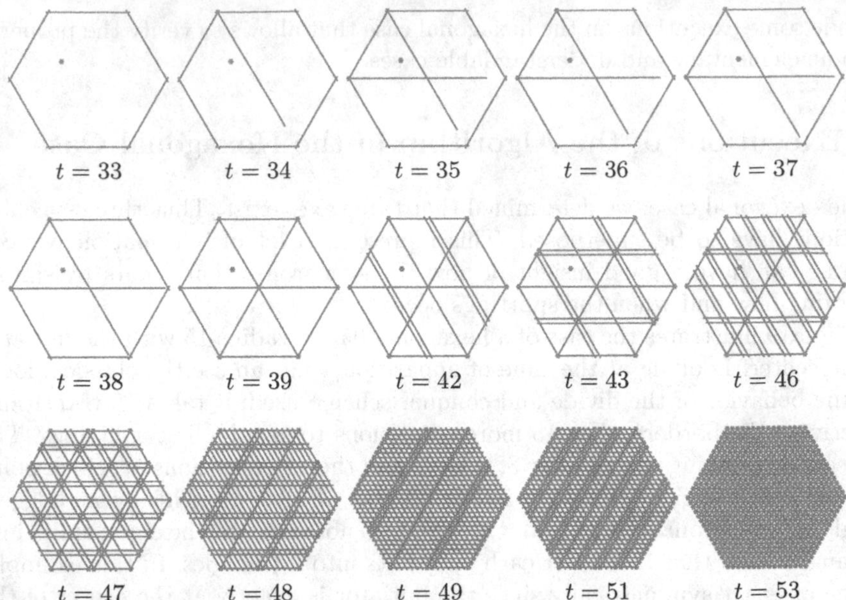

Fig. 10. Splittings of an hexagonal ball of radius 15 with the initiator's position indicated by the isolated point. All configurations where borders appear are shown. The independence of the axes is even clearer.

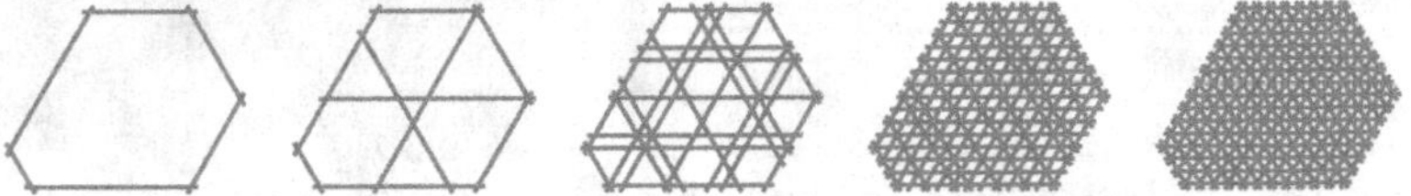

Fig. 11. Splittings of a trimmed hexagonal $R^H_{18\times14\times14}$

6 Synchronization Time

An important thing to discuss is the synchronization time. In the unidimensional case, if we denote by l the length of the line (in number of hops, not in number of cells), and we denote by p the distance of initiator to the nearest border, the synchronization occurs after $2l - p + 1$ transitions. Here, we superposed many axis synchronizations. Reminding that the global synchronization occurs when the latest axis synchronizes, we obviously obtain the following formula:

$$T_s = \max_{d \in D}\{2l_d - p_d + 1\}. \tag{2}$$

Then we recover the minimal synchronization time in all the considered case, *i.e.* Moore rectangle, and von Neumann diamond being the most known for the bidimensional case.

7 Conclusion

In [4,5] we presented an algorithm that solves the G-FSSP on various shapes in dimension 1 and 2. Even if it was easy to understand how to extend it to higher dimensions, we asked if our solution was usable to solve the G-FSSP on 2D shapes in the hexagonal topology, which is *a priori* less obvious (remind that no one had proposed a solution up to now). This was obtained by the identification of some properties of the synchronized shapes that permits to determine the right values of some parameters to the algorithm that are related to the topology. We do not have a formal proof of our claims yet, but we experimented successfully everything that is presented here. All the characterizations and properties we talked about can be proved, but this will be the main thread of a work to come. We claim that we have a very generic solution that is able to synchronize many regular shapes of any dimensions with various topologies in minimal-time. Characterizing all the shapes that our solution captures is now a challenge. We also think that it is possible to decorrelate in some way the axes to the neighborhood and to "choose" more independently the axes. Of course, this will necessitate to understand well the relations in between the ν's and the neighborhood.

References

1. Balzer, R.: An 8-state minimal time solution to the firing squad synchronization problem. Inf. Control **10**, 22–42 (1967)
2. Grasselli, A.: Synchronization of cellular arrays: the firing squad problem in two dimensions. Inf. Control **28**, 113–124 (1975)
3. Kobayashi, K.: The firing squad synchronization problem for two-dimensional arrays. Inf. Control **34**, 177–197 (1977)
4. Maignan, L., Yunès, J.-B.: A spatio-temporal algorithmic point of view on firing squad synchronisation problem. In: Sirakoulis, G.C., Bandini, S. (eds.) ACRI 2012. LNCS, vol. 7495, pp. 101–110. Springer, Heidelberg (2012)
5. Maignan, L., Yunès, J.B.: Moore and von Neumann neighborhood n-dimensional generalized firing squad solutions using fields. In: AFCA 2013 Workshop, CANDAR 2013 Conference, Matsuyama, Japan, 4–6 December 2013
6. Mazoyer, J.: A six-state minimal time solution to the firing squad synchronization problem. Theoret. Comput. Sci. **50**, 183–238 (1987)
7. Moore, E.E.: Sequential Machines, Selected Papers, pp. 213–214. Addison-Wesley, Reading (1964)
8. Moore, E.E., Langdon, G.: A generalized firing squad problem. Inf. Control **12**, 212–220 (1968)
9. Noguchi, K.: Simple 8-state minimal time solution to the firing squad synchronization problem. Theoret. Comput. Sci. **314**(3), 303–334 (2004)
10. Róka, Z.: The firing squad synchronization problem on Cayley graphs. In: Hájek, Petr, Wiedermann, Jiří (eds.) MFCS 1995. LNCS, vol. 969, pp. 402–411. Springer, Heidelberg (1995)
11. Romani, F.: Cellular automata synchronization. Inf. Sci. **10**, 299–318 (1976)

12. Schmidt, H., Worsch, T.: The firing squad synchronization problem with many generals for one-dimensional ca. In: Levy, J.J., Mayr, E.W., Mitchell, J.C. (eds.) TCS 2004. IFIP, vol. 155, pp. 111–124. Springer, Heidelberg (2004)
13. Settle, A., Simon, J.: Smaller solutions for the firing squad. Theoret. Comput. Sci. **276**(1), 83–109 (2002)
14. Shinahr, I.: Two- and three-dimensional firing-squad synchronization problems. Inf. Control **24**, 163–180 (1974)
15. Szwerinski, H.: Time-optimum solution of the firing-squad-synchronization-problem for n-dimensional rectangles with the general at an arbitrary position. Theoret. Comput. Sci. **19**, 305–320 (1982)
16. Umeo, H.: Recent developments in firing squad synchronization algorithms for two-dimensional cellular automata and their state-efficient implementations. In: AFL, pp. 368–387 (2011)
17. Yamakawi, T., Amesara, T., Umeo, H.: A note on three-dimensional firing squad synchronization algorithm. In: ITC-CSCC, pp. 773–776 (2008)

Strict Majority Bootstrap Percolation on Augmented Tori and Random Regular Graphs: Experimental Results

P. Moisset de Espanés[1,3(✉)] and I. Rapaport[1,2]

[1] Centro de Modelamiento Matemático (UMI 2807 CNRS), Universidad de Chile, Santiago, Chile
pablo.moisset@gmail.com
[2] Departamento de Ingeniería Matemática, Universidad de Chile, Santiago, Chile
[3] Centro de Biotecnología y Bioingeniería, Universidad de Chile, Santiago, Chile

Abstract. We study the strict majority bootstrap percolation process on graphs. Vertices may be active or passive. Initially, active vertices are chosen independently with probability p. Each passive vertex v becomes active if at least $\lceil \frac{deg(v)+1}{2} \rceil$ of its neighbors are active (and thereafter never changes its state). If at the end of the process all vertices become active then we say that the initial set of active vertices percolates on the graph. We address the problem of finding graphs for which percolation is likely to occur for small values of p. For that purpose we study percolation on two topologies. The first is an $n \times n$ toroidal grid augmented with a universal vertex. Also, each vertex v in the torus is connected to all nodes whose distance to v is less than or equal to a parameter r. The second family contains all random regular graphs of even degree, also augmented with a universal node. We compare our computational results to those obtained in previous publications for r-rings and random regular graphs.

1 Introduction

Consider the following deterministic process on a graph $G = (V, E)$. Initially, every vertex in V can be either *active* or *passive*. A passive vertex can become active depending on the state of its neighbors. Once active, a vertex cannot change its state. Such a process is called *bootstrap percolation*. In Sect. 2, we will describe some families of graphs and transition rules that have been already studied and what is known about the resulting processes.

The set of active vertices grows monotonically. Therefore, for a finite graph, a fixed point has to be reached after a finite number of steps. If the fixed point is such that all vertices have become active, then we say that the initial set of active vertices *percolates* on G.

This work has been partially supported by CONICYT via Basal in Applied Mathematics (I.R.), Núcleo Milenio Información y Coordinación en Redes ICM/FIC RC130003 (I.R).

T. Isokawa et al. (Eds.): AUTOMATA 2014, LNCS 8996, pp. 97–105, 2015.
DOI: 10.1007/978-3-319-18812-6_8

The basic question is to determine the ratio of initial active vertices one needs to choose randomly in order to percolate the whole graph with high probability. More precisely, suppose that the elements of the initial set of active vertices $A \subseteq V$ are chosen independently with probability p. The problem consists in finding values of p for which percolation of A is likely to occur. The least p for which percolation will happen with probability greater than or equal to 1/2 will be called the *critical probability.*

In the *(simple) majority bootstrap percolation* [1], each passive vertex v becomes active if at least $\lceil \frac{deg(v)}{2} \rceil$ of its neighbors are active, where $deg(v)$ denotes the degree of node v in G. In the present paper we study the *strict majority bootstrap percolation* process. In this case, each passive node v becomes active if it has strictly more active than passive neighbors. More precisely, it will change if at least $\lceil \frac{deg(v)+1}{2} \rceil$ of its neighbors are active. Note that if $deg(v)$ is odd, the rules for the strict and simple majority bootstrap percolation process coincide. Our decision to use strict majority, as opposed to the simple version, is related to our augmentation of a graph with a *universal vertex*, i.e. one that is connected to every other vertex in the graph. Intuitively, the simple majority percolation process in the augmented graph is somehow equivalent to the strong majority process in the original one.

A natural question to ask about the strict majority bootstrap percolation process is what graphs result in the critical probability being small. This problem, which motivates the present work, has not been addressed yet. Nevertheless, it is possible to conclude, from a paper of Balogh and Pittel [2], that the critical probability of the strict majority bootstrap percolation for random 7-regular graphs is 0.269.

Here we test empirically two different families of graphs. The first class is the set of augmented 2D-tori. The other family is the set of augmented random k-regular graphs. The results of the numerical experiments, in Sect. 3, show that for the augmented 2D-torus, the estimated critical probability (call it p_c) is about 0.185. For the augmented random d-regular graph, we obtain unexpectedly high values for p_c. For "small" values of d, that is $d \leq 16$, we obtain $p_c > 0.33$. This is surprising (especially when $d = 4$) because the relatively high girth of the graphs and a simple characterization of the vertices that will remain passive suggests that the value for p_c should be small.

2 Related and Previous Work

A common activation rule in literature is as follows: A passive vertex changes to the active state if at least k of its neighbors are already active. The resulting process is known as *k-neighbor bootstrap percolation*, and was proposed by Chalupa et al. [3]. Since its introduction this percolation process has mainly been studied in the d-dimensional grid $[n]^d = \{1, \ldots, n\}^d$ [4–7]. The precise definition of *critical probability* that has been used is the following:

$$p_c([n]^d, k) = \inf\{p \in [0,1] \colon \mathbb{P}\left(A \text{ percolates on } [n]^d\right) \geq 1/2\}. \tag{1}$$

The result of [9] is the culmination of many efforts aiming to obtain a sharp threshold for $p_c([n]^d, k)$. The result states that for every $d \geq k \geq 2$:

$$p_c([n]^d, k) = \left(\frac{\lambda(d,k) + o(1)}{\log_{(k-1)} n}\right)^{d-k+1},$$

where $\lambda(d,k) < \infty$ for every $d \geq k \geq 2$. Bootstrap percolation has also been studied on other graphs such as high dimensional tori [1,10–13], infinite trees [14–16] and random regular graphs [2,17].

In [18] the authors gave explicit constructions of two (families of) graphs for which the critical probability is also small (but higher than 0.269). The idea behind these constructions is the following. Consider a regular graph of even degree G. Let $G * u$ denote the graph G augmented with a single universal vertex u. The strict majority bootstrap percolation dynamics on $G * u$ has two phases. In the *first phase*, assuming that vertex u is not initially active, the dynamics restricted to G corresponds to the strict majority bootstrap percolation. If more than half of the vertices of G become active, then the universal vertex u also becomes active, and the *second phase* begins. In this new phase, the dynamics restricted to G follows the simple majority bootstrap percolation (and full activation becomes much more likely to occur). This justifies our interest in the strict majority activation rule.

The two augmented graphs studied in [18] were the *wheel* $\mathrm{W}_n = u * R_n$ and the *toroidal grid plus a universal vertex* $\mathrm{TW}_n = u * R_n^2$ (where R_n is the ring on n vertices and R_n^2 is the toroidal grid on n^2 vertices). For a family of graphs $\mathcal{G} = (G_n)_n$, the following parameter was defined (A again denotes the initial set of active nodes, however now the dynamics is driven by the strict majority bootstrap percolation process):

$$p_c^+(\mathcal{G}) = \inf\left\{p \in [0,1] \colon \liminf_{n\to\infty} \mathbb{P}\left(A \,\text{percolates on}\, G_n\right) = 1\right\}. \quad (2)$$

Note that in the last definition the limit of the probability has to be equal to 1. This seems to be in conflict with the definition in Eq. 1, in which we demand the probability of percolation to be greater than 1/2. There is no contradiction, though. Considering $\liminf_{n\to\infty} \mathbb{P}\left(A \text{ percolates on}\, G_n\right)$ as function of p, it is easy to prove that its value will transition from 0 to 1 at $p_c^+(\mathcal{G})$, i.e. it is a step function. Thus, the definition in Eq. 2 could be rewritten demanding the limit to be greater than 1/2.

Now consider the families $\mathcal{W} = (\mathrm{W}_n)_n$ and $\mathcal{TW} = (\mathrm{TW}_n)_n$. It was proved in [18] that $p_c^+(\mathcal{W}) = 0.4030...$, where 0.4030... is the unique root in the interval $[0,1]$ of the equation $x + x^2 - x^3 = \frac{1}{2}$. For the toroidal case it was shown that $0.35 \leq p_c^+(\mathcal{TW}) \leq 0.372$.

Computing the critical probability of the (one-dimensional) wheel is a trivial task. Nevertheless, if we increase the *radius* of the vertices from 1 to any other constant, then the situation becomes much more complicated. More precisely, let $R_n(r)$ be the ring where every vertex is connected to its r closest vertices to the left and to its r closest vertices to the right. Obviously, $R_n = R_n(1)$.

Kiwi et al. [19] studied the strict majority bootstrap percolation process in a generalization of the wheel that is called *r-wheel* $\mathrm{W}_n(r) = u * R_n(r)$. A peculiarity of the model in this paper is that the initial state of the universal vertex is always set to 0. This is somewhat arbitrary, but simplifies the analysis and allows to find an upper bound for $p_c^+(\mathcal{W}(r))$ when the universal vertex can be initialized randomly. The main result in [19] is that for the class of *r-wheels* $\mathcal{W}(r)$,

$$\lim_{r\to\infty} p_c^+(\mathcal{W}(r)) = 1/4.$$

This is the smallest critical probability that has been proved for any class of graphs. We would like to point out that the deterministic counterpart of both the simple majority and the strict majority bootstrap percolation processes have been intensively studied. In fact, bounds have been derived for the minimum number of vertices one needs to activate in order to end up activating the whole graph. These sets of vertices are called *irreversible dynamic monopolies* or *irreversible dynamos* [20–29].

3 Experiments and Results

The purpose of our experiments is to estimate $p_c^+(\mathcal{G})$ for a given $\mathcal{G}$. Informally, we choose an n which is "large enough", create $G \in \mathcal{G}$ of size n. We then activate vertices with probability p (forcing the universal vertex to 0, following [19]) and simulate the strict majority bootstrap percolation process on it until it reaches a fixed point. We then analyze the fixed point and determine whether the initial set percolates on G. We can repeat the experiment several times and compute the fraction of replicas that resulted in percolation on G (call it f). Since f is an estimation of the probability of the initial set percolating on G, we can try different values of p until $f \approx 1/2$. We will refer to this particular value of p as p_c. This will be our estimation of $p_c^+(\mathcal{G})$. The goal of our simulation is finding a family of grpahs for which $p_c^+(\mathcal{G}) < 1/4$.

For our simulations we used an in-house program written in C. The total amount of CPU time needed to generate the results we are presenting was approximately 10 days.

3.1 Augmented Toroidal Grid

By analogy with the generalization of the wheel in [19], we define an augmented torus. Let R_n^2 be as before and let $R_n^2(r)$ be the graph so every node v is connected to all vertices whose Moore distance from v is less than or equal to r. Now $\mathrm{TW}_n(r) = u * R_n^2(r)$. We finally define the class of r-tori $\mathcal{TW}(r) = (\mathrm{TW}_n(r))_n$. Intuitively, they are tori of $n \times n$ size, with vertices connected to all other vertices at distances no greater than r. Besides, there is the universal vertex connected to all other nodes in the grid.

For the experiments, we run our simulator for $r = 1, 2, 3$. For each value of r we tried different values of p and measured f. As it is well known, some percolation problems are hard to study using simulations, because the asymptotic behavior of the system as (say) n grows is not apparent until n is so large that simulation is not feasible. As a simple (heuristical) test, we run our simulations for $n = 2000$ and $n = 4000$. By comparing the estimations of p_c we obtained from both variants we can have a rough idea of the reliability of our results.

Due to running time constraints we had to adjust the number of replicas we used to compute f. For $r = 1, n = 2000$ we run 100 replicas per value of p (that is, a single data point in Fig. 1). For $r = 1, n = 4000$ we used 20 replicas per point. For $r = 2, n = 2000$ we computed 50 replicas per point and for $r = 2, n = 4000$ we did 20 replicas per point. Similarly, for $r = 3$ and $n = 2000, 400$ we had 100 and 25 replicas per point respectively.

Figures 1, 2 and 3 describe the $r = 1, 2$ and 3 cases respectively.

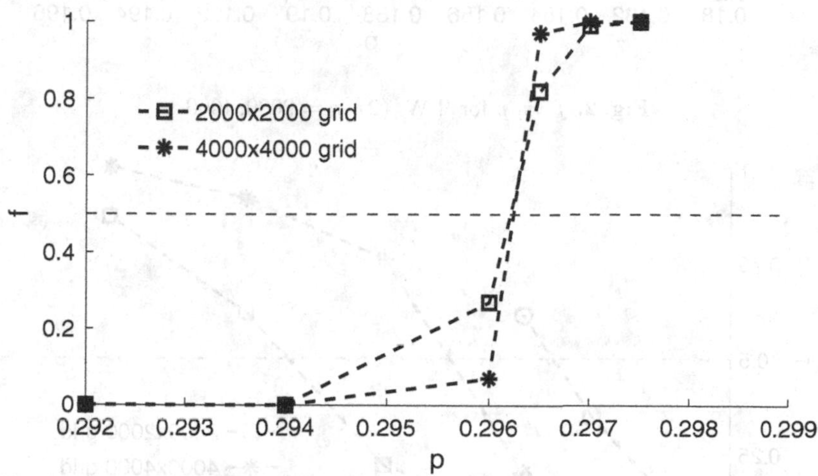

Fig. 1. f vs. p for $\mathrm{TW}_n(1)$. $n = 2000, 4000$

3.2 Random Regular Graphs

Since they have been also heavily studied, we run experiments using random regular graphs. There is another powerful motivation though. Consider a 4-regular graph. It is easy to prove that if there is a cycle where all vertices belonging to it are passive, they will all remain passive under the dynamics imposed by the by the strict majority activation rule. Moreover, this condition characterizes precisely the set of vertices that never become active. Since random regular graphs have a "large" girth, in a probabilistic sense, the intuition is that with high probability, those cycles will have at least one active node unless, of course, p is very small. This intuition led us to hope for a very small p_c.

Given n and k, generating k-regular graphs with n vertices (with uniform probability) is a very challenging computational task. The intuitive and simple algorithms are slow while faster methods are very cumbersome to implement.

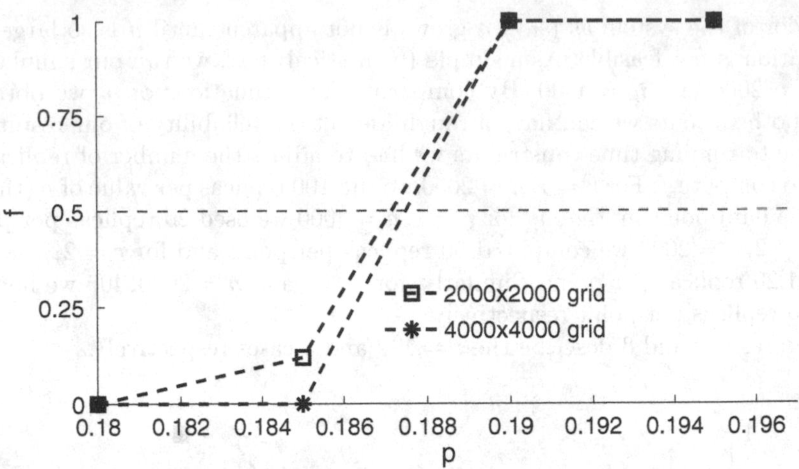

Fig. 2. f vs. p for $\mathrm{TW}_n(2)$. $n = 2000, 4000$

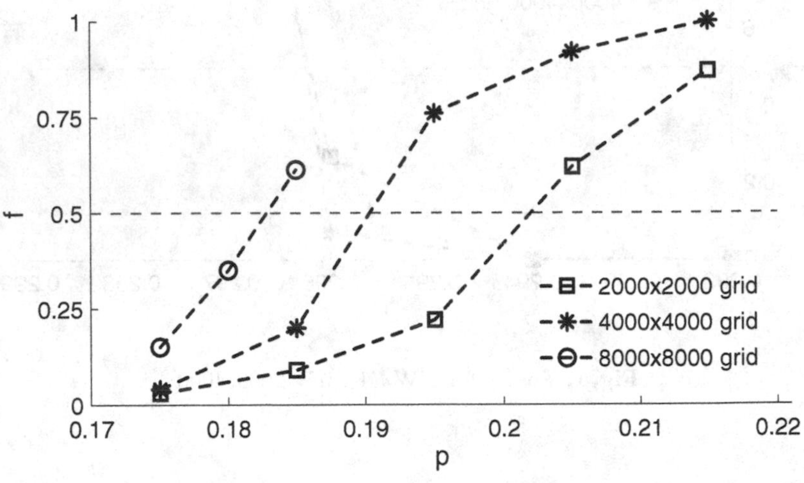

Fig. 3. f vs. p for $\mathrm{TW}_n(3)$. $n = 2000, 4000$

For an introduction to the problem algorithms see [30]. To reduce development time we used some existing code written by Golan Pundak, uploaded to MATLAB central. This function generates a k regular random graph with n vertices using the pairing model, also described in [30]. The graphs generated by this code were fed into our simulator.

The running times for generating each graph were long. The extreme case was $k = 50, n = 100000$: it takes 2 days of CPU time to create a single graph. Therefore we adopted the following strategy: for $n = 100000$, for $k = 4, 8, 16, 50$, we generated a single graph. That is, we generated four graphs in total. For each one of these graphs we estimated the value of p_c and the results are displayed in Fig. 4.

As a matter of fact we obtained the analogous results for $n = 2000$ and $n = 10000$. The values we computed for p_c changed very little with n. The differences where in the third or fourth significative digits. Therefore the resulting plots would have been almost the same as Fig. 4 and hence we omitted them.

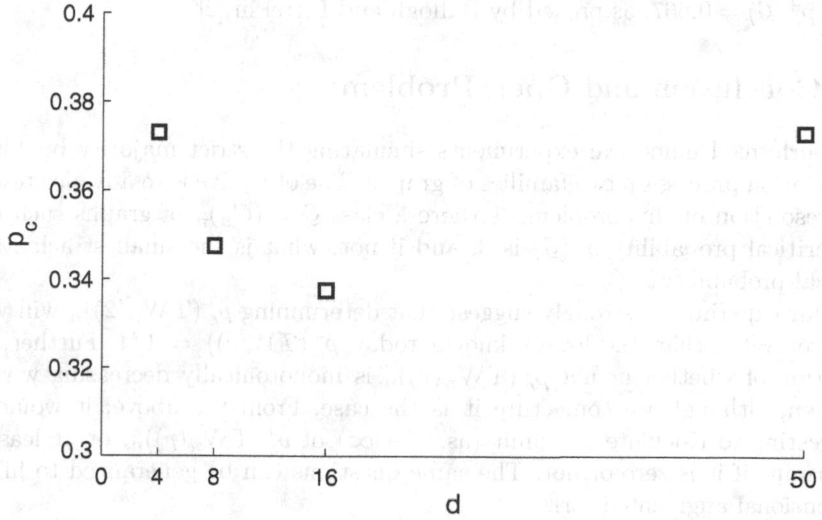

Fig. 4. p_c vs d for d-regular random graphs with $n = 100000$.

3.3 Analysis of the Simulations

Our experiments for $\mathcal{TW}(r)$ show a $p_c \approx 0.2963$ for $r = 1$, and $p_c \approx 0.187$ for $r = 2$. Since the estimations were very similar regardless of the values of n, our heuristic suggests n was large enough for the simulations to capture the asymptotic behavior. Therefore p_c should be a reasonable approximation to p_c^+. When $r = 3$ there is a bigger discrepancy between the $n = 2000$ and $n = 4000$ runs than before. For the former, $p_c \approx 0.19$. For the latter, $p_c \approx 0.20$. We suspect $p_c < 0.185$ if n is large enough. This is based on some preliminary simulation results, but considering it would require weeks of CPU time (with the current software) to explore the $r = 3, n = 8000$ case we do not expect the approach based on direct simulations to scale up much more.

Nonetheless, obtaining estimations below 0.19 is encouraging as they suggest $\mathcal{G} = (\mathrm{TW}_n(2))_n$ is a good candidate for having the new lowest known $p_c^+(\mathcal{G})$. Further, the successive values for p_c we obtained when increasing r were 0.2963, 0.187 and 0.185. Although the last one is still dubious, this points to a decreasing monotonicity of $p_c^+(\mathcal{TW}(r))$ w.r.t. r. Based on these simulations and previous results in [19], we expect it to be the case.

For the random d-regular graphs (see Fig. 4), we note three features in the results. The first one is that the estimations for p_c are larger than what we obtained for the augmented tori or has been proved for wheels. This is surprising since our heuristic argument suggested the opposite had to happen. Another feature is the similarity of p_c values for different d's. Besides, there is the lack of monotonicity in p_c w.r.t. d. We are unable at this time to explain these phenomena. Finally, we see how our addition of the universal vertex can dramatically affect the value of the critical probability. For our model, when $d = 4$, we obtain $p_c \approx 0.37$. This contrasts with the case without the universal vertex, were $p_c^+(\mathcal{G}) = 0.667$, as proved by Ballogh and Pittel in [2].

4 Conclusion and Open Problems

We performed numerical experiments simulating the strict majority bootstrap percolation process on two families of graphs. The objective is to advance toward the resolution of this problem: Is there a class $\mathcal{G} = (G_n)_n$ of graphs such that the critical probability $p_c^+(\mathcal{G})$ is 0, and if not, what is the smallest achievable critical probability?

Our experiments strongly suggest that determining $p_c^+(\mathrm{TW}_n(2))_n$ will yield a lower value than the lowest known today $p_c^+(\mathcal{TW}(r)) = 1/4$. Further, the question of whether or not $p_c^+(\mathrm{TW}_n(r))_n$ is monotonically decreasing w.r.t. r is open, although we conjecture it is the case. From the above, it would be interesting to calculate the limit (as $r \to \infty$) of $p_c^+(\mathrm{TW}_n(r))_n$, or at least to determine if it is zero or not. The same questions can be generalized to higher dimensional augmented tori.

Finally, in spite of the k-random regular graphs failing dramatically at yielding a small value for p_c, it would be interesting to know why the intuition was invalid, why the value of p_c almost did not change for different values of k and determine whether $p_c^+(\mathcal{G})$ is not monotonic.

References

1. Balogh, J., Bollobás, B., Morris, R.: Majority bootstrap percolation on the hypercube. Comb. Probab. Comput. **18**, 17–51 (2009)
2. Balogh, J., Pittel, B.: Bootstrap percolation on the random regular graph. Random Struct. Algorithms **30**(1–2), 257–286 (2007)
3. Chalupa, J., Leath, P.L., Reich, G.R.: Bootstrap percolation on a Bethe lattice. J. Phys. C Solid State Phys. **12**, L31–L35 (1979)
4. Aizenman, A., Lebowitz, J.: Metastability effects in bootstrap percolation. J. Phys. A Math. Gen. **21**, 3801–3813 (1988)
5. Balogh, J., Bollobás, B., Morris, R.: Bootstrap percolation in three dimensions. Ann. Probab. **37**(4), 1329–1380 (2009)
6. Cerf, R., Manzo, F.: The threshold regime of finite volume bootstrap percolation. Stoch. Process. Appl. **101**, 69–82 (2002)
7. Holroyd, A.: Sharp metastability threshold for two-dimensional bootstrap percolation. Probab. Theor. Relat. Fields **125**(2), 195–224 (2003)
8. Dubhashi, D.P., Panconesi, A.: Concentration of Measure for the Analysis of Randomized Algorithms. Cambridge University Press, Cambridge (2009)
9. Balogh, J., Bollobás, B., Duminil-Copin, H., Morris, R.: The sharp threshold for bootstrap percolation in all dimensions. Trans. Am. Math. Soc. **364**, 2667–2701 (2012)

10. Balogh, J., Bollobás, B.: Bootstrap percolation on the hypercube. Prob. Theory Rel. Fields **134**, 624–648 (2006)
11. Balogh, J., Bollobás, B., Morris, R.: Bootstrap percolation in high dimensions. Comb. Probab. Comput. **19**(5–6), 643–692 (2010)
12. Van der Hofstad, R., Slade, G.: Asymptotic expansions in n^{-1} for percolation critical values on the n-cube and $\mathbb{Z}^n$. Random Struct. Algorithms **27**(3), 331–357 (2005)
13. Van der Hofstad, R., Slade, G.: Expansion in n^{-1} for percolation critical values on the n-cube and $\mathbb{Z}^n$: the first three terms. Comb. Probab. Comput. **15**(5), 695–713 (2006)
14. Balogh, J., Peres, Y., Pete, G.: Bootstrap percolation on infinite trees and non-amenable groups. Comb. Probab. Comput. **15**, 715–730 (2006)
15. Biskup, M., Schonmann, R.H.: Metastable behavior for bootstrap percolation on regular trees. J. Statist. Phys. **136**, 667–676 (2009)
16. Fontes, L.R., Schonmann, R.H.: Bootstrap percolation on homogeneous trees has 2 phase transitions. J. Statist. Phys. **132**, 839–861 (2008)
17. Janson, S.: On percolation in random graphs with given vertex degrees. Electron. J. Probab. **14**, 86–118 (2009)
18. Rapaport, I., Suchan, K., Todinca, I., Verstraete, J.: On dissemination thresholds in regular and irregular graph classes. Algorithmica **59**, 16–34 (2011)
19. Kiwi, M., Moisset de Espanés, P., Rapaport, I., Rica, S., Theyssier, G.: Strict majority bootstrap percolation in the r-wheel. Inf. Process. Lett. **114**(6), 277–281 (2014)
20. Adams, S.S., Bootha, P., Troxell, D.S., Zinnen, S.L.: Modeling the spread of fault in majority-based network systems: dynamic monopolies in triangular grids. Discrete Appl. Math. **160**(1011), 1624–1633 (2012)
21. Adams, S.S., Troxell, D.S., Zinnen, S.L.: Dynamic monopolies and feedback vertex sets in hexagonal grids. Comput. Math. Appl. **62**(11), 4049–4057 (2011)
22. Berger, E.: Dynamic monopolies of constant size. J. Comb. Theor. Ser. B **88**(2), 191–200 (2001)
23. Dreyer, P.A., Roberts, F.S.: Irreversible k-threshold processes: graph-theoretical threshold models of the spread of disease and of opinion. Discrete Appl. Math **157**(7), 1615–1627 (2009)
24. Flocchini, P., Geurts, F., Santoro, N.: Optimal irreversible dynamos in chordal rings. Discrete Appl. Math. **113**(1), 23–42 (2001)
25. Flocchini, R., Kralovic, A., Roncato, P., Ruzicka, N.: Santoro on time versus size for monotone dynamic monopolies in regular topologies. J. Discrete Algorithms **1**(2), 129–150 (2003)
26. Flocchini, P., Lodi, E., Luccio, F., Pagli, L., Santoro, N.: Dynamic monopolies in tori. Discrete Appl. Math. **137**(2), 197–212 (2004)
27. Luccio, F., Pagli, L., Sanossian, H.: Irreversible dynamos in butterflies. In: Proceedings of the 6th International Colloquium on Structural Information and Communication Complexity, pp. 204–218 (1999)
28. Morris, R.: Minimal percolating sets in bootstrap percolation. Electron. J. Comb. **16**(1), 20 (2009). Research Paper 2
29. Peleg, D.: Local majorities, coalitions and monopolies in graphs: a review. Theor. Comput. Sci. **282**, 231–257 (2002)
30. Wormald, N.: Models of random regular graphs. In: Lamb, J.D., Preece, D.A. (eds.) Surveys in Combinatorics, pp. 239–298. Cambridge University Press, Cambridge (1999)

Language Recognition by Reversible Partitioned Cellular Automata

Kenichi Morita[✉]

Hiroshima University, Higashi-Hiroshima 739–8527, Japan
km@hiroshima-u.ac.jp

Abstract. We investigate the language accepting capability of one-dimensional reversible partitioned cellular automata (RPCAs). It is well known that bounded cellular automata (CAs) are equivalent to deterministic linear-bounded automata (DLBAs) in their language accepting capability. Here, we prove RPCAs are also equivalent to them by showing a construction method of an RPCA that simulates a given DLBA. Thus, the reversibility constraint does not decrease the ability of PCAs.

1 Introduction

One-dimensional cellular automata (CAs) as language acceptors have been extensively studied until now, and fast recognition algorithms as well as their properties have been investigated (see, e.g., a survey [1]). Smith [8] showed deterministic CAs whose space is bounded by the input length are equivalent to deterministic linear-bounded automata (DLBA) in their accepting capability if computing time is not bounded. On the other hand, Kutrib and Malcher [2] studied reversible CA acceptors, and derived basic properties of real-time ones.

In this paper, we study how the constraint of reversibility affects the accepting capability of bounded CAs in the case computing time is not bounded. For this purpose, we consider the following two sub-problems. The first one is how a DLBA is converted into an equivalent reversible DLBA (RDLBA). The second one is how an RDLBA is simulated by a reversible bounded CA. For the first problem, Lange, McKenzie and Tapp [3] showed that a DLBA can be simulated by an RDLBA. However, their method is complex, and it is difficult to give a practical procedure of conversion. Here, we give a much simpler conversion method based on the one shown in [6]. For the second problem, we use the framework of a deterministic partitioned cellular automaton (PCA), since it makes design of reversible CAs easier. In [4,7], it is shown that a reversible Turing machine (RTM) is simulated by a reversible PCA (RPCA). However, there, the configuration size of the RPCA was not bounded, and thus a new technique is required to simulate an RDLBA in a bounded RPCA. Here, we propose a formulation of an RPCA acceptor, and give a conversion method of an RDLBA into an RPCA that simulates the former in the cellular space whose working space is always bounded by the input length plus 2. By above, any given DLBA can be converted into an RPCA acceptor that simulates the former. Hence, the

T. Isokawa et al. (Eds.): AUTOMATA 2014, LNCS 8996, pp. 106–120, 2015.
DOI: 10.1007/978-3-319-18812-6_9

language accepting capability of bounded PCAs does not decrease, even if the reversibility constraint is added.

2 Reversible Partitioned Cellular Automaton (RPCA)

Definition 1. A 1-dimensional 3-neighbor deterministic partitioned cellular automaton (PCA) *as an acceptor of a language is defined by* $P = ((L, C, R), f, (\#, \#, \#), r_s, \Sigma, A)$. *Here,* L, C,*and* R *are nonempty finite sets of states of left, center, and right parts of a cell, and thus the state set of a cell is* $Q = L \times C \times R$. *A mapping* $f : Q \to Q$ *is a* local function, $(\#, \#, \#) \in Q$ *is a quiescent state that satisfies* $f(\#, \#, \#) = (\#, \#, \#)$, $r_s \in R$ is a *start state,* $\Sigma \subset C$ *is an input alphabet, and* $A \subset L$ *is a set of* accepting states.

Let $p_L : Q \to L$ be the projection such that $p_L(l, c, r) = l$ for all $(l, c, r) \in Q$. The projections $p_C : Q \to C$ and $p_R : Q \to R$ are also defined similarly. Let $\mathrm{Conf}(Q)$ be the set of all configurations over Q, i.e., $\mathrm{Conf}(Q) = \{\alpha \mid \alpha : \mathbb{Z} \to Q\}$, where $\mathbb{Z}$ is the set of all integers. The *global function* $F : \mathrm{Conf}(Q) \to \mathrm{Conf}(Q)$ of P induced by f is defined as the one that satisfies the following:

$$\forall \alpha \in \mathrm{Conf}(Q), \forall x \in \mathbb{Z}\ (F(\alpha)(x) = f(p_L(\alpha(x+1)), p_C(\alpha(x)), p_R(\alpha(x-1)))).$$

Let F^t denote the operation of applying F repeatedly t times $(t = 0, 1, \ldots)$.

In a PCA P, the next state of each cell is determined by the present state of the left part of the right-neighboring cell, the center part of this cell, and the right part of the left-neighboring cell. Note that a state in L (R, respectively) can be regarded as a "signal" to the left-neighboring (right-neighboring) cell. An equation $f(l, c, r) = (l', c', r')$, where $(l, c, r), (l', c', r') \in Q$, is called a *rule* of P.

Definition 2. Let $P = ((L, C, R), f, (\#, \#, \#), r_s, \Sigma, A, N)$ *be a* PCA. P *is called locally reversible iff the local function* f *is injective, and called globally reversible iff the global function* F *induced by* f *is injective.*

Proposition 1. *[7] Any PCA* P *is locally reversible iff it is globally reversible.*

As stated in Proposition 1, local and global reversibility are equivalent in PCAs. Hence, in the following, we shall design a locally reversible PCA to obtain a globally reversible one, and it is simply called a *reversible* PCA (RPCA).

In the following, we assume a PCA (or RPCA) P satisfies the condition (P1) below so that the number of non-quiescent cells does not exceeds $n + 2$ throughout a computation process, where n is the length of an input.

(P1) If a cell of P is in the state $\#$ in the center part, then it bounces any signal l (r, respectively) from the right (left), and sends back a signal r' (l') to the right (left): $\forall l \in L, \exists r' \in R\ (f(l, \#, \#) = (\#, \#, r'))$ and $\forall r \in R, \exists l' \in L\ (f(\#, \#, r) = (l', \#, \#))$.

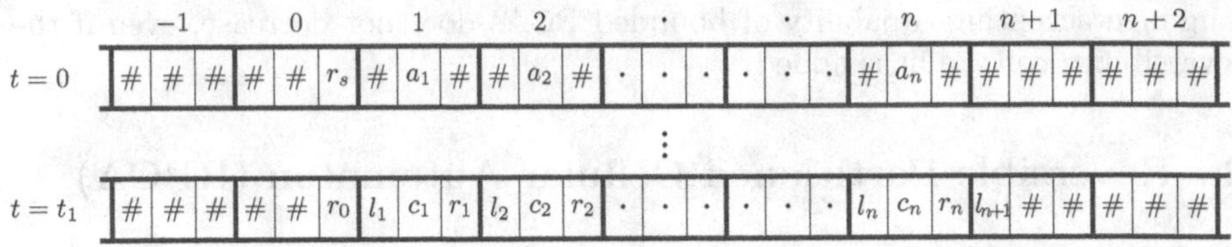

Fig. 1. An initial configuration α_w $(t = 0)$ of a PCA with an input $w = a_1a_2 \cdots a_n$, and an accepting configuration $(t = t_1)$ where $p_L(F^{t_1}(\alpha_w)(1)) = l_1 \in A$.

Definition 3. Let $P = ((L, C, R), f, (\#, \#, \#), r_s, \Sigma, A, N)$ *be a*PCA*, and* $w = a_1a_2 \cdots a_n \in \Sigma^n$ $(n = 1, 2, \ldots)$ *be an input word. The configuration* α_w *defined below is called an* initial configuration of P *with* w.

$$\alpha_w(x) = \begin{cases} (\#, \#, r_s) & \text{if } x = 0 \\ (\#, a_x, \#) & \text{if } 1 \leq x \leq n \\ (\#, \#, \#) & \text{if } x < 0 \text{ or } x > n \end{cases}$$

We sayw is accepted by P *if* $\exists t_1 > 0$ $(p_L(F^{t_1}(\alpha_w)(1)) \in A)$. The language *accepted by* P is: $L(P) = \{w \in \Sigma^* \mid \exists t_1 > 0\ (p_L(F^{t_1}(\alpha_w)(1)) \in A)\}$.

An initial configuration and an accepting configuration are illustrated in Fig. 1. Here, we assume an infinite array of cells. But, since the condition (P1) holds, only $n+2$ cells are used in a computation. In the case of usual CA acceptors border cells at the positions 0 and $n+1$ do not change their states (see [1]). But, in PCA acceptors, the right part of the left border cell, and the left part of the right border cell may change their states.

3 Reversible Linear-Bounded Automaton (RLBA)

Lange, McKenzie and Tapp [3] showed that the complexity class of deterministic space $S(n)$ is equal to that of reversible space $S(n)$. From this, we obtain equivalence of a deterministic linear-bounded automaton (DLBA) and a reversible DLBA (RDLBA) by letting $S(n) = n$. But, their method is complex, and it is difficult to get a concrete description of the RDLBA. Here, we show a simpler method of converting a DLBA into an RDLBA based on the method in [6].

In this paper, a linear-bounded automaton (LBA) is defined as a 2-track LBA shown in Fig. 2 rather than a standard 1-track LBA, because in the proof of Lemma 2, which gives a method of converting an irreversible LBA to a reversible one, it is required that an input word is kept unchanged throughout its computation. It is easy to see a 2-track LBA can simulate a 1-track LBA, and vice versa by a straightforward method, and thus they are equivalent.

Definition 4. A 2-track linear-bounded automaton *(LBA) consists of a finite-state control, a read-write head, and a tape with an input track and a storage*

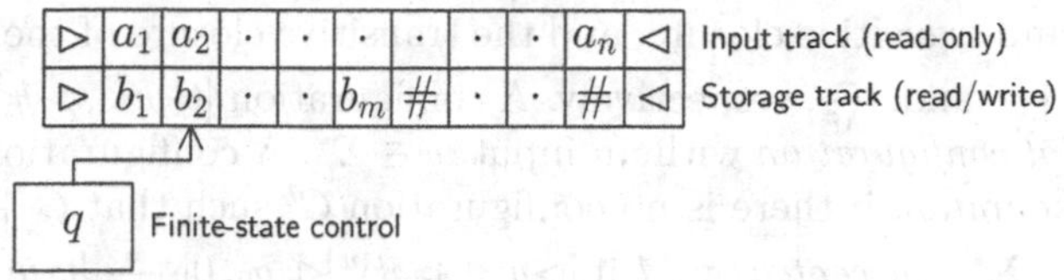

Fig. 2. A 2-track linear-bounded automaton (LBA).

track (Fig. 2). It is defined by $M = (Q, \Sigma, \Gamma, \delta, \triangleright, \triangleleft, \#, q_0, A, N)$. *$Q$ is a nonempty finite set of states, Σ is a nonempty finite set of input symbols for the input track, and Γ is a nonempty finite set of storage symbols for the storage track. $\triangleright$ and $\triangleleft$ are left and right endmarkers of each track of the tape such that* $\{\triangleright, \triangleleft\} \cap (\Sigma \cup \Gamma) = \emptyset$, and $\# \in \Gamma$ *is a blank symbol for the storage track.* $q_0\,(\in Q)$ *is the initial state, and* $A\,(\subset Q)$ and $N\,(\subset Q)$ *are sets of accepting and non-accepting states that satisfy* $A \cap N = \emptyset$. *δ is a subset of* $(Q \times ((\Sigma \times \Gamma^2 \cup \{[\triangleright, [\triangleright, \triangleright]], [\triangleleft, [\triangleleft, \triangleleft]]\}) \cup \{-1, 0, +1\}) \times Q)$ *that determines the transition relation on M' s configurations. Here,* $-1, 0,$ *and* $+1$ *stand for left-shift, no-shift, and right-shift of the head, respectively. In what follows, we also use* $-$ and $+$ *instead of* -1 *and* $+1$ *for simplicity. Note that only reading is permitted on the input track, while both reading and writing are allowed on the storage track.*

Each element $r = [p, x, q] \in \delta$ is called a *rule* of M in the triple form, where $x = [a, [b, c]] \in \Sigma \times \Gamma^2 \cup \{[\triangleright, [\triangleright, \triangleright]], [\triangleleft, [\triangleleft, \triangleleft]]\}$ or $x = d \in \{-, 0, +\}$. A rule of the form $[p, [a, [b, c]], q]$ is called a *read-write rule*, and means if M is in the state p and reads an input symbol a and a storage symbol b, then rewrites the latter to c, and enters the state q. Here, $\triangleright$ and $\triangleleft$ should not be rewritten to any other symbol. A rule of the form $[p, d, q]$ is called a *shift rule*, and means if M is in the state p, then shifts the head to the direction d, and enters the state q.

Let $q \in Q$, $w \in \Sigma^*$, $v \in \Gamma^*$ such that $|v| = |w|$, and $h \in \{0, 1, \ldots, |w| + 1\}$. Then, $[\triangleright w \triangleleft, \triangleright v \triangleleft, q, h]$ is called a *computational configuration* (or simply a *configuration*) of M with an input w. It means that the contents of the input track and the storage track are w and v, the finite-state control is in the state q, and the head position is h, where the position of $\triangleright$ is 0.

Let S be a set of symbols. A partial function $s : S^+ \times \mathbb{N} \to S$ is defined as follows, where $\mathbb{N}$ is the set of all non-negative integers. If $x = x_0 x_1 \cdots x_{n-1}$ $(x_i \in S)$, then $s(x, j) = x_j$ for $0 \le j < n$, and $s(x, j)$ is undefined for $j \ge n$. Hence, $s(x, j)$ gives the j-th symbol of x, where the leftmost symbol is the 0-th.

The *transition relation* $\vdash_{\overline{M}}$ between a pair of configurations $[\triangleright w \triangleleft, \triangleright v \triangleleft, q, h]$ and $[\triangleright w \triangleleft, \triangleright v' \triangleleft, q', h']$ is defined as follows.

$$[\triangleright w \triangleleft, \triangleright v \triangleleft, q, h] \vdash_{\overline{M}} [\triangleright w \triangleleft, \triangleright v' \triangleleft, q', h'] \;\text{ iff (1) or (2) holds.}$$

(1) $[q, [s(\triangleright w \triangleleft, h), [s(\triangleright v \triangleleft, h), s(\triangleright v' \triangleleft, h')]], q'] \in \delta \;\wedge\; h' = h \;\wedge$
$\forall j\, (0 \le j \le |v| + 1 \;\wedge\; j \ne h \;\Rightarrow\; s(\triangleright v' \triangleleft, j) = s(\triangleright v \triangleleft, j))$

(2) $[q, h' - h, q'] \in \delta \;\wedge\; v' = v$

The reflexive and transitive closure, and the transitive closure of the relation $\vdash_{M}$ is denoted by $\vdash_{M}^{*}$ and $\vdash_{M}^{+}$, respectively. A configuration $[\rhd w \lhd, \rhd \#^{|w|} \lhd, q_0, 0]$ is called an *initial configuration* with an input $w \in \Sigma^*$. A configuration C is called a *halting configuration* if there is no configuration C' such that $C \vdash_{M} C'$.

We say $w \in \Sigma^*$ is *accepted* by M if $[\rhd w \lhd, \rhd \#^{|w|} \lhd, q_0, 0] \vdash_{M}^{*} [\rhd w \lhd, \rhd v \lhd, q, h]$ for some $q \in A$, $v \in \Gamma^{|w|}$, and $h \in \{0, 1, \ldots, |w|+1\}$. The *language* accepted by M is the set of all words accepted by M, and denoted by $L(M)$.

$$\begin{array}{l} L(M) = \{w \in \Sigma^* \mid [\rhd w \lhd, \rhd \#^{|w|} \lhd, q_0, 0] \vdash_{M}^{*} [\rhd w \lhd, \rhd v \lhd, q, h] \;\text{ for some} \\ \qquad\qquad\qquad\qquad q \in A,\; v \in \Gamma^{|w|}, \text{ and } h \in \{0, 1, \ldots, |w|+1\} \;\} \end{array}$$

The set N of non-accepting states is not used in the definition of acceptance. But, it is convenient to specify it for the later construction of reversible LBAs.

Definition 5. *An LBA* $M = (Q, \Sigma, \Gamma, \delta, \rhd, \lhd, \#, q_0, A, N)$*is called a* deterministic LBA *(DLBA) iff the following* determinism condition *holds.*

$$\begin{array}{l} \forall\, r_1 = [p, x, q] \in \delta,\; \forall\, r_2 = [p', x', q'] \in \delta : \\ \;(r_1 \neq r_2 \;\wedge\; p = p') \Rightarrow\; (x \notin \{-, 0, +\} \;\wedge\; x' \notin \{-, 0, +\} \;\wedge \\ \;\;\forall\, [a, [b, c]], [a'[b', c']] \in \Sigma \times \Gamma^2 \cup \{[\rhd, [\rhd, \rhd]], [\lhd, [\lhd, \lhd]]\} \\ \;\;\;(x = [a, [b, c]] \;\wedge\; x' = [a', [b', c']] \;\Rightarrow\; [a, b] \neq [a', b'])) \end{array}$$

It means that for any two distinct rules r_1 and r_2 *in* δ, *if the present states pand* p' *are the same, then they are both read-write rules, and the pairs of the input symbols and the read storage symbols* $[a, b]$ *and* $[a', b']$ *are different.*

Definition 6. *An LBA* $M = (Q, \Sigma, \Gamma, \delta, \rhd, \lhd, \#, q_0, A, N)$ *is called a* reversible LBA *(RLBA) iff the following* reversibility condition *holds.*

$$\begin{array}{l} \forall\, r_1 = [p, x, q] \in \delta,\; \forall\, r_2 = [p', x', q'] \in \delta : \\ \;(r_1 \neq r_2 \;\wedge\; q = q') \Rightarrow\; (x \notin \{-, 0, +\} \;\wedge\; x' \notin \{-, 0, +\} \;\wedge \\ \;\;\forall\, [a, [b, c]], [a'[b', c']] \in \Sigma \times \Gamma^2 \cup \{[\rhd, [\rhd, \rhd]], [\lhd, [\lhd, \lhd]]\} \\ \;\;\;(x = [a, [b, c]] \;\wedge\; x' = [a', [b', c']] \;\Rightarrow\; [a, c] \neq [a', c'])) \end{array}$$

It means that for any two distinct rules r_1 *and* r_2 *in* δ, *if the next states* q *and* q' *are the same, then they are both read-write rules and the pairs of the input symbols and the written storage symbols* $[a, c]$ *and* $[a', c']$ *are different.*

A rule $[p, x, q]$ is called a *deterministic rule* (*reversible rule*, respectively), if there is no rule $[p', x', q']$ such that the pair $([p, x, q], [p', x', q'])$ violates the determinism (reversibility) condition.

A reversible and deterministic LBA is denoted by RDLBA. In the following, we consider only DLBAs and RDLBAs. From the definition, it is easily seen that if M is deterministic, then for every configuration C of M there is at most one configuration C' such that $C \vdash_{M} C'$. Likewise, if M is reversible, then for every configuration C of M there is at most one configuration C' such that $C' \vdash_{M} C$.

We define a *computation graph* $G_{M,w} = (V, E)$ of M with an input $w \in \Sigma^*$ as follows. Let $\mathrm{Conf}(M, w)$ be the set of all configurations of M with w, i.e.,

$\mathrm{Conf}(M,w) = \{[\rhd w\lhd, \rhd v\lhd, q, h] \mid q \in Q \wedge v \in \Gamma^{|w|} \wedge h \in \{0,1,\ldots,|w|+1\}\}$. The set $V(\subset \mathrm{Conf}(M,w))$ of nodes is the smallest set that contains the initial configuration $[\rhd w\lhd, \rhd\#^{|w|}\lhd, q, h]$, and satisfies the following condition: $\forall C_1, C_2 \in \mathrm{Conf}(M,w)\,((C_1 \in V \wedge (C_1 \vdash_{\overline{M}} C_2 \vee C_2 \vdash_{\overline{M}} C_1)) \Rightarrow C_2 \in V)$. Namely, V is the set of all configurations connected to the initial configuration, and is finite. The set E of directed edges is: $E = \{(C_1, C_2) \mid C_1, C_2 \in V \wedge C_1 \vdash_{\overline{M}} C_2\}$. If M is deterministic, then outdegree of each node in V is either 0 or 1, where a node of outdegree 0 corresponds to a halting configuration. On the other hand, if M is reversible, then indegree of each node in V is either 0 or 1.

In the following, we assume, without loss of generality, any given DLBA $M = (Q, \Sigma, \Gamma, \delta, \rhd, \lhd, \#, q_0, A, N)$ satisfies the following conditions (C1)–(C6) for the later convenience. In fact, M is easily modified so that it satisfies them.

(C1) The initial state q_0 does not appear as the third component of a rule in δ: $\forall [q, x, q'] \in \delta\ \ (q' \neq q_0)$.

(C2) M performs read-write and shift operations alternately. Hence, Q is written as $Q = Q_{\mathrm{rw}} \cup Q_{\mathrm{sf}}$ for some Q_{rw} and Q_{sf} such that $Q_{\mathrm{rw}} \cap Q_{\mathrm{sf}} = \emptyset$, and δ satisfies the following condition:

$$\forall\, [p, x, q] \in \delta \quad ((x \in \Sigma \times \Gamma^2 \cup \{[\rhd,[\rhd,\rhd]],[\lhd,[\lhd,\lhd]]\} \Rightarrow p \in Q_{\mathrm{rw}} \wedge q \in Q_{\mathrm{sf}}) \wedge (x \in \{-,0,+\} \Rightarrow p \in Q_{\mathrm{sf}} \wedge q \in Q_{\mathrm{rw}}))$$

We can easily modify M so that it satisfies the above condition by adding new states to it. Each element of Q_{rw} and Q_{sf} is called a *read-write state* and a *shift state*, respectively. We further assume $q_0 \in Q_{\mathrm{rw}}$, and $A \cup N \subset Q_{\mathrm{sf}}$, though each state in $A \cup N$ makes no further move as in (C3).

(C3) Every state in $A \cup N$ is a halting state in Q_{sf}, and vice versa: $\forall q \in Q\ \ (q \in A \cup N \Leftrightarrow q \in Q_{\mathrm{sf}} \wedge \neg\exists [q, x, q'] \in \delta)$.

(C4) If M reads a left (right, respectively) endmarker, then in the next step the shift direction of the head is to the right (left):

$$\begin{aligned}&\forall p, r \in Q_{\mathrm{rw}},\ \forall q \in Q_{\mathrm{sf}},\\ &\forall [a,[b,c]] \in (\Sigma \times \Gamma^2 \cup \{[\rhd,[\rhd,\rhd]],[\lhd,[\lhd,\lhd]]\}),\ \forall d \in \{-,0,+\}\\ &\quad ([p,[a,[b,c]],q],[q,d,r] \in \delta \Rightarrow (a = \rhd \Rightarrow b = c = \rhd \wedge d = +) \wedge\\ &\qquad\qquad (a = \lhd \Rightarrow b = c = \lhd \wedge d = -))\end{aligned}$$

Likewise, if M reads a left (right, respectively) endmarker, then in the previous step the shift direction of the head is to the left (right):

$$\begin{aligned}&\forall p, r \in Q_{\mathrm{sf}},\ \forall q \in Q_{\mathrm{rw}},\\ &\forall [a,[b,c]] \in (\Sigma \times \Gamma^2 \cup \{[\rhd,[\rhd,\rhd]],[\lhd,[\lhd,\lhd]]\}),\ \forall d \in \{-,0,+\}\\ &\quad ([r,d,q],[q,[a,[b,c]],p] \in \delta \Rightarrow (a = \rhd \Rightarrow b = c = \rhd \wedge d = -) \wedge\\ &\qquad\qquad (a = \lhd \Rightarrow b = c = \lhd \wedge d = +))\end{aligned}$$

(C5) Just after M starts to move, it confirms the storage track contains only blank symbols #s. It is done by replacing the rule $[q_0,[\rhd,[\rhd,\rhd]],q]$ by

$[q_0,[\rhd,[\rhd,\rhd]],q_{0,1}],\ \ [q_{0,1},+,q_{0,2}], [q_{0,2},[a,[\#,\#]],q_{0,1}],$
$[q_{0,2},[\lhd,[\lhd,\lhd]],q_{0,3}], [q_{0,3},-,q_{0,4}], [q_{0,4},[a,[\#,\#]],q_{0,3}], [q_{0,4},[\rhd,[\rhd,\rhd]],q]$.

Here, $q_{0,1}, q_{0,2}, q_{0,3}, q_{0,4}$ are new states, and the rules $[q_{0,2},[a,[\#,\#]],q_{0,1}]$ and $[q_{0,4},[a,[\#,\#]],q_{0,3}]$ are added for each $a \in \Sigma$. Note that there is only one rule that has q_0 as the first component since (C1) and (C2) hold.

We define the following functions to give the condition (C6) below: prev-rw : $Q_{\rm rw} \to 2^{Q_{\rm sf}\times\{-,0,+\}}$, prev-sf : $Q_{\rm sf} \times (\Sigma\times\Gamma \cup \{[\triangleright,\triangleright],[\triangleleft,\triangleleft]\}) \to 2^{Q_{\rm rw}\times(\Gamma\cup\{\triangleright,\triangleleft\})}$, $\deg_{\rm rw} : Q_{\rm rw} \to \mathbb{N}$, and $\deg_{\rm sf} : Q_{\rm sf} \times (\Sigma\times\Gamma \cup \{[\triangleright,\triangleright],[\triangleleft,\triangleleft]\}) \to \mathbb{N}$ as follows, where $Q_{\rm rw}$ and $Q_{\rm sf}$ are the sets given in (C2).

$$
\begin{aligned}
\text{prev-rw}(q) &= \{[p,d] \mid p \in Q_{\rm sf} \ \wedge\ d \in \{-,0,+\} \ \wedge\ [p,d,q] \in \delta\} \\
\text{prev-sf}(q,a,c) &= \{[p,b] \mid p \in Q_{\rm rw} \ \wedge\ b \in (\Gamma \cup \{\triangleright,\triangleleft\}) \ \wedge\ [p,[a,[b,c]],q] \in \delta\} \\
\deg_{\rm rw}(q) &= |\text{prev-rw}(q)| \\
\deg_{\rm sf}(q,a,c) &= |\text{prev-sf}(q,a,c)|
\end{aligned}
$$

Assume M is in the configuration $[\triangleright w\triangleleft, \triangleright v\triangleleft, q, h]$. If q is a read-write state (shift state, respectively), then $\deg_{\rm rw}(q)$ ($\deg_{\rm sf}(q, s(\triangleright w\triangleleft, h), s(\triangleright v\triangleleft, h))$) gives the total number of previous configurations of $[\triangleright w\triangleleft, \triangleright v\triangleleft, q, h]$. Each element $[p,d] \in$ prev-rw(q) ($[p,b] \in$ prev-sf$(q, s(\triangleright w\triangleleft, h), s(\triangleright v\triangleleft, h))$, respectively) gives a previous state and a shift direction (a previous state and a previous storage symbol). If M is an RDLBA, then $\deg_{\rm rw}(q) \leq 1$ and $\deg_{\rm sf}(q,a,c) \leq 1$ hold for any $q \in Q$, and $(a,c) \in (\Sigma\times\Gamma \cup \{[\triangleright,\triangleright],[\triangleleft,\triangleleft]\})$.

(C6) M satisfies $\deg_{\rm rw}(q) \leq 1$ for all $q \in Q_{\rm rw}$. If otherwise, we modify M as follows. If there is a pair of shift rules $[p, d_1, q]$ and $[p', d_2, q]$ in δ, then add a new state q' in Q, remove $[p', d_2, q]$ from δ, and add rules $[p', d_2, q']$ and $[q', [a,[b,c]], r]$ for each $[q, [a,[b,c]], r] \in \delta$. Hence, $\deg_{\rm sf}(r,a,c)$ increases, but $\deg_{\rm rw}(q)$ decreases. Repeat this procedure until no such pair exits.

We first show Lemma 1 stating that an RDLBA always halts. It is proved in a similar manner to the case of a reversible multi-head finite automaton [5].

Lemma 1. *Let $M = (Q, \Sigma, \Gamma, \delta, \triangleright, \triangleleft, \#, q_0, A, N)$ be an RDLBA that satisfies (C1). Then, it eventually halts for any input $w \in \Sigma^*$.*

Proof. Let $C_0 \mathrel{|\!\!\frac{}{M}} C_1 \mathrel{|\!\!\frac{}{M}} C_2 \mathrel{|\!\!\frac{}{M}} \cdots$ be a computation of M starting from the initial configuration $C_0 = [\triangleright w\triangleleft, \triangleright\#^{|w|}\triangleleft, q_0, 0]$ with an input $w \in \Sigma^*$. First, we show M never loops for any w. Assume, on the contrary, it loops, i.e., there exists a pair of integers (i,j) such that $0 \leq i < j$ and $C_i = C_j$. Let (i_0, j_0) be the pair such that i_0 is the least integer among such (i,j)-pairs. By the condition (C1), there is no configuration C_{-1} that satisfy $C_{-1} \mathrel{|\!\!\frac{}{M}} C_0$. Hence, $C_0 \neq C_{i_0} = C_{j_0}$, and thus $i_0 > 0$. Therefore $C_{i_0-1} \neq C_{j_0--1}$. But, since $C_{i_0-1} \mathrel{|\!\!\frac{}{M}} C_{i_0}$, $C_{j_0-1} \mathrel{|\!\!\frac{}{M}} C_{j_0}$, and $C_{i_0} = C_{j_0}$ hold, it contradicts the assumption M is reversible. Therefore, M never loops. On the other hand, the total number of configurations reachable from C_0 is bounded by $|Q| \cdot |\Gamma|^{|w|} \cdot (|w|+2)$. Hence, M halts for any input w. □

We now give a method of converting a DLBA to an RDLBA in Lemma 2.

Lemma 2. *Let $M = (Q, \Sigma, \Gamma, \delta, \triangleright, \triangleleft, \#, q_0, A, N)$ be a DLBA. We can construct an RDLBA $M^\dagger = (Q^\dagger, \Sigma, \Gamma, \delta^\dagger, \triangleright, \triangleleft, \#, q_0, \{\hat{q}_0^{\rm b}\}, \{q_0^{\rm b}\})$ such that the following holds, and thus $L(M^\dagger) = L(M)$.*

$$
\begin{aligned}
\forall w \in \Sigma^* \ (&(w \in L(M) \ \Rightarrow\ [\triangleright w\triangleleft, \triangleright\#^{|w|}\triangleleft, q_0, 0] \mathrel{|\!\!\frac{+}{M^\dagger}} [\triangleright w\triangleleft, \triangleright\#^{|w|}\triangleleft, \hat{q}_0^{\rm b}, 0]) \ \wedge \\
&(w \notin L(M) \ \Rightarrow\ [\triangleright w\triangleleft, \triangleright\#^{|w|}\triangleleft, q_0, 0] \mathrel{|\!\!\frac{+}{M^\dagger}} [\triangleright w\triangleleft, \triangleright\#^{|w|}\triangleleft, q_0^{\rm b}, 0]))
\end{aligned}
$$

Proof. In our construction, $M^\dagger$ traverses the computation graph $G_{M,w}$ from the initial configuration of M with an input w to find an accepting one as shown in Fig. 3. We assume M satisfies the conditions (C1)–(C6). We further assume the sets Q, and $\Gamma \cup \{\rhd, \lhd\}$ are totally ordered, and the elements of the set prev-sf(q, a, c) is sorted by these orders. Thus, we express it by an ordered list as below. Note that since M satisfies (C6), $|\text{prev-rw}(q)| \leq 1$ holds for all $q \in Q_{\text{rw}}$.

$$\text{prev-sf}(q,a,c) = [[p_1, b_1], \ldots, [p_k, b_k]], \text{ where } k = \deg_{\text{sf}}(q,a,c)$$

Then, $Q^\dagger = \{q, \hat{q}, q^{\text{b}}, \hat{q}^{\text{b}} \mid q \in Q\}$, and $\delta^\dagger$ is defined as below.

$$\begin{aligned}
\delta^\dagger &= \delta_1 \cup \cdots \cup \delta_4 \cup \hat{\delta}_1 \cup \cdots \cup \hat{\delta}_4 \cup \delta_A \cup \delta_N \\
\delta_1 &= \{ [q^{\text{b}}, [a,[c,b_1]], p_1^{\text{b}}], [p_1, [a,[b_1,b_2]], p_2^{\text{b}}], [p_2, [a,[b_2,b_3]], p_3^{\text{b}}], \ldots, \\
&\qquad [p_{k-1}, [a,[b_{k-1},b_k]], p_k^{\text{b}}], [p_k, [a,[b_k,c]], q] \mid \\
&\qquad q \in Q_{\text{sf}} \wedge (a,c) \in (\Sigma \times \Gamma \cup \{(\rhd,\rhd),(\lhd,\lhd)\}) \wedge \deg_{\text{sf}}(q,a,c) \geq 1 \\
&\qquad \wedge \text{prev-sf}(q,a,c) = [[p_1,b_1],\ldots,[p_k,b_k]], \text{ where } k = \deg_{\text{sf}}(q,a,c) \} \\
\delta_2 &= \{ [q^{\text{b}}, -d, p^{\text{b}}], [p, d, q] \mid q \in Q_{\text{rw}} \wedge \text{prev-rw}(q) = [[p,d]] \} \\
\delta_3 &= \{ [q^{\text{b}}, [a,[c,c]], q] \mid q \in Q_{\text{sf}} - (A \cup N) \\
&\qquad \wedge (a,c) \in (\Sigma \times \Gamma \cup \{(\rhd,\rhd),(\lhd,\lhd)\}) \wedge \deg_{\text{sf}}(q,a,c) = 0 \} \\
\delta_4 &= \{ [q, [a,[b,b]], q^{\text{b}}] \mid q \in Q_{\text{rw}} - \{q_0\} \\
&\qquad \wedge (a,b) \in (\Sigma \times \Gamma \cup \{(\rhd,\rhd),(\lhd,\lhd)\}) \wedge \neg \exists c \exists p\, ([q,[a,[b,c]],p] \in \delta) \} \\
\hat{\delta}_i &= \{ [\hat{p}, x, \hat{q}] \mid [p,x,q] \in \delta_i \} \; (i = 1, \ldots, 4) \\
\delta_A &= \{ [q, 0, \hat{q}^{\text{b}}] \mid q \in A \} \cup \{ [\hat{q}, 0, q^{\text{b}}] \mid q \in A \} \\
\delta_N &= \{ [q, 0, q^{\text{b}}] \mid q \in N \} \cup \{ [\hat{q}, 0, \hat{q}^{\text{b}}] \mid q \in N \}
\end{aligned}$$

$Q^\dagger$ has four types of states. They are of the forms $q, \hat{q}, q^{\text{b}}$ and $\hat{q}^{\text{b}}$. The states without a superscript (i.e., q and $\hat{q}$) are for forward computation, while those with a superscript "b" (i.e., q^{b} and $\hat{q}^{\text{b}}$) are for backward computation. The states with "^" (i.e., $\hat{q}$ and $\hat{q}^{\text{b}}$) are the ones indicating that an accepting configuration of M was found in the process of traversal, while those without "^" (i.e., q and q^{b}) are for indicating no accepting configuration has been found so far.

$\delta_1, \ldots, \delta_4$ are the sets of rules for the states without "^", and $\hat{\delta}_1, \ldots, \hat{\delta}_4$ are the ones of corresponding rules for the states with "^". δ_1 and $\hat{\delta}_1$ are for searching the graph $G_{M,w}$ at a shift state of M. See, for example, the node with a shift state q_3 in Fig. 3 (a). By the rules in δ_1 and $\hat{\delta}_1$, the graph $G_{M,w}$ is searched by the states of $M^\dagger$ from $\hat{q}_3^{\text{b}}$ to $\hat{q}_5^{\text{b}}$, from $\hat{q}_5$ to $\hat{q}_0^{\text{b}}$, from q_0 to q_6^{b}, and from q_6 to q_3. δ_2 and $\hat{\delta}_2$ are for searching $G_{M,w}$ at a read-write states of M. For example, see the node with a read-write state q_1 in Fig. 3 (a). By these rules the graph is searched from $\hat{q}_1^{\text{b}}$ to $\hat{q}_3^{\text{b}}$, and from q_3 to q_1. δ_3 and $\hat{\delta}_3$ are for turning the direction of search from backward to forward in $G_{M,w}$ for a shift state. See, for example, the node with the shift state q_9 in Fig. 3 (a), where the state of $M^\dagger$ changes from $\hat{q}_9^{\text{b}}$ to $\hat{q}_9$. δ_4 and $\hat{\delta}_4$ are for turning the direction from forward to backward in for halting configuration with a read-write state. There is no example of this type in Fig. 3. But, if the configuration with q_2 were such a one, then the state of $M^\dagger$ changes from q_2 to q_2^{b}. δ_A (δ_N, respectively) is for turning the search direction from forward to backward for accepting (non-accepting) states. In addition, each rule in δ_A makes $M^\dagger$ change the state from a one without "^" to the corresponding one with "^". Note that the sets of rules

$\{[\hat{q}, 0, q^{\rm b}] \mid q \in A\} \subset \delta_A$ and $\{[\hat{q}, 0, \hat{q}^{\rm b}] \mid q \in N\} \subset \delta_N$ are not used to simulate M, but for keeping symmetry between the states with "^" and those without "^".

We can verify $M^\dagger$ is deterministic and reversible. For example, consider the rules in δ_1. Since prev-sf$(q, a, c) = [[p_1, b_1], \ldots, [p_k, b_k]]$ ($k = \deg_{\rm sf}(q, a, c) \geq 1$), there are rules $[p_1, [a, [b_1, c], q]], [p_2, [a, [b_2, c], q]], \ldots, [p_k, [a, [b_k, c], q]]$ in δ of M. First, $[q^{\rm b}, [a, [c, b_1]], p_1^{\rm b}] \in \delta_1$ is a deterministic rule, because it is the sole rule of the form $[q^{\rm b}, [a, [c, x]], y^{\rm b}]$ (for some $x \in \Gamma \cup \{\triangleright, \triangleleft\}$ and $y \in Q$) for the combination (q, a, c). It is also a reversible rule, since $[p_1, [a, [b_1, c], q]] \in \delta$ is a deterministic rule. Second, $[p_i, [a, [b_i, b_{i+1}]], p_{i+1}^{\rm b}] \in \delta_1$ ($i = 1, \ldots, k-1$) is deterministic, since $[p_i, [a, [b_i, c], q]] \in \delta$ is deterministic. It is reversible, since $[p_{i+1}, [a, [b_{i+1}, c], q]] \in \delta$ is deterministic. Third, $[p_k, [a, [b_k, c]], q] \in \delta_1$ is deterministic, since $[p_k, [a, [b_k, c], q]] \in \delta$ is deterministic. It is also reversible, since it is the sole rule of the form $[x, [a, [y, c]], q] \in \delta_1$ (for some $x \in Q$ and $y \in \Gamma \cup \{\triangleright, \triangleleft\}$) for the combination (q, a, c). It is also easy to verify that other rules in $\delta^\dagger$ are deterministic and reversible.

We can also verify that the constructed $M^\dagger$ also satisfies the conditions (C1)–(C6) except (C4) (since there are rules of the form $[p, 0, q]$ in δ_A and δ_N). For example, (C2) can be verified from the following fact: if $q, \hat{q} \in Q^\dagger_{\rm rw}$ ($q, \hat{q} \in Q^\dagger_{\rm sf}$, respectively), then $q^{\rm b}, \hat{q}^{\rm b} \in Q^\dagger_{\rm sf}$ ($q^{\rm b}, \hat{q}^{\rm b} \in Q^\dagger_{\rm rw}$).

Now, consider the case where M finally halts in a configuration $C_{\rm h}$. Then $G_{M,w}$ becomes a finite tree with the root $C_{\rm h}$. Given the input w, $M^\dagger$ starts to search $G_{M,w}$. As explained above, from each node, $M^\dagger$ visits all of its child nodes one after another, and thus $M^\dagger$ will perform a depth-first search of a tree (Fig. 3 (a)). Note that the search starts not from the root of the tree but from the leaf node $[\triangleright w \triangleleft, \triangleright \#^{|w|} \triangleleft, q_0, 0]$. Since each node of $G_{M,w}$ is identified by the configuration of M of the form $[\triangleright w \triangleleft, \triangleright v \triangleleft, q, h]$, it is easy for $M^\dagger$ to keep it by the configuration of $M^\dagger$ itself.

If $M^\dagger$ enters an accepting state of M, say $q_{\rm a}$, which is the root of the tree while traversing the tree, then $M^\dagger$ goes to the state $\hat{q}_{\rm a}^{\rm b}$ by a rule in δ_A, and continues the depth-first search. After that, $M^\dagger$ uses the states of the form $\hat{q}$ and $\hat{q}^{\rm b}$ indicating that the input w should be accepted. $M^\dagger$ will eventually reach the initial configuration of M by its configuration $[\triangleright w \triangleleft, \triangleright \#^{|w|} \triangleleft, \hat{q}_0^{\rm b}, 0]$. Thus, $M^\dagger$ halts and accepts the input.

If $M^\dagger$ enters a halting state of M other than the accepting states, then by a rule in $\delta_N \cup \delta_4$, and then by rules in $\delta_1 \cup \delta_2 \cup \delta_3$ it continues the depth-first search without entering a state of the form $\hat{q}$. Also in this case, $M^\dagger$ will finally reach the initial configuration of M by its configuration $[\triangleright w \triangleleft, \triangleright \#^{|w|} \triangleleft, q_0^{\rm b}, 0]$. Thus, $M^\dagger$ halts and rejects the input.

We can see $M^\dagger$ halts either in the configuration $[\triangleright w \triangleleft, \triangleright \#^{|w|} \triangleleft, \hat{q}_0^{\rm b}, 0]$ or $[\triangleright w \triangleleft, \triangleright \#^{|w|} \triangleleft, q_0^{\rm b}, 0]$ by the following reasons. First, $M^\dagger$ does not halt in a state other than $\hat{q}_0^{\rm b}$ and $q_0^{\rm b}$, since $\delta^\dagger$ is so designed that $M^\dagger$ continues the traversal at any node of $G_{M,w}$ such that M's state is not q_0. Second, $M^\dagger$ does not halt in a configuration $[\triangleright w' \triangleleft, \triangleright v \triangleleft, \hat{q}_0^{\rm b}, h]$ or $[\triangleright w' \triangleleft, \triangleright v \triangleleft, q_0^{\rm b}, h]$ for some $w' \in \Sigma^*$ such that $w' \neq w$, $v \in \Gamma^{|w'|}$ and $h \in \{0, \ldots, |w'| + 1\}$, since input symbols are not rewritten. Note that, if M rewrites input symbols, then $G_{M,w}$

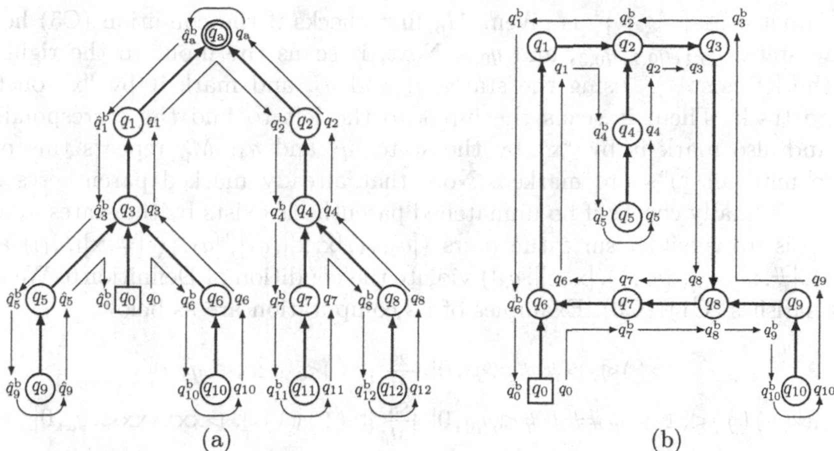

Fig. 3. Examples of computation graphs $G_{M,w}$ of an DLBA M. Each node represents a configuration of M, though only a state of the finite-state control is written in a circle. The node labeled by q_0 represents the initial configuration of M. An RDLBA $M^\dagger$ traverses these graphs along thin arrows using its configurations, and finally halts. (a) A case M halts in an accepting state q_a. (b) A case M loops forever.

may have two or more initial configurations, and thus $M^\dagger$ does not traverse $G_{M,w}$ entirely even if it is a tree. Third, $M^\dagger$ does not halt in a configuration $[\rhd w\lhd, \rhd v\lhd, \hat{q}_0^\mathrm{b}, h]$ or $[\rhd w\lhd, \rhd v\lhd, q_0^\mathrm{b}, h]$ for some $v \in \Gamma^{|w|}$ and $h \neq 0$. Since the initial configuration of M is $[\rhd w\lhd, \rhd \#^{|w|}\lhd, q_0, 0]$, and (C1) holds, we can assume there is no rule of the form $[q_0, [a, [b, c]], q]$ with $[a, [b, c]] \neq [\rhd, [\rhd, \rhd]]$ in δ. Hence, $[\rhd w\lhd, \rhd v\lhd, q_0, h]$ with $h \neq 0$ is not a node of $G_{M,w}$. Fourth, the case that $M^\dagger$ halts in $[\rhd w\lhd, \rhd v\lhd, \hat{q}_0^\mathrm{b}, 0]$ or $[\rhd w\lhd, \rhd v\lhd, q_0^\mathrm{b}, 0]$ for some $v \neq \#^{|w|}$ is also inhibited. If it starts from $[\rhd w\lhd, \rhd v\lhd, q_0, 0]$ with $v \neq \#^{|w|}$, it halts in $q_{0,2}$, because of (C5). Hence, $[\rhd w\lhd, \rhd v\lhd, q_0, 0]$ with $v \neq \#^{|w|}$ is not a node of $G_{M,w}$.

Next, consider the case where M enters a loop. Then $G_{M,w}$ is not a tree, but a finite graph (Fig. 3 (b)). In this case, since there is no accepting configuration in $G_{M,w}$, $M^\dagger$ never reaches an accepting state of M no matter how $M^\dagger$ visits the nodes of $G_{M,w}$ (it may not visit all the nodes of $G_{M,w}$). Thus, $M^\dagger$ uses only the states without "$\hat{\ }$". Since M satisfies the condition (C1), $M^\dagger$ eventually halts by Lemma 1. By the same argument as in the case $G_{M,w}$ is a tree, $M^\dagger$ must halt in the configuration $[\rhd w\lhd, \rhd \#^{|w|}\lhd, q_0^\mathrm{b}, 0]$. By above, the theorem holds. □

Example 1. Consider a DLBA M_p that accepts all well-formed parentheses.

$$
\begin{aligned}
M_\mathrm{p} &= (Q, \{\ (,\ )\ \}, \{\#, \mathrm{x}\}, \delta, \rhd, \lhd, \#, q_0, \{q_\mathrm{a}\}, \{q_\mathrm{r}\}) \\
Q &= \{q_0, q_{0,1}, q_{0,2}, q_{0,3}, q_{0,4}, q_1, q_2, q_3, q_4, q_5, q_6, q_\mathrm{a}, q_\mathrm{r}\} \\
\delta &= \{\, [q_0, [\rhd, [\rhd, \rhd]], q_{0,1}],\ [q_{0,1}, +, q_{0,2}],\ [q_{0,2}, [\ (, [\#, \#]], q_{0,1}],\ [q_{0,2}, [\ ), [\#, \#]], q_{0,1}], \\
&\quad [q_{0,2}, [\lhd, [\lhd, \lhd]], q_{0,3}],\ [q_{0,3}, -, q_{0,4}],\ [q_{0,4}, [\ (, [\#, \#]], q_{0,3}],\ [q_{0,4}, [\ ), [\#, \#]], q_{0,3}], \\
&\quad [q_{0,4}, [\rhd, [\rhd, \rhd]], q_1],\ [q_1, +, q_2],\ [q_2, [\ (, [\#, \#]], q_1],\ [q_2, [\ (, [\mathrm{x}, \mathrm{x}]], q_1], \\
&\quad [q_2, [\ ), [\mathrm{x}, \mathrm{x}]], q_1],\ [q_2, [\ ), [\#, \mathrm{x}]], q_3],\ [q_2, [\lhd, [\lhd, \lhd]], q_5],\ [q_3, -, q_4], \\
&\quad [q_4, [\ (, [\mathrm{x}, \mathrm{x}]], q_3],\ [q_4, [\ ), [\mathrm{x}, \mathrm{x}]], q_3],\ [q_4, [\ (, [\#, \mathrm{x}]], q_1],\ [q_4, [\rhd, [\rhd, \rhd]], q_\mathrm{r}], \\
&\quad [q_5, -, q_6],\ [q_6, [\ (, [\mathrm{x}, \mathrm{x}]], q_5],\ [q_6, [\ ), [\mathrm{x}, \mathrm{x}]], q_5],\ [q_6, [\ (, [\#, \#]], q_\mathrm{r}], \\
&\quad [q_6, [\rhd, [\rhd, \rhd]], q_\mathrm{a}]\ \}
\end{aligned}
$$

If an input $w \in \{\,(,\,)\,\}^*$ is given, M_p first checks if the condition (C5) holds by the states $q_{0,1}, q_{0,2}, q_{0,3}$, and $q_{0,4}$. Next, it scans the input to the right to find the leftmost ")" using the states q_1 and q_2, and mark it by "x" on the storage track. Then, it scans the input to the left to find the corresponding "(", and also mark it by "x" by the states q_3 and q_4. M_p repeats this procedure until all ")"s are marked. Note that already marked parentheses are ignored. It finally checks if no unmatched parenthesis exists by the states q_5 and q_6. M_p is irreversible, since the pairs $([q_2, [\,(, [\mathrm{x},\mathrm{x}]], q_1], [q_4, [\,(, [\#,\mathrm{x}]], q_1])$ and $([q_2, [\,), [\#,\mathrm{x}]], q_3], [q_4, [\,), [\mathrm{x},\mathrm{x}]], q_3])$ violate the condition of Definition 6. We can see it satisfies (C1)–(C6). Examples of its computation are as below.

$$[\rhd(\,)\lhd,\ \rhd\#\#\lhd, q_0, 0] \mathrel{\Big|\!\!\frac{29}{M_\mathrm{p}}} [\rhd(\,)\lhd,\ \rhd\mathrm{xx}\lhd, q_\mathrm{a}, 0]$$
$$[\rhd(\,(\,)\,(\,)\,)\lhd,\ \rhd\#\#\#\#\#\#\lhd, q_0, 0] \mathrel{\Big|\!\!\frac{85}{M_\mathrm{p}}} [\rhd(\,(\,)\,(\,)\,)\lhd,\ \rhd\mathrm{xxxxxx}\lhd, q_\mathrm{a}, 0]$$
$$[\rhd(\,(\,)\,(\,)\lhd,\ \rhd\#\#\#\#\#\lhd, q_0, 0] \mathrel{\Big|\!\!\frac{55}{M_\mathrm{p}}} [\rhd(\,(\,)\,(\,)\lhd,\ \rhd\#\mathrm{xxxx}\lhd, q_\mathrm{r}, 1]$$

An RDLBA $M_\mathrm{p}^\dagger$ that simulates M_p obtained by the method in Lemma 2 is:

$$M_\mathrm{p}^\dagger = (Q^\dagger, \{\,(,\,)\,\}, \{\#,\mathrm{x}\}, \delta^\dagger, \rhd, \lhd, \#, q_0, \{\hat{q}_0^\mathrm{b}\}, \{q_0^\mathrm{b}\}),$$

where $Q^\dagger = \{q, \hat{q}, q^\mathrm{b}, \hat{q}^\mathrm{b} \mid q \in Q\}$. $\delta^\dagger$ has 152 rules, and is not described here.

Examples of computing processes of $M_\mathrm{p}^\dagger$ are as follows.

$$[\rhd(\,)\lhd,\ \rhd\#\#\lhd, q_0, 0] \mathrel{\Big|\!\!\frac{71}{M_\mathrm{p}^\dagger}} [\rhd(\,)\lhd,\ \rhd\#\#\lhd, \hat{q}_0^\mathrm{b}, 0]$$
$$[\rhd(\,(\,)\,(\,)\,)\lhd,\ \rhd\#\#\#\#\#\#\lhd, q_0, 0] \mathrel{\Big|\!\!\frac{739}{M_\mathrm{p}^\dagger}} [\rhd(\,(\,)\,(\,)\,)\lhd,\ \rhd\#\#\#\#\#\#\lhd, \hat{q}_0^\mathrm{b}, 0]$$
$$[\rhd(\,(\,)\,(\,)\lhd,\ \rhd\#\#\#\#\#\lhd, q_0, 0] \mathrel{\Big|\!\!\frac{239}{M_\mathrm{p}^\dagger}} [\rhd(\,(\,)\,(\,)\lhd,\ \rhd\#\#\#\#\#\lhd, q_0^\mathrm{b}, 0]$$

4 Simulating RDLBA by RPCA

Lemma 3. *For any DLBA $M = (Q, \Sigma, \Gamma, \delta, \rhd, \lhd, \#, q_0, A, N)$, we can construct an RPCA P_M such that $L(P_M) = L(M)$.*

Proof. Let $M^\dagger = (Q^\dagger, \Sigma, \Gamma, \delta^\dagger, \rhd, \lhd, \#, q_0, \{\hat{q}_0^\mathrm{b}\}, \{q_0^\mathrm{b}\})$ be the RDLBA converted from M by the method given in Lemma 2. Here, we design P_M so that it simulates $M^\dagger$. The simulation method is based on the one given in [4,7], but here P_M should be constructed so that it satisfies the condition (P1).

From the method shown in Lemma 2 it is easy to see that $M^\dagger$ also satisfies the condition (C2) as well as M. Let $Q^\dagger_\mathrm{rw}$ and $Q^\dagger_\mathrm{sf}$ be the sets of read-write states and shift states, respectively, where $Q^\dagger = Q^\dagger_\mathrm{rw} \cup Q^\dagger_\mathrm{sf}$, and $Q^\dagger_\mathrm{rw} \cap Q^\dagger_\mathrm{sf} = \emptyset$. Let $Q^\dagger_-, Q^\dagger_0$, and $Q^\dagger_+$, which are subsets of $Q^\dagger_\mathrm{rw}$, be as follows: $Q^\dagger_- = \{q \mid \exists p\,([p, -, q] \in \delta^\dagger)\}$, $Q^\dagger_0 = \{q \mid \exists p\,([p, 0, q] \in \delta^\dagger)\}$, and $Q^\dagger_+ = \{q \mid \exists p\,([p, +, q] \in \delta^\dagger)\}$. Since $M^\dagger$ satisfies the reversibility condition and (C1), $Q^\dagger_-, Q^\dagger_0$, and $Q^\dagger_+$ are mutually disjoint, and $(Q^\dagger_- \cup Q^\dagger_0 \cup Q^\dagger_+) \cap \{q_0, \hat{q}_0\} = \emptyset$. Note that, here we assume there is no "useless" state in Q of M that never appears as the third component of a rule except q_0. Thus, $Q^\dagger_{\rm rw} = Q^\dagger_- \cup Q^\dagger_0 \cup Q^\dagger_+ \cup \{q_0, \hat{q}_0\}$ holds.

P_M is defined as follows.

$$P_M = ((L, C, R), f, (\#, \#, \#), r_{\rm s}, \Sigma, \{\hat{l}_{\rm h}\})$$
$$L = Q^\dagger_- \cup \{\#\}$$
$$C = \Sigma \cup \Sigma \times (\Gamma - \{\#\}) \cup \Sigma \times \Gamma \times (Q^\dagger_0 \cup Q^\dagger_{\rm sf} - \{q^{\rm b}_0, \hat{q}^{\rm b}_0\}) \cup \{\#\}$$
$$R = Q^\dagger_+ \cup \{\#\}$$

$r_{\rm s}(\in R)$ is the state such that $\exists p\,([q_0, [\rhd, [\rhd, \rhd]], p], [p, +, r_{\rm s}] \in \delta^\dagger)$.
$\hat{l}_{\rm h}(\in L)$ is the state such that $[\hat{l}_{\rm h}, [\rhd, [\rhd, \rhd]], \hat{q}^{\rm b}_0] \in \delta^\dagger$.

Note that $r_{\rm s}$ is the state of $M^\dagger$ that appears two steps after q_0, and $\hat{l}_{\rm h}$ is the state that appears just before $\hat{q}^{\rm b}_0$.

The local function $f : L \times C \times R \to L \times C \times R$ is defined as follows. Here, the notation $[a, b]$ in (b), (d), (e) and (g) represents the combination of symbols as it is, if $b \neq \#$. But, $[a, \#]$ (i.e., in the case $b = \#$) stands for the symbol $a \in \Sigma$. This is only for simplifying the description of the local function f.

1. Rules of P_M for the case a cell does not change its state.
   (a) For each $a \in (\Sigma \cup \Sigma \times (\Gamma - \{\#\}) \cup \{\#\})$, $f(\#, a, \#) = (\#, a, \#)$.
2. Rules of P_M for simulating shift rules of $M^\dagger$.
   (b) For each $p \in Q^\dagger_{\rm sf}$, $q \in Q^\dagger_-$, and $(a, b) \in \Sigma \times \Gamma$,
   if $[p, -, q] \in \delta^\dagger$, then $f(\#, [a, b, p], \#) = (q, [a, b], \#)$.
   (c) For each $p \in Q^\dagger_{\rm sf}$, $q \in Q^\dagger_0$, and $(a, b) \in \Sigma \times \Gamma$,
   if $[p, 0, q] \in \delta^\dagger$, then $f(\#, [a, b, p], \#) = (\#, [a, b, q], \#)$.
   (d) For each $p \in Q^\dagger_{\rm sf}$, $q \in Q^\dagger_+$, and $(a, b) \in \Sigma \times \Gamma$,
   if $[p, +, q] \in \delta^\dagger$, then $f(\#, [a, b, p], \#) = (\#, [a, b], q)$.
3. Rules of P_M for simulating read-write rules of $M^\dagger$.
   (e) For each $p \in Q^\dagger_-$, $q \in Q^\dagger_{\rm sf}$, and $(a, b, c) \in \Sigma \times \Gamma^2$,
   if $[p, [a, [b, c]], q] \in \delta^\dagger$, then $f(p, [a, b], \#) = (\#, [a, c, q], \#)$.
   (f) For each $p \in Q^\dagger_0$, $q \in Q^\dagger_{\rm sf}$, and $(a, b, c) \in \Sigma \times \Gamma^2$,
   if $[p, [a, [b, c]], q] \in \delta^\dagger$, then $f(\#, [a, b, p], \#) = (\#, [a, c, q], \#)$.
   (g) For each $p \in Q^\dagger_+$, $q \in Q^\dagger_{\rm sf}$, and $(a, b, c) \in \Sigma \times \Gamma^2$,
   if $[p, [a, [b, c]], q] \in \delta^\dagger$, then $f(\#, [a, b], p) = (\#, [a, c, q], \#)$.
4. Rules of P_M for simulating the movements of $M^\dagger$ at the left and the right endmarkers. Here, $H^\dagger = A \cup N \cup \hat{A} \cup \hat{N}$, where $\hat{A} = \{\hat{q} \mid q \in A\}$ and $\hat{N} = \{\hat{q} \mid q \in N\}$. By the rules in (h) and (i) ((j) and (k), respectively), two (four) steps of $M^\dagger$'s movements are simulated by one step of P_M.
   (h) For each $p_1 \in Q^\dagger_-$, $p_2 \in Q^\dagger_{\rm sf} - H^\dagger$, and $p_3 \in Q^\dagger_+$,
   if $[p_1, [\rhd, [\rhd, \rhd]], p_2], [p_2, +, p_3] \in \delta^\dagger$, then $f(p_1, \#, \#) = (\#, \#, p_3)$.
   (i) For each $p_1 \in Q^\dagger_+$, $p_2 \in Q^\dagger_{\rm sf} - H^\dagger$, and $p_3 \in Q^\dagger_-$,
   if $[p_1, [\lhd, [\lhd, \lhd]], p_2], [p_2, -, p_3] \in \delta^\dagger$, then $f(\#, \#, p_1) = (p_3, \#, \#)$.
   (j) For each $p_1 \in Q^\dagger_-$, $p_2 \in H^\dagger$, $p_3 \in Q^\dagger_0$, $p_4 \in Q^\dagger_{\rm sf} - H^\dagger$, and $p_5 \in Q^\dagger_+$,
   if $[p_1, [\rhd, [\rhd, \rhd]], p_2], [p_2, 0, p_3], [p_3, [\rhd, [\rhd, \rhd]], p_4], [p_4, +, p_5] \in \delta^\dagger$,
   then $f(p_1, \#, \#) = (\#, \#, p_5)$.

(k) For each $p_1 \in Q^\dagger_+$, $p_2 \in H^\dagger$, $p_3 \in Q^\dagger_0$, $p_4 \in Q^\dagger_{\rm sf} - H^\dagger$, and $p_5 \in Q^\dagger_-$, if $[p_1, [\lhd, [\lhd, \lhd]], p_2], [p_2, 0, p_3], [p_3, [\lhd, [\lhd, \lhd]], p_4], [p_4, -, p_5] \in \delta^\dagger$, then $f(\#, \#, p_1) = (p_5, \#, \#)$.

5. Rules of P_M for the cases $M^\dagger$ halts. Since the RPCA P_M cannot halt, here we set f to generate the signals q_0 and $\hat{q}_0$ by the signals $l_{\rm h}$ and $\hat{l}_{\rm h}$. By these rules, P_M finally goes back to the initial configuration, and repeats its computation indefinitely. However, note that, any P_M necessarily goes back to the initial configuration whatever the injection f is.
   (l) $f(\hat{l}_{\rm h}, \#, \#) = (\#, \#, \hat{r}_{\rm s})$, and $f(l_{\rm h}, \#, \#) = (\#, \#, r_{\rm s})$.

Though f is defined only on a subset of $L \times C \times R$ by (a)–(l), we can verify it is injective on this set, since $M^\dagger$ is reversible. From this partial function we can easily make an injective total function f by appropriately determining undefined values of f. Hence, P_M is an RPCA.

If an input $w \in \Sigma^*$ is given, P_M starts its computation from the initial configuration α_w (in Definition 3). Then, P_M simulates $M^\dagger$ step by step by the rules (b)–(g). Movements of $M^\dagger$ at the left and right border cells are simulated by (h)–(k). Hence, $\exists\, t_1 > 0\ (p_L(F^{t_1}(\alpha_w)(1)) = \hat{l}_{\rm h})$ holds iff $w \in L(M^\dagger)$. Thus, $L(P_M) = L(M^\dagger) = L(M)$ is concluded. □

Let $\mathcal{L}(\mathcal{A})$ denote the class of languages accepted by the class of acceptors $\mathcal{A}$. From Lemmas 2 and 3, and the fact that PCAs can be easily simulated by DLBAs (since the condition (P1) is assumed), the following theorem is obtained.

Theorem 1. $\mathcal{L}$(RPCA) $= \mathcal{L}$(PCA) $= \mathcal{L}$(RDLBA) $= \mathcal{L}$(DLBA).

Example 2. Consider the DLBA $M_{\rm p}$ in Example 1. An RPCA $P_{M_{\rm p}}$ such that $L(P_{M_{\rm p}}) = L(M_{\rm p})$ is given below. $P_{M_{\rm p}}$ simulates the RDLBA $M^\dagger_{\rm p}$ constructed by the method shown in Lemma 3.

$$P_{M_{\rm p}} = ((L, C, R), f, (\#, \#, \#), q_{0,2}, \{\,(,\,)\,\}, \{\hat{q}^{\rm b}_{0,1}\})$$
$$L = Q^\dagger_- \cup \{\#\}$$
$$C = \{\,(,\,)\,\} \cup \{\,(,\,)\,\} \times \{{\rm x}\} \cup \{\,(,\,)\,\} \times \{{\rm x}, \#\} \times (Q^\dagger_0 \cup Q^\dagger_{\rm sf} - \{q^{\rm b}_0, \hat{q}^{\rm b}_0\}) \cup \{\#\}$$
$$R = Q^\dagger_+ \cup \{\#\}$$

In $M^\dagger_{\rm p}$, $|Q^\dagger| = 52$, $|Q^\dagger_{\rm rw}| = |Q^\dagger_{\rm sf}| = 26$, $|Q^\dagger_-| = 10$, $|Q^\dagger_0| = 4$, and $|Q^\dagger_+| = 10$. Therefore, $|L| = 11$, $|C| = 117$, and $|R| = 11$. Hence, the number of states of a cell, and that of rules of $P_{M_{\rm p}}$ are both 14157. However, the number of rules that are actually used to simulate $M^\dagger_{\rm p}$ is only 203. Here, we omit to describe f, but from Fig. 4 we can observe how the rules are applied.

Figure 4 shows an example of a computing process of $P_{M_{\rm p}}$ with the input $w =$ ( ). $P_{M_{\rm p}}$ accepts the input at time $t = 56$. Note that the initial state q_0, and the accepting state $\hat{q}^{\rm b}_0$ of $M^\dagger_{\rm p}$ do not appear in $P_{M_{\rm p}}$, since a few steps of $M^\dagger_{\rm p}$ at the left and right endmarkers are simulated by one step of $P_{M_{\rm p}}$. From $t = 57$ to 113, P_M performs essentially the same computing process as the one from $t = 0$ to 56, except that the states with "ˆ" and those without "ˆ" are swapped. At time $t = 114$, $P_{M_{\rm p}}$ becomes the initial configuration again, and

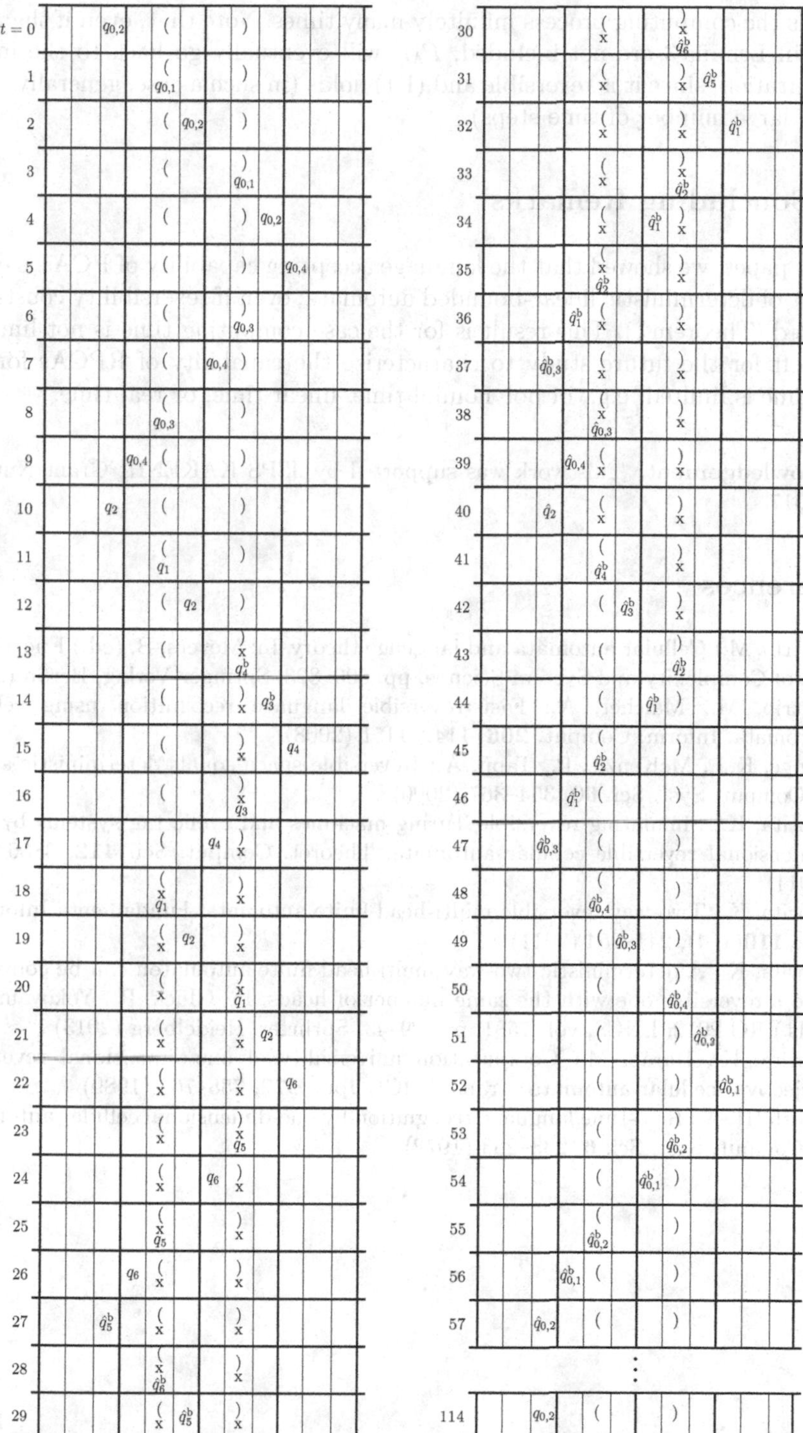

Fig. 4. A computing process of RPCA P_{M_p} with the input $w = ()$. It is accepted at $t = 56$, since $\hat{q}^b_{0,1}$ is an accepting state. Here, the state # is indicated by a blank.

repeats the computing process infinitely many times. Note that, even if the rules of (l) in Lemma 3 are not included, P_{M_p} will eventually go back to the initial configuration, since it is reversible and (P1) holds (in such a case, generally, after a very large number of time steps).

5 Concluding Remarks

In this paper, we showed that the language accepting capability of PCAs is equal to that of deterministic linear-bounded automata, even if reversibility constraint is added (Theorem 1). This result is for the case computing time is not limited. It is left for the future study to characterize the capability of RPCAs for the case time is limited, e.g., in polynomial time, linear time, or real time.

Acknowledgement. This work was supported by JSPS KAKENHI Grant Number 24500017.

References

1. Kutrib, M.: Cellular automata and language theory. In: Meyers, B. (ed.) Encyclopedia of Complexity and System Science, pp. 800–823. Springer-Verlag, Berlin (2009)
2. Kutrib, M., Malcher, A.: Fast reversible language recognition using cellular automata. Inform. Comput. **206**, 1142–1151 (2008)
3. Lange, K.J., McKenzie, P., Tapp, A.: Reversible space equals deterministic space. J. Comput. Syst. Sci. **60**, 354–367 (2000)
4. Morita, K.: Simulating reversible Turing machines and cyclic tag systems by one-dimensional reversible cellular automata. Theoret. Comput. Sci. **412**, 3856–3865 (2011)
5. Morita, K.: Two-way reversible multi-head finite automata. Fundamenta Informaticae **110**(1–4), 241–254 (2011)
6. Morita, K.: A deterministic two-way multi-head finite automaton can be converted into a reversible one with the same number of heads. In: Glück, R., Yokoyama, T. (eds.) RC 2012. LNCS, vol. 7581, pp. 29–43. Springer, Heidelberg (2013)
7. Morita, K., Harao, M.: Computation universality of one-dimensional reversible (injective) cellular automata. Trans. IEICE Jpn. **E72**, 758–762 (1989)
8. Smith III, A.: Real-time language recognition by one-dimensional cellular automata. J. Comput. Syst. Sci. **6**, 233–253 (1972)

Complexity of Conjugacy, Factoring and Embedding for Countable Sofic Shifts of Rank 2

Ville Salo and Ilkka Törmä(✉)

TUCS – Turku Centre for Computer Science, University of Turku, Turku, Finland
{vosalo,iatorm}@utu.fi

Abstract. In this article, we study countable sofic shifts of Cantor-Bendixson rank at most 2. We prove that their conjugacy problem is complete for GI, the complexity class of graph isomorphism, and that the existence problems of block maps, factor maps and embeddings are NP-complete.

Keywords: Sofic shift · SFT · Topological conjugacy · Graph isomorphism · Complexity class

1 Introduction

The computational complexity class GI is defined as the set of decision problems reducible to the graph isomorphism problem in polynomial time. The class is one of the strongest candidates for an NP-intermediate class, that is, one that lies strictly between P and NP. It contains a plethora of other isomorphism problems of finite objects, like multigraphs, hypergraphs, labeled or colored graphs, finite automata and context-free grammars, most of which are GI-complete. The classical reference for the subject is [14].

In the field of symbolic dynamics, which studies sets of infinite sequences of symbols as topological dynamical systems, there is a fundamental isomorphism problem whose decidability has been open for some decades: the conjugacy problem of shifts of finite type. A shift of finite type is a class of sequences defined by finitely many forbidden patterns that must never occur, and a conjugacy is a homeomorphism that commutes with the shift transformation, or in combinatorial terms, a bijection between shifts of finite type defined by a local rule. The most common version of this problem further restricts to *mixing* shifts of finite type, whose dynamics is intuitively the most random and unpredictable. See [4] for a review of the problem (and many others).

In this article, we take a different approach, and study the conjugacy problem of *countable sofic shifts*. Sofic shifts are a generalization of shifts of finite type, and the class of countable shifts of finite type can be seen as the polar opposite of the mixing class, as they are very well-structured and combinatorial. Their properties have previously been studied at least in [1,2,10–12] (although usually somewhat indirectly).

T. Isokawa et al. (Eds.): AUTOMATA 2014, LNCS 8996, pp. 121–134, 2015.
DOI: 10.1007/978-3-319-18812-6_10

A useful tool in the study of countable sofic shifts (and topological spaces in general) is the Cantor-Bendixson rank. Every countable sofic shift has such a rank, which is a number $n \in \mathbb{N}$, and we study the first few levels of this hierarchy in this article. Rank 1 countable sofic shifts are the finite ones, and the conjugacy problem for them is very easy (Proposition 2). Rank 2 countable sofic shifts are the first non-trivial case, and our main result states that the conjugacy problem of rank 2 countable SFTs and sofic shifts is GI-complete (with respect to polynomial-time many-one reductions), when the shift spaces are given by right-resolving symbolic edge shifts. Using the same methods, we also prove that the existence of block maps, factor maps and embeddings between rank 2 countable sofic shifts is NP-complete. Of course, corresponding hardness results follow for general SFTs, since countable SFTs of rank 2 are a (very small) subcase. However, we are not able to extract any corollaries for the usual case of mixing SFTs.

Note that it is of course GI-complete to check whether two given edge shifts are isomorphic in the sense that the graphs defining them are isomorphic. This is not equivalent to conjugacy of the edge shifts, as shown in Example 1. The graph representations we use are more canonical representations of the shift spaces, and very specific to the rank 2 case.

2 Definitions

Let A be a finite set, called the *alphabet*, whose elements are called *symbols*. We equip the set $A^{\mathbb{Z}}$ with the product topology and define the *shift map* $\sigma : A^{\mathbb{Z}} \to A^{\mathbb{Z}}$ by $\sigma(x)_i = x_{i+1}$ for all $x \in A^{\mathbb{Z}}$ and $i \in \mathbb{Z}$. The pair $(A^{\mathbb{Z}}, \sigma)$ is a dynamical system, called the *full shift over* A. For a word $w \in A^*$ and $x \in A^{\mathbb{Z}}$, we say that w *occurs in* x, denoted $w \sqsubset x$, if there exists $i \in \mathbb{Z}$ with $x_{[i,i+|w|-1]} = w$.

A topologically closed and σ-invariant subset $X \subset A^{\mathbb{Z}}$ is called a *shift space*. Alternatively, a shift space is defined by a set $F \subset A^*$ of *forbidden patterns* as $X = \{x \in A^{\mathbb{Z}} \mid \forall w \in F : w \not\sqsubset x\}$. If F is finite, then X is a *shift of finite type*, or *SFT* for short, and if F is a regular language, then X is a *sofic shift*. For $n \in \mathbb{N}$, we denote $\mathcal{B}_n(X) = \{w \in A^n \mid x \in X, w \sqsubset x\}$, and define the *language* of X as $\mathcal{B}(X) = \bigcup_{n \in \mathbb{N}} \mathcal{B}_n(X)$. We also denote by $\mathcal{P}(X) = \{x \in X \mid \exists p \in \mathbb{N} : \sigma^p(x) = x\}$ the set of σ-periodic points of X. We say x and y are left asymptotic if $x_i = y_i$ for all small enough i, and right asymptotic if this holds for all large enough i.

A shift space is uniquely determined by its language, so for a language L such that $w \in L$ always implies $uwv \in L$ for some nonempty words $u, v \in A^*$ (often called an *extendable* language), we denote $X = \mathcal{B}^{-1}(L)$, where X is the unique shift space such that $\mathcal{B}(X) = \{w \mid \exists u, v \in A^* : uwv \in L\}$. For a configuration $x \in A^{\mathbb{Z}}$, we write $\mathcal{O}_\sigma(x) = \{\sigma^n(x) \mid n \in \mathbb{Z}\}$ for the *σ-orbit of* x, and $\overline{X}$ for the topological closure of X, when X is a subset of $A^{\mathbb{Z}}$.

A continuous function $f : X \to Y$ between shift spaces satisfying $\sigma|_Y \circ f = f \circ \sigma|_X$ is a *block map*. Alternatively, a block map is defined by a *local function* $\hat{f} : \mathcal{B}_{2r+1}(X) \to \mathcal{B}_1(Y)$, where $r \in \mathbb{N}$ is called a *radius* of f, as $f(x)_i = \hat{f}(x_{[i-r,i+r]})$. Block maps with radius 0 are called *symbol maps* and identified with their local functions. Sofic shifts are exactly the images of SFTs under block maps. The standard reference for shift spaces and block maps is [9].

If a block map $f : X \to Y$ is bijective, it is known that its inverse is also a block map, and then f is called a *conjugacy* between X and Y. A surjective block map $f : X \to Y$ is called a *factor map* from X to Y, and such an injection is called an *embedding*. The problem of deciding whether two SFTs are conjugate is known as the *strong shift equivalence problem*, and its decidability has been open for several decades. See [4] for more information on this and other open problems in symbolic dynamics.

We include a full definition of Cantor-Bendixson rank for completeness, although we only need this concept for natural numbers in the case of sofic shifts. Let X be a topological space. The *Cantor-Bendixson derivative* of X is the set $X' = \{x \in X \mid \overline{X \setminus \{x\}} = X\} \subset X$. In other words, X' is exactly X minus its isolated points. For every ordinal λ, we define the λ'th iterated derivative of X, denoted $X^{(\lambda)}$, as follows.

- If $\lambda = 0$, then $X^{(\lambda)} = X$.
- If $\lambda = \beta + 1$, then $X^{(\lambda)} = (X^{(\beta)})'$.
- If λ is a limit ordinal, then $X^{(\lambda)} = \bigcap_{\beta<\lambda} X^{(\beta)}$.

The smallest ordinal λ such that $X^{(\lambda)} = X^{(\lambda+1)}$ is called the *Cantor-Bendixson rank* of X, and denoted $\mathrm{rank}(X)$. If X is a shift space, then it is countable if and only if $X^{(\mathrm{rank}(X))} = \emptyset$. In this case, the *rank* of a point $x \in X$, denoted $\mathrm{rank}_X(x)$, is the least ordinal λ such that $x \notin X^{(\lambda)}$. It is not hard to show that if X is a shift space, then $X^{(\lambda)}$ is a shift space for all ordinals λ.

By a *graph* we understand a tuple $G = (V, E)$, where $V = \mathcal{V}(G)$ is a finite set of *vertices* and $E = \mathcal{E}(G)$ a set of *edges*, which are two-element subsets of V (so self-loops and multiple edges are not allowed). A *labeled graph* is a triple $G = (V, E, \pi)$, where $\mathcal{E}(G) = E$ is now a set of tuples (e, ℓ) with e an edge and $\ell \in L$ its *label*, and $\pi = \pi_G : E \to L$ is the *labeling function* given by $\pi(e, \ell) = \ell$. For a set C, a *C-colored graph* has its vertices colored with elements of C so that no adjacent vertices have the same color. Directed versions of all types of graphs have tuples as edges, instead of sets, and may have self-loops. Finally, a (directed) *multigraph* is similar to a (directed) graph, but its edges form a multiset, so multiple edges between two vertices are allowed.

Homomorphisms of C-colored graphs must preserve the colors. For a fixed graph H which is not bipartite, it is NP-complete to decide whether there exists a homomorphism from a given graph G to H, by a result of Hell and Nešetřil [6]. Likewise, for some classes of graphs H, it is NP-complete whether an edge-surjective homomorphism (also known as a *compaction*) exists from a given graph G to H [13]. Deciding the existence of edge-injective homomorphisms between two graphs is NP-complete [3], but not if one of them is fixed.

Every SFT is conjugate to an *edge shift*, the SFT X defined by a directed multigraph G over the alphabet of edges $\mathcal{E}(G)$ as follows. A set of forbidden patterns for X is given by the pairs of edges ee' such that the target of e differs from the source of e', or in other words, X is the set of edges of all bi-infinite walks in G. Similarly, every sofic shift is conjugate to a *symbolic edge shift*, the image of an edge shift under a symbol map $\pi : \mathcal{E}(G) \to A$. Equivalently, a symbolic edge shift consists of the labels of all bi-infinite walks in a labeled directed graph. A symbolic edge shift is called *right-resolving* if for each vertex $v \in G$, any distinct edges that start from v have different labels.

The *graph isomorphism problem* is the problem of deciding whether two graphs, encoded as lists of edges, are isomorphic. The set of decision problems polynomial-time reducible to the graph isomorphism problem is denoted GI. It is known that $\mathsf{P} \subseteq \mathsf{GI} \subseteq \mathsf{NP}$. Examples of GI-complete isomorphism problems include those of directed graphs, labeled graphs and $\{0,1\}$-colored graphs. The classical reference for GI is [14]. In this paper, hardness and completeness with respect to a complexity class are taken with respect to standard polynomial time many-one reductions.

3 Countable Sofic Shifts

In this section, we give some background on countable sofic shifts and countable SFTs, and present their basic properties. As a conclusion, we obtain a combinatorial characterization of rank 2 sofic shifts in Corollary 2. The point of this section is mainly to put our results into place in the theory of symbolic dynamics. Readers interested in the complexity theoretic result only can take the definition of a rank 2 sofic shift to be the second condition listed in Corollary 2, and otherwise skip this section.

Lemma 1 (Proposition 3.8 of [12]). *All sofic shifts have finite Cantor-Bendixson rank.*

Lemma 2 (Corollary of Lemma 4.8 of [10]). *A shift space $X \subset A^{\mathbb{Z}}$ is a countable sofic shift if and only if it can be presented as a finite union of shift spaces of the form*

$$\mathcal{X}(u_0, \ldots, u_m, v_1, \ldots, v_m) = \mathcal{B}^{-1}(u_0^* v_1 u_1^* \cdots u_{n-1}^* v_m u_m^*),$$

where $u_i \in A^+$ and $v_i \in A^*$, and each configuration ${}^\infty u_i v_{i+1} u_{i+1}{}^\infty$ is aperiodic.

Intuitively, the configurations of a countable sofic shift consist of long periodic areas, with 'disturbances' of bounded length in between. The traditional application of symbolic dynamics is the encoding of information in a restricted medium, and from this viewpoint, countable sofic shifts are extremely restricted, as the asymptotic amount of information per coordinate in a configuration is zero.

Definition 1. *Let $X \subset A^{\mathbb{Z}}$ be a countable sofic shift, and let T be a finite set of tuples over A^* such that $X = \bigcup_{t \in T} \mathcal{X}(t)$ and the conditions of Lemma 2 hold. Then the set T is called a* combinatorial representation *of X.*

We remark that a nonempty countable sofic shift has infinitely many different combinatorial representations. Using the notation of Lemma 2, we write $n(u_0, \ldots, u_m, v_1, \ldots, v_m) = m$. The following lemma relates the rank of a countable sofic shift to its combinatorial representation.

Lemma 3. *Let $X \subset A^{\mathbb{Z}}$ be a nonempty countable sofic shift with the combinatorial representation T. Then*

$$\operatorname{rank}(X) = 1 + \max\{n(t) \mid t \in T\}.$$

Proof. First, we need to show that if $X, Y \subset A^{\mathbb{Z}}$ are shift spaces with ranks $m, n \in \mathbb{N}$, respectively, then the (not necessarily disjoint) union $X \cup Y$ has Cantor-Bendixson rank $\max\{m, n\}$. This follows directly from the well-known property $(X \cup Y)' = X' \cup Y'$ of the derivative operator.

From this, we obtain by induction that the Cantor-Bendixson rank of a finite union of finite-rank shift spaces is just the maximal rank of the components. It is then enough to show that the Cantor-Bendixson rank of a shift space of the form $\mathcal{X}(u_0, \ldots, u_m, v_1, \ldots, v_m)$ is precisely $m+1$, and we proceed by induction. It is clear that the rank is 1 if $m = 0$, since the shift space is finite but nonempty. On the other hand, it is not hard to show that

$$\mathcal{X}(u_0, \ldots, u_m, v_1, \ldots, v_m)' = \mathcal{X}(u_1, \ldots, u_m, v_2, \ldots, v_m) \cup \mathcal{X}(u_0, \ldots, u_{m-1}, v_1, \ldots, v_{m-1}),$$

from which the claim follows. □

We state some well-known characterizations of finite shift spaces, and then list some characterizations of the rank 2 case.

Corollary 1. *The following are equivalent for a nonempty shift space X:*

- *X contains only periodic points,*
- *X is finite,*
- *X has rank 1,*
- *X is a countable SFT (and/or sofic shift) of rank 1,*
- *X is a finite union of shift spaces of the form $\mathcal{X}(u) = \mathcal{B}^{-1}(u^*)$.*

Corollary 2. *The following are equivalent for an infinite shift space X:*

- *X is a countable sofic shift of rank 2,*
- *X is a finite union of shift spaces of the form $\mathcal{X}(u_0, u_1, v) = \mathcal{B}^{-1}(u_0^* v u_1^*)$ (where ${}^{\infty}u_0 v u_1{}^{\infty}$ may or may not be periodic),*
- *X is a countable shift space of rank 2,*
- *every configuration in X is either periodic or isolated.*

Proof. The first and second conditions are equivalent by Lemma 3. The third and fourth are equivalent by the definition of rank and the previous corollary, and the first trivially implies the third.

We give a proof sketch for the fact that a countable shift space of rank 2 satisfies the second condition, which concludes the proof. If $X \subset A^{\mathbb{Z}}$ is such a shift space, then X' has rank 1, and is thus an SFT by the previous corollary. By Lemma 2.6 in [2], $X \setminus X'$ then consists of finitely many orbits. Then, $X = \mathcal{O}_\sigma(x^1) \cup \cdots \mathcal{O}_\sigma(x^k) \cup Y$, where $Y \subset A^{\mathbb{Z}}$ is a finite shift space of periodic configurations, none of the configurations $x^i \in X$ are periodic, and the orbits $\mathcal{O}_\sigma(x_i)$ are pairwise disjoint. Since every x^i is isolated in X (as it is not in X'), there exists a word $w^{(i)} \in A^*$ which occurs in x_i at exactly one position, and occurs in none of the x_j for $j \neq i$. Now, note that the shift space

$$X_i^R = \overline{\{\sigma^n(x^i) \mid n \in \mathbb{N}\}}$$

(the shift space generated by the right tail of x^i) is a subset of X and does not contain any of the isolating patterns $w^{(j)}$ for $j \in [1, k]$. It is then a subset of Y, which implies that it is actually the orbit of a single periodic configuration, and x^i then in fact has a periodic right tail.[1] Similarly, x^i has a periodic left tail, from which the claim follows. □

4 Structure Graphs

Every SFT is conjugate to an edge shift, and if the graphs defining two edge shifts are isomorphic, then the SFTs are conjugate. It is clearly GI-complete, in general, to check whether two SFTs are conjugate in this particular way. We show that even in the rank 2 case, two SFTs can be conjugate even though the graphs defining their edge shifts are not isomorphic.[2]

Example 1. Let X be the edge shift of the directed graph $\circlearrowleft a \to b \circlearrowright$, and let Y be that of $\circlearrowleft a \to b \to c \circlearrowright$. The graphs are not isomorphic, but the edge shifts are easily seen to be conjugate by the block map $f : X \to Y$ defined by

$$f(x)_i = \begin{cases} (a,a), \text{ if } x_i = (a,a), \\ (a,b), \text{ if } x_i = (a,b), \\ (b,c), \text{ if } x_{i-1} = (a,b), \\ (c,c), \text{ if } x_{i-1} = (b,b). \end{cases}$$

We now define the structure graph of a rank 2 countable sofic shift, which is a certain labeled directed graph. Corollary 3 shows that this graph is canonical up to renaming the vertices.

Definition 2. *Let X be a rank 2 countable sofic shift. Define the labeled directed graph $G(X) = (V, E, \pi)$ as follows. First, $V = \mathcal{P}(X)$ is the set of σ-periodic points of X. For all $x \in \mathcal{P}(X)$, add an edge $x \to \sigma(x)$ into E with the label $\circlearrowleft$, called a* rotation edge. *Then, for each pair of configurations $x, y \in \mathcal{P}(X)$ such that the set $C_{(x,y)} = \{z \in X \mid \exists n \in \mathbb{N} : z_{(-\infty,-n]} = x_{(-\infty,-n]}, z_{[n,\infty)} = y_{[n,\infty)}\}$ is nonempty, add an edge $e = (x, y)$ into E with the label $\pi(e) = |\{\mathcal{O}_\sigma(z) \mid z \in C_e\}|$, called a* transition edge. *We call $G(X)$ the* structure graph *of X.*

[1] There is a common period $p \in \mathbb{N}$ for the configurations in Y, and if this period breaks infinitely many times in the right tail of x, then X_i^R is not contained in Y.

[2] From Proposition 2, one can extract that in the rank 1 case, conjugacy of edge shifts *is* equivalent to the graphs defining them being isomorphic.

A homomorphism between two structure graphs $G(X)$ and $G(Y)$ is a graph homomorphism $\tau : G(X) \to G(Y)$ that satisfies

$$\tau^{-1}(\pi_{G(Y)}^{-1}(\circlearrowright)) = \pi_{G(X)}^{-1}(\circlearrowright),$$

that is, τ respects the property of being a rotation edge. A bijective homomorphism is called an isomorphism.

Note that the structure graph is finite and transition edges have finite labels, as there are finitely many σ-orbits in a rank 2 countable sofic shift. Also, the inverse function of an isomorphism of structure graphs is itself an isomorphism.

Example 2. Let $X = \mathcal{B}^{-1}(0^*10^* + 0^*(12)^* + 0^*(13)^* + (12)^*(1+2)(13)^*)$, a rank 2 countable sofic shift. Then $\mathcal{P}(X) = \{{}^\infty0^\infty, {}^\infty(12)^\infty, {}^\infty(21)^\infty, {}^\infty(13)^\infty, {}^\infty(31)^\infty\}$, and the structure graph $G(X)$ is the one depicted in Fig. 1.

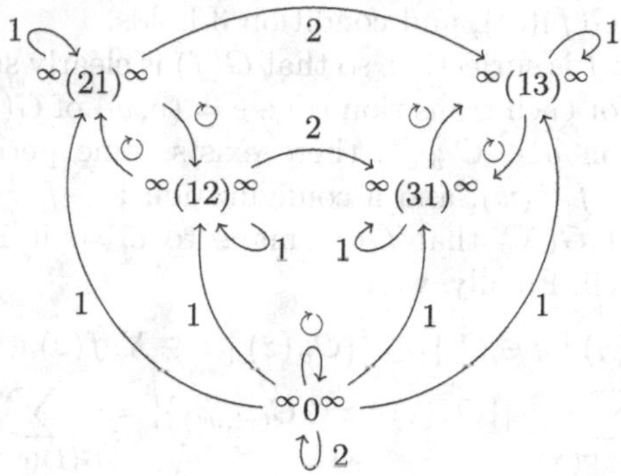

Fig. 1. The structure graph of the countable sofic shift X of Example 2.

Next, we show that the structure graph is functorial: block maps between two shift spaces correspond to homomorphisms between their structure graphs.

Proposition 1. *For every block map $f : X \to Y$ between rank 2 countable sofic shifts, there exists a homomorphism $G(f) : G(X) \to G(Y)$ between their structure graphs such that $G(\mathrm{id}_X) = \mathrm{id}_{G(X)}$ for all X, and $G(g \circ h) = G(g) \circ G(h)$ for all $g : Y \to Z$ and $h : X \to Y$.*

Proof. Let $f : X \to Y$ be as stated, and define $G(f) : G(X) \to G(Y)$ as follows. For each $x \in \mathcal{P}(X)$, let $G(f)(x) = f(x) \in \mathcal{P}(Y) = \mathcal{V}(G(Y))$. Then for any rotation edge $e : x \to \sigma(x)$ in $\mathcal{E}(G(X))$, there exists a rotation edge $e' : f(x) \to \sigma(f(x))$ in $\mathcal{E}(G(Y))$, so let $G(f)(e) = e'$. Finally, for any transition edge $e : x \to y$ with label $k > 0$, the set $C_{(x,y)}$ is nonempty, which implies that $C_{(f(x),f(y))}$ is also nonempty. Thus $e' = (f(x), f(y))$ is a transition edge of $G(Y)$ with some label $\ell > 0$, and we again let $G(f)(e) = e'$.

It is easy to see that $G(f)$ is a homomorphism between the structure graphs, and that $G(\mathrm{id}_X) = \mathrm{id}_{G(X)}$ holds. Proving the equation $G(g \circ h) = G(g) \circ G(h)$ is simply a matter of expanding the definitions. □

The operation G that sends block maps to structure graph homomorphisms preserves injectivity and surjectivity in the following sense.

Lemma 4. *A homomorphism $\tau : G(X) \to G(Y)$ of structure graphs*
1. *always has a G-preimage,*
2. *has an injective G-preimage if and only if it is edge-injective, and every transition edge e of $G(X)$ satisfies $\pi(e) \leq \pi(\tau(e))$,*
3. *has a surjective G-preimage if and only if it is edge-surjective, and every transition edge e of $G(Y)$ satisfies $\sum_{\tau(e')=e} \pi(e') \geq \pi(e)$,*
4. *has a bijective G-preimage if and only if it is edge-bijective and preserves the labels of transition edges.*

Proof. First, we prove that if $f : X \to Y$ is injective, then condition 2 holds for $G(f)$. The edge-injectivity of $G(f)$ follows immediately. For each transition edge $e = (v, w)$ of $G(X)$ with label $k > 0$, the function from $\{\mathcal{O}_\sigma(y) \mid y \in C_e\}$ to $\{\mathcal{O}_\sigma(z) \mid z \in C_{G(f)(e)}\}$ defined by $\mathcal{O}_\sigma(y) \mapsto \mathcal{O}_\sigma(f(y))$ is injective, since f is. Thus we have $k \leq \pi(G(f)(e))$, and condition 3 holds.

Suppose next that f is surjective, so that $G(f)$ is clearly surjective on vertices and rotation edges. For each transition edge $e = (v, w)$ of $G(Y)$ with label $k > 0$ and each configuration $y \in C_{(v,w)}$, there exists some periodic configurations $v' \in f^{-1}(v)$ and $w' \in f^{-1}(w)$, and a configuration $z \in f^{-1}(y) \cap C_{(v',w')}$. Then (v', w') is an edge of $G(X)$ that $G(f)$ maps to e, so it is surjective on the transition edges as well. Finally, we have

$$\begin{aligned} k = |\{\mathcal{O}_\sigma(y) \mid y \in C_e\}| &\leq |\{\mathcal{O}_\sigma(z) \mid z \in X, f(z) \in C_e\}| \\ &= \sum_{\substack{v',w' \in \mathcal{P}(X) \\ G(f)(v',w')=e}} |\{\mathcal{O}_\sigma(z) \mid z \in C_{(v',w')}\}| = \sum_{G(f)(e')=e} \pi(e'). \end{aligned}$$

If f is bijective, this and the previous case together show that condition 4 holds.

Finally, we construct a G-preimage $f : X \to Y$ for τ with the desired properties. We must of course have $f(x) = \tau(x)$ for every periodic configuration $x \in \mathcal{P}(X)$, which is well-defined since $\tau(\sigma(x)) = \sigma(\tau(x))$. Let then $x \in X$ be aperiodic, and let $y, z \in \mathcal{P}(X)$ be such that $x \in C_{(y,z)}$. Then $G(X)$ has a transition edge $e = (y, z)$ with some label $k > 0$. Let $e' = \tau(e) = (y', z')$. Now e' has some label $\ell > 0$, so that $C_{e'}$ is also nonempty. We choose some $x' \in C_{e'}$ and define $f(x) = x'$, and extend f to $\mathcal{O}_\sigma(x)$ by defining $f(\sigma^n(x)) = \sigma^n(x')$ for all $n \in \mathbb{Z}$. For this, note that x is isolated in X. If condition 2 holds, there are enough orbits in $\bigcup_{e \in \tau^{-1}(e')} C_e$ to guarantee that every $x' \in C_{e'}$ can be given an f-preimage, and if condition 3 holds, then there are enough orbits in $C_{e'}$ to guarantee that every $x \in C_{(y,z)}$ can be given a different f-image.

The definition of f is now complete, and it is easy to see that it is continuous and shift-invariant, thus a block map. Moreover, it follows immediately from the definition of f that $G(f) = \tau$. □

As a corollary of the above, we obtain the following.

Corollary 3. *Let X and Y be countable rank 2 sofic shifts. Then X and Y are conjugate if and only if $G(X)$ is obtained from $G(Y)$ by renaming its vertices.*

5 Complexity Classes of Conjugacy, Factoring, Embedding and Block Map Existence

In this section, we present our results on the computational complexity of different decision problems related to countable rank 1 and rank 2 sofic shifts. If one is only interested in decidability, then it is irrelevant what kind of encodings we use for shift spaces $X \subset A^{\mathbb{Z}}$, since there are computable transformations between all reasonable encodings. However, for finding out the precise complexity class, there are some subtleties in how the algorithm receives the shift space as input. There are several possibilities:

1. Every sofic shift can be encoded by a finite list $F \subset B^*$ of forbidden words that define an SFT over the alphabet B, and a symbol map $f : B \to A$. For SFTs, we can take $B = A$ and $f = \mathrm{id}_A$.
2. Every sofic shift is the symbolic edge shift defined by a (possibly right-resolving) labeled graph. For SFTs, up to conjugacy, we can take the symbol map to be the identity map, and obtain edge shifts given by adjacency matrices. This is the standard encoding of SFTs in the conjugacy problem.
3. Countable sofic shifts can be encoded by combinatorial representations.
4. Countable sofic shifts of rank at most 2 can be encoded by structure graphs.

We show that, up to polynomial-time reductions, encodings 2 and 4 are equivalent in the rank 2 case, if we assume right-resolvingness, so it makes no difference which one we choose.

Lemma 5. *For countable sofic shifts of rank at most 2, the representations by right-resolving symbolic edge shifts and structure graphs are equivalent up to polynomial-time reductions.*

Proof. First, let G be a right-resolving labeled graph of size n encoding a countable rank 2 sofic shift $X \subset A^{\mathbb{Z}}$. We construct the structure graph of X, and for this, we may assume that G is the minimal right-resolving representation of X (which can be computed in polynomial time from a given right-resolving labeled graph, see Sect. 4 of [9] for details). In particular, since X is countable, the cycles of G are disjoint, and we can enumerate them as $C_0, \dots, C_{c-1}$, and if $(q_i^0, \dots, q_i^{m_i-1})$ are the vertices of the cycle C_i, then $\sum_{i=0}^{c-1} m_i \leq n$. Also, if $u_i \in A^{m_i}$ is the label of the cycle C_i, then ${}^\infty u_i^\infty$ has least period m_i, for otherwise we could replace C_i by a shorter cycle and obtain a smaller presentation for X.

Call a path in G *transitional* if it contains no edges of any cycle. Then the length of a transitional path is at most n. Now, let $M \in \mathbb{N}^{\mathcal{V}(G) \times \mathcal{V}(G)}$ be the matrix defined by $M(q_i^r, q_i^{r+1}) = 0$ for all $i \in [0, c-1]$ and $r \in [0, m_i - 1]$, and $M(v, w) = |\{e : v \to w \mid e \in \mathcal{E}(G)\}|$ for all other vertices $v, w \in \mathcal{V}(G)$. Note that since G is right-resolving, the edges in the above set have distinct labels. The number of transitional paths of a given length $\ell \in \mathbb{N}$ between two vertices $v, w \in \mathcal{V}(G)$ is then exactly $M^\ell(v, w)$, and their labels are also distinct.

For each periodic configuration ${}^\infty u^\infty \in X$, there are at most two cycles in G with the label u, one with outgoing and one with incoming transitional paths, for otherwise we could replace two such cycles with a single one and obtain a smaller right-resolving representation. Now, the vertices of the structure graph $G(X)$ are the periodic configurations $\sigma^r({}^\infty u_i^\infty)$ for $i \in [0, c-1]$ and $r \in [0, m_i - 1]$, and its transitional edges are exactly $e : x \to y$ with labels

$$\pi(e) = \sum_{\substack{x=\sigma^r({}^\infty u_i^\infty) \\ y=\sigma^s({}^\infty u_j^\infty)}} \sum_{\ell=1}^{n} \sum_{k=0}^{\operatorname{lcm}(m_i,m_j)-1} |M^\ell(q_i^{r+k}, q_j^{s+k+\ell})|,$$

plus 1 in the case $x = y$ to account for the periodic point itself. Thus $G(X)$ can be computed from G in polynomial time.

Next, we take the structure graph $G(X)$ for X, and construct a right-resolving labeled graph G whose shift space Y is conjugate to X. From $G(X)$ we can easily extract the periodic orbits of X, which we denote by $\mathcal{O}_\sigma({}^\infty u_i^\infty)$ for $i \in [0, c-1]$, where $u_i \in A^+$. For all $i \in [0, c-1]$ and $r \in [0, |u_i|-1]$, we add to G two vertices p_i^r and q_i^r, and two edges $e : q_i^r \to q_i^{r+1}$ and $e' : p_i^r \to p_i^{r+1}$ with the same labels a_i^r. The labels of the cycles of G, and thus the periodic points of Y, are thus $a_i = a_i^0 \cdots a_i^{|u_i|-1}$ for $i \in [0, c-1]$.

Let then $e : \sigma^r({}^\infty u_i^\infty) \to \sigma^s({}^\infty u_j^\infty)$ be a transitional edge in the structure graph $G(X)$, and let $\pi(e) = \sum_{\ell=0}^{d-1} 2^{k_\ell}$ be the binary representation of its label, where $k_0 < \cdots < k_{d-1}$. For each $\ell \in [0, d-1]$, we add to G the subgraph $G_e = q_i^r \to v_e^0 \rightrightarrows v_e^1 \rightrightarrows \cdots \rightrightarrows v_e^{k_\ell} \to w_e^0 \to \cdots \to w_e^p \to p_j^s$ whose length divides $|u_i|$ and $|u_j|$. Apart from the vertices q_i^r and p_j^s, the subgraphs G_e for different transitional edges e are disjoint, and their edges have distinct labels. Then G is a right-resolving labeled graph with exactly $\pi(e)$ transitional paths from q_i^r to p_j^s of length dividing $|u_i|$ and $|u_j|$. Every configuration of Y which is left asymptotic to $\sigma^r({}^\infty a_i^\infty)$ and right asymptotic to $\sigma^s({}^\infty a_i^\infty)$ contains the label of one of the paths in G_e. This implies that $G(Y)$ is obtained from $G(X)$ by renaming each vertex $\sigma^r({}^\infty u_i^\infty)$ to $\sigma^r({}^\infty a_i^\infty)$, and then X and Y are conjugate by Corollary 3. It is clear that the construction of G can be done in polynomial time. □

We can also show a similar result for forbidden words and general symbolic edge shifts, although we omit the proof.

Lemma 6. *For countable sofic shifts of rank at most* 2, *the representations by symbolic edge shifts and forbidden words are equivalent up to polynomial-time reductions.*

It is known [8] that computing the number of words of a given length accepted by a given nondeterministic finite automaton is complete in a complexity class known as #P, which contains NP and is believed to be much larger than it. Thus, under reasonable complexity assumptions, there is no polynomial-time algorithm for computing the structure graph of a given symbolic edge shift, if the input need not be right-resolving. We do not know the exact complexity of the conjugacy problem, if the inputs are given in this form. The hardness results are still valid, and the problems are all decidable in this case as well.

The next example shows that the combinatorial representation is not equivalent to the other three, since there is an exponential blowup.

Example 3. Any combinatorial representation of the rank 2 countable SFT defined by the right-resolving labeled graph

$$\overset{0}{\circlearrowleft} q_0 \underset{2}{\overset{1}{\rightrightarrows}} q_1 \underset{2}{\overset{1}{\rightrightarrows}} q_2 \underset{2}{\overset{1}{\rightrightarrows}} \cdots \underset{2}{\overset{1}{\rightrightarrows}} q_k \overset{3}{\circlearrowright}$$

clearly contains at least 2^k terms, as each term only represents one σ-orbit.

In what follows, we assume that in the decision problems, all countable SFTs and sofic shifts are encoded by their structure graphs, and we will do so without explicit mention.

We first solve the case of rank 1. As one might imagine, there are fast and simple algorithms in this case.

Proposition 2. *Conjugacy, and existence of block maps, factor maps, and embeddings between countable sofic shifts of Cantor-Bendixson rank 1 is in* P.

Proof. Every such shift space X is a finite union of periodic orbits of some least periods $p_1, \ldots, p_\ell \in \mathbb{N}$, which can be computed from the structure graph in polynomial time. Let Y be another one with least periods $q_1, \ldots, q_m \in \mathbb{N}$. Clearly, X and Y are conjugate if and only if $(p_1, \ldots, p_\ell) = (q_1, \ldots, q_m)$, if the periods are given in ascending order. A block map from X to Y exists if and only if, for every $i \in [1, \ell]$, there exists $j \in [1, m]$ with $q_j | p_i$, which is equivalent to the condition that the orbit of X with period p_i can be mapped onto the orbit of Y with period q_j. An embedding from X to Y must map every orbit of X to an orbit of Y of the same period, so one exists if and only if there exists an injection $\alpha : [1, \ell] \to [1, m]$ with $p_i = q_{\alpha(i)}$ for all $i \in [1, \ell]$. These checks are easy to do in polynomial time.

The interesting case is factoring. For this, construct a bipartite graph G with

$$\mathcal{V}(G) = \{L\} \times [1, \ell] \cup \{R\} \times [1, m],$$

and $((L, i), (R, j)) \in \mathcal{E}(G)$ if and only if $q_j | p_i$. It is easy to see that there exists a factor map from X to Y if and only if there exists a block map from X to Y, and G has a matching of size m (that is, we can find separate preimages for all the orbits of Y). Computing a matching of maximal size – and thus the maximal size itself – is well-known to be in P, see for example Sect. 5.2 in [5]. □

Now, we give our main result: the complexity of conjugacy of rank 2 countable SFTs (and sofic shifts).

Theorem 1. *Conjugacy of countable sofic shifts or SFTs of Cantor-Bendixson rank at most* 2 *is* GI*-complete.*

Proof. Corollary 3 states that conjugacy is equivalent to the equivalence problem of structure graphs under vertex renaming. This problem, on the other hand, is easily reducible to the isomorphism problem of directed graphs (associate to each label k a distinct small number $m_k \geq 3$, and replace every edge $e : x \to y$ with label k by m_k parallel paths of length m_k), which is GI-complete [14]. Thus the conjugacy problem is in GI.

To prove completeness, we reduce the color-preserving isomorphism problem of $\{0,1\}$-colored graphs to the conjugacy problem of SFTs; the claim then follows, as the former is GI-complete [14]. Let thus $G = (V, E, \pi)$ be a $\{0,1\}$-colored graph with the coloring $\pi : V \to \{0,1\}$. We may assume that G contains no isolated vertices. Define a rank 2 countable SFT by

$$X_G = \bigcup_{\substack{\{u,v\} \in \mathcal{E}(G) \\ \pi(u)=0}} \mathcal{B}^{-1}(u^* v^*).$$

After renaming the vertices, the structure graph of X_G is exactly G, except that each vertex v has gained two self-loops labeled $\circlearrowright$ and 1, and each edge $\{u,v\}$ where u is colored with 0 has gained the label 1. Thus, two $\{0,1\}$-colored graphs G and H are isomorphic by a color-preserving isomorphism if and only if the structure graphs of X_G and X_H are equivalent up to renaming the vertices. By Corollary 3, this is equivalent to the conjugacy of X_G and X_H. □

With the same ideas, we obtain many NP-complete problems, at least for countable sofic shifts.

Theorem 2. *Existence of embeddings between countable sofic shifts of Cantor-Bendixson rank at most* 2 *is* NP*-complete. Also, there exist countable rank* 2 *sofic shifts X and Y such that for a given countable rank* 2 *sofic shift Z, existence of block maps from Z to X, and of factor maps from Z to Y, are* NP*-complete problems.*

Proof. Proposition 1 and Lemma 4 imply that all three problems are in NP, since the conditions given in Lemma 4 are easy to check in polynomial time for a given structure graph homomorphism.

We prove the completeness of all three problems using the same construction. For all graphs G, we define a countable rank 2 sofic shift

$$X_G = \bigcup_{\{u,v\} \in \mathcal{E}(G)} \mathcal{B}^{-1}((\#u)^*(\#v)^*) \cup \mathcal{B}^{-1}((\#u)^*(v\#)^*),$$

where $\# \notin \mathcal{V}(G)$ is a new symbol.

For two graphs G and H, we show a correspondence between graph homomorphisms $\phi : G \to H$ and block maps $f : X_G \to X_H$. First, for each homomorphism ϕ, we define a block map f_ϕ as the symbol map $f_\phi(\#) = \#$ and $f_\phi(v) = \phi(v)$ for all $v \in \mathcal{V}(G)$, and by the definition of X_G and X_H, it is a well-defined block map from X_G to X_H. Second, for a block map f, we define a homomorphism ϕ_f by $\phi_f(v) = w$ if and only if $f({}^\infty(\#v)^\infty) \in \mathcal{O}_\sigma({}^\infty(\#w)^\infty)$.

Then $\{u, v\} \in \mathcal{E}(G)$ implies that ${}^{\infty}(\#u)(\#v)^{\infty}, {}^{\infty}(\#u)(v\#)^{\infty} \in X_G$, and since X_H contains no points of period 1, the f-image of at least one the configurations is aperiodic. But this implies $\{\phi_f(u), \phi_f(v)\} \in \mathcal{E}(H)$ by the definition of X_H, so that ϕ_f is indeed a graph homomorphism.

It is easy to see that surjectivity or injectivity of ϕ (on both vertices and edges) implies the same property for f_ϕ, and analogously for f and ϕ_f. The claim then directly follows from the corresponding NP-completeness results for graph homomorphisms, compactions and edge-injective homomorphisms found in [6],[13], and [3], respectively. □

6 Further Discussion

In this article, we have studied the conjugacy problem of countable SFTs and sofic shifts, and have shown that the special case of Cantor-Bendixson rank 2 is decidable. The classical formulation of the conjugacy problem of SFTs only considers mixing SFTs of positive entropy, which are uncountable, and conceptually very far from countable SFTs. Even though our results do not directly advance the study of this notoriously difficult problem, they show that related decision problems can be computable, and even have a relatively low computational complexity.

A natural continuation of this research would be to extend the results to countable sofic shifts of higher ranks, possibly for all countable sofic shifts. We suspect that for rank 3 countable sofic shifts, the problem is no longer in GI, as distances between two disturbances can encode infinitely many essentially different configurations. However, we also believe it to be decidable, possibly even in NP, as any conjugacy has a finite radius and must thus consider distant disturbances separately. The problem is then essentially combinatorial, and finding a suitable representation for the shift spaces, similar to the structure graph, might be the key to determining its complexity class.

Of course, a lot of tools have been developed for tackling the mixing case, and it could be that these tools easily decide conjugacy in the countable case. For example, it is well-known that a weaker type of conjugacy called shift equivalence is decidable in high generality, so it would be enough to show that in the case of countable SFTs, this is equivalent to conjugacy (although we have not been able to show this). Thus, we explicitly state our interest:

Question 1. Is the conjugacy of countable SFTs decidable?

In the usual case of mixing (and uncountable) SFTs and sofics, the decidability of conjugacy has not yet been solved. However, there might be an easy way to show that the conjugacy problem is, say, NP-hard. We are not aware of such investigations in the literature. Such a view might be helpful in finding ways to encode computation in instances of the conjugacy problem. Such a way would presumably need to be found in order to show that the problem is undecidable, but might also be useful (or at least interesting) if it turns out to be decidable.

Finally, we note that in the case of multidimensional SFTs, the conjugacy problem is undecidable. In fact, it was even shown in [7] that for all two-dimensional SFTs X, it is undecidable whether a given SFT Y is conjugate to it (and they also determine the complexity of finding factor maps).

References

1. Ballier, A., Durand, B., Jeandel, E.: Structural aspects of tilings. In: Weil, P., Albers, S. (eds.) Proceedings of the 25th Annual Symposium on the Theoretical Aspects of Computer Science, Bordeaux, France, pp. 61–72. IBFI Schloss Dagstuhl, February 2008
2. Ballier, A., Jeandel, E.: Structuring multi-dimensional subshifts. ArXiv e-prints, September 2013
3. Biedl, T.: The complexity of domino tiling. In: Proceedings of the 17th Canadian Conference on Computational Geometry, pp. 187–190 (2005)
4. Boyle, M.: Open problems in symbolic dynamics. In: Geometric and Probabilistic Structures in Dynamics. Contemp. Math., vol. 469, pp. 69–118. Amer. Math. Soc., Providence (2008)
5. Gibbons, A.: Algorithmic Graph Theory. Cambridge University Press, Cambridge (1985)
6. Hell, P., Nešetřil, J.: On the complexity of H-coloring. J. Combin. Theory Ser. B **48**(1), 92–110 (1990)
7. Jeandel, E., Vanier, P.: Hardness of conjugacy and factorization of multidimensional subshifts of finite type. CoRR, abs/1204.4988 (2012)
8. Kannan, S., Sweedyk, E., Mahaney, S.: Counting and random generation of strings in regular languages. In: Proceedings of the Sixth Annual ACM-SIAM Symposium on Discrete Algorithms (San Francisco, CA, 1995), pp. 551–557. ACM, New York (1995)
9. Lind, D., Marcus, B.: An introduction to symbolic dynamics and coding. Cambridge University Press, Cambridge (1995)
10. Pavlov, R., Schraudner, M.: Classification of sofic projective subdynamics of multidimensional shifts of finite type (submitted)
11. Salo, V., Törmä, I.: Computational aspects of cellular automata on countable sofic shifts. In: Rovan, B., Sassone, V., Widmayer, P. (eds.) MFCS 2012. LNCS, vol. 7464, pp. 777–788. Springer, Heidelberg (2012)
12. Salo, V., Törmä, I.: Constructions with countable subshifts of finite type. Fundamenta Informaticae **126**(2–3), 263–300 (2013)
13. Vikas, N.: Computational complexity of graph compaction. ProQuest LLC, Ann Arbor (1997). Thesis (Ph.D.)-Simon Fraser University (Canada)
14. Zemlyachenko, V.N., Korneenko, N.M., Tyshkevich, R.I.: The graph isomorphism problem. Zap. Nauchn. Sem. Leningrad. Otdel. Mat. Inst. Steklov. (LOMI), **118**, 83–158, 215 (1982). The theory of the complexity of computations, I

Plane-Walking Automata

Ville Salo and Ilkka Törmä(✉)

TUCS – Turku Centre for Computer Science, University of Turku, Turku, Finland
{vosalo,iatorm}@utu.fi

Abstract. In this article, we study classes of multidimensional subshifts defined by multihead finite automata, in particular the hierarchy of classes of subshifts defined as the number of heads grows. The hierarchy collapses on the third level, where all co-recursively enumerable subshifts are obtained in every dimension. We also compare these classes to SFTs and sofic shifts. We are unable to separate the second and third level of the hierarchy in one and two dimensions, and suggest a related open problem for two-counter machines.

Keywords: Plane-walking automaton · Multihead automaton · Subshift

1 Introduction

In this article, we discuss multihead finite automata on infinite multidimensional configurations, which we call plane-walking automata, and use them to define classes of subshifts. Our model is based on the general idea of a graph-walking automaton. In this model, the automaton is placed on one of the nodes of a graph with colored nodes, and it repeatedly reads the color of the current node, updates its internal state, and steps to an adjacent node. The automaton eventually enters an accepting or rejecting state, or runs forever without making a decision. Usually, we collect the graphs that it accepts, or the ones that it does not reject, and call this collection the language of the automaton. We restrict our attention to machines that are deterministic, although an interesting continuation of our research would be to consider nondeterministic or alternating machines.

Well-known such models include the two-way deterministic finite automata (2DFA) walking back-and-forth on a finite word, and tree-walking automata traversing a tree. See [7] for a survey on multihead automata on words, and the references in [2] for information on tree-walking automata. In multiple dimensions, our automata are based on the concept of picture-walking (or 4-way) automata for accepting picture languages, defined in [1] and surveyed in [10,11].

The first question about subshifts accepted by plane-walking automata is how this class relates to existing classes of subshifts. In particular, we compare the class of subshifts accepted by a one-head deterministic automaton to SFTs and sofic shifts, two well-known classes in the theory of subshifts. They correspond, in some sense, to local languages and regular languages of finite words, since an

T. Isokawa et al. (Eds.): AUTOMATA 2014, LNCS 8996, pp. 135–148, 2015.
DOI: 10.1007/978-3-319-18812-6_11

SFT is defined by local rules, and a sofic shift is a letter-to-letter projection of an SFT. It is well-known that in the one-dimensional finite case, graph-walking automata with a single head (2DFA) define precisely the regular languages. However, for more complicated graphs, deterministic graph-walking automata often define a smaller class than the one containing letter-to-letter projections of local languages (which is often considered the natural generalization of regularity): deterministic tree-walking automata do not define all regular tree languages [3] and deterministic picture-walking automata do not accept all recognizable picture languages [6]. We show in Theorem 1 that this is also the case for a one-head deterministic plane-walking automaton in the multidimensional case: the class of subshifts defined is strictly between SFTs and sofic shifts.

Already in [1], the basic model of picture-walking automata was augmented by multiple heads,[1] and we similarly consider classes of subshifts defined by multihead plane-walking automata. In [1, Theorem 3], it was shown that the hierarchy obtained as the number of heads grows is infinite in the case of pictures (by a diagonalization argument). Similar results are known for one-dimensional words [8] and trees [4]. In the case of subshifts, we show that the hierarchy collapses to the third level, which is precisely the class of subshifts whose languages are co-recursively enumerable. In particular, it properly contains the class of sofic shifts. However, we are not able to separate the second and third levels in the case of one or two dimensions, although we find it very likely that they are distinct. We discuss why this problem appears hard to us, suggest a possible separating language, and state a related open problem for two-counter machines.

2 Preliminary Notions

In this article, a *(d-dimensional) pattern* is a function $P : D \to \Sigma$, where $D = D(P) \subset \mathbb{Z}^d$ is the *domain* of P, and Σ is a finite *alphabet*. A full pattern with domain $\mathbb{Z}^d$ is called a *configuration (over Σ)*, and other patterns have finite domains unless otherwise noted. The restriction of a pattern P to a smaller domain D is denoted by $P|_D$. We say that a pattern P *occurs at* $\boldsymbol{v} \in \mathbb{Z}^d$ in another pattern P', if we have $\boldsymbol{u} + \boldsymbol{v} \in D(P')$ and $P'_{\boldsymbol{u}+\boldsymbol{v}} = P_{\boldsymbol{u}}$ for all $\boldsymbol{u} \in D(P)$. For $s \in \Sigma$, we denote by $|P|_s$ the number of occurrences of s in P.

A *subshift* is a set $X \subset \Sigma^{\mathbb{Z}^d}$ of configurations defined by a set F of *forbidden patterns* – a configuration $x \in \Sigma^{\mathbb{Z}^d}$ is in X if and only if none of the patterns of F occur in it. If F is finite, then X is a *subshift of finite type*, or SFT for short, and if F is recursively enumerable, then X is *co-RE* or Π^0_1. If the domain of every pattern in F is of the form is $\{\boldsymbol{0}, \boldsymbol{e}_i\}$, where $\boldsymbol{e}_1, \dots, \boldsymbol{e}_d$ is the natural basis of $\mathbb{Z}^d$, then X is a *tiling system*. A *sofic shift* is obtained by renaming the symbols of an SFT, or equivalently a tiling system. If it is decidable whether a given pattern occurs in some configuration of X, then X is *recursive*.

Unless otherwise noted, we always use the binary alphabet $\Sigma = \{0, 1\}$.

[1] Strictly speaking, they were augmented by markers, but the difference is small.

3 Choosing the Machines

The basic idea in this article is to define subshifts by deterministic and multihead finite automata as follows: Given a configuration $x \in \Sigma^{\mathbb{Z}^d}$, we initialize the heads of the automaton on some of its cells, and let them run indefinitely, moving around and reading the contents of x. If the automaton halts in a rejecting state, then we consider x to be rejected, and otherwise it is accepted.

After this high-level idea has been established, there are multiple a priori inequivalent ways of formalizing it, and we begin with a discussion of such choices. Much of this freedom is due to the fact that many different definitions and variants of multihead finite automata exist in the literature, both in the case of finite or infinite pictures and one-dimensional words (see [7] and references therein).

Heads or markers? A multihead automaton can be defined as having multiple heads capable of moving around the input, or as having one mobile head and several immobile markers that the head can move around. In the latter case, one must also decide whether the markers are indistinguishable or distinct, and whether they can store information or not. In this article, we choose the former approach of having multiple mobile heads.

Global control or independent heads? Next, we must choose how the heads of our machines interact. The traditional approach is to have a single global state that controls each head, but in our model, this could be considered 'physically infeasible', as the heads may travel arbitrarily far from each other. For this reason, and in order not to have too strong a model, the heads of our automata are independent, and can interact only when they lie in the same cell.

Synchronous or asynchronous motion? Now that the heads have no common memory, we need to decide whether they still have a common perception of time, that is, whether they can synchronize their motion. In the synchronous updating scheme, the heads update their states and positions at the same time, so that the distance between two heads moving in the same direction stays constant. The other option is asynchronous updating, where the heads may update at different paces, possibly nondeterministically. We choose the synchronous scheme, as it is easier to formalize and enables us to shoot carefully synchronized signals, which we feel are the most interesting aspect of multihead plane-walking automata.

Next, we need to decide how exactly a plane-walking automaton defines a subshift. Recall that a subshift is defined by a possibly infinite set of finite forbidden patterns in a translation-invariant way. In our model, the forbidden patterns should be exactly those that support a rejecting run of the automaton.

How do we start? First, we could always initialize our automata at the origin $\mathbf{0} \in \mathbb{Z}^d$, decide the acceptance of a configuration based on this single run, and restrict to automata that define translation-invariant sets. Second, we may quantify over all coordinates of $\mathbb{Z}^d$, initialize all the heads at the same coordinate, and reject if some choice leads to rejection. In the third option, we quantify over all k-tuples of coordinates, and place the k heads in them independently. The first definition is not very satisfying, since most one-head automata would have to be discarded, and of the remaining two, we choose the former, as it is more restrictive. We also quantify over a set of initial states, so that our subshift classes are closed under finite intersection, and accordingly seem more natural.

How do we end? Finally, we have a choice of what constitutes as a rejecting state. Can a single head cause the whole computation to reject, or does every head have to reject at the same time, and if that is the case, are they further required to be at the same position? We again choose the most restrictive option.

All of the above models are similar, in that by adding a few more heads or counters, one can usually simulate an alternative definition. Sometimes, one can even show that two models are equivalent. For example, [1, Theorem 2.3] states that being able to distinguish markers is not useful in the case of finite pictures; however, the argument seems impossible to apply to plane-walking automata.

To recap, our definition of choice is the *deterministic k-head plane-walking finite automaton with local information sharing, synchronous updating, quantification over single initial coordinate and initial state, and rejection with all heads at a single coordinate*, with the (necessarily ambiguous) shorthand kPWDFA.

4 Definitions

We now formally define our machines, runs, acceptance conditions and the subshifts they define. For this section, let the dimension d be fixed.

Definition 1. *A kPWDFA is a 5-tuple $A = (Q, \Sigma, \delta, I, R)$, where $Q = Q_1 \times \cdots \times Q_k$ is the finite set of* global states, *the Q_i are the* local states, *Σ is the* alphabet, *and $\delta = (\delta_1, \ldots, \delta_k)$ is the list of* transition functions

$$\delta_j : S_j \times \Sigma \to Q_j \times \mathbb{Z}^d,$$

where $S_j = Q'_1 \times \cdots \times Q'_{j-1} \times Q_j \times Q'_{j+1} \times \cdots \times Q'_k$, and $Q'_i = Q_i \cup \{?\}$. We call $I \subset Q$ the set of initial states, *and $R \subset Q$ the set of* rejecting states.

Note that all functions above are total.

Definition 2. *Let $A = (Q, \Sigma, \delta, I, R)$ be a kPWDFA. An* instantaneous description *or* ID *of A is an element of $\mathrm{ID}_A = (\mathbb{Z}^d)^k \times Q$. Given a configuration $x \in \Sigma^{\mathbb{Z}^d}$, we define the* update function *$A_x : \mathrm{ID}_A \to \mathrm{ID}_A$. Namely, given $c = (\boldsymbol{v}^1, \ldots, \boldsymbol{v}^k, q_1, \ldots, q_k) \in \mathrm{ID}_A$, we define $A_x(c)$ as follows. If $(q_1, \ldots, q_k) \in R$ and $\boldsymbol{v}^1 = \cdots = \boldsymbol{v}^k$, then we say c is* rejecting, *and $A_x(c) = c$. Otherwise, $A_x(c) = (\boldsymbol{w}^1, \ldots, \boldsymbol{w}^k, p_1, \ldots, p_k)$, where $\boldsymbol{w}^j = \boldsymbol{v}^j + \boldsymbol{u}^j$ and*

$$\delta_j(q'_1, \ldots, q'_{j-1}, q_j, q'_{j+1}, \ldots, q'_k, x_{\boldsymbol{v}^j}) = (p_j, \boldsymbol{u}^j),$$

where we write $q'_i = q_i$ if $\boldsymbol{v}^i = \boldsymbol{v}^j$, and $q'_i = ?$ otherwise. The run of A on $x \in \Sigma^{\mathbb{Z}^d}$ from $c \in \mathrm{ID}_A$ *is the infinite sequence $A_x^\infty(c) = (A_x^n(c))_{n \in \mathbb{N}}$. We say the run is* accepting *if no $A_x^n(c)$ is rejecting. We define the* subshift of A *by*

$$S(A) = \{x \in \Sigma^{\mathbb{Z}^d} \mid \forall q = (q_1, \ldots, q_k) \in I, \boldsymbol{v} \in \mathbb{Z}^d : A_x^\infty(\boldsymbol{v}, \ldots, \boldsymbol{v}, q) \text{ is accepting.}\}$$

We now define our hierarchy of interest:

Definition 3. *We refer to the class of all d-dimensional SFTs (sofc shifts) over the alphabet* $\Sigma = \{0,1\}$ *as simply* SFT^d (sofic^d, *respectively). For* $k > 0$, *define*

$$S_k^d = \{S(A) \mid A \text{ is a } d\text{-dimensional } kPWDFA.\}$$

It is easy to see that $S_k^d \subset S_{k+1}^d$ for all $k > 0$, and that every S_k^d only contains Π_1^0 subshifts. Since a deterministic finite state automaton can clearly check any local property, we also have $\mathrm{SFT}^d \subset S_1^d$.

Remark 1. We note some robustness properties. While the definition only allows information sharing when several heads lie in the same cell, we may assume that heads can communicate if they are at most t cells away from each other. Namely, if we had a stronger k-head automaton where such behavior is allowed, then we could simulate its computation step by $\Theta(kt^d)$ steps of a kPWDFA where the heads visit, one by one, the $\Theta(t^d)$ cells at most t steps away from them, and remember which other heads they saw in which states. Also, while we allow the machines to move by any finite vector, we may assume these vectors all have length 0 or 1 by simulating a step of length r by r steps of length 1. Finally, the classes S_k^d are closed under conjugacy, rotation, mirroring and intersection.

To compare these classes, we need to define a few subshifts and classes of subshifts. In most of our examples, the configurations contain the symbol 0 in all but a bounded number of coordinates.

Definition 4. *The* d-dimensional n-sunny side up subshift *is the* d*-dimensional subshift* $X_n^d \subset \{0,1\}^{\mathbb{Z}^d}$ *with forbidden patterns* $\{P \mid |P|_1 > n\}$. *A* d*-dimensional subshift is* n -sparse *if it is a subshift of* X_n^d, *and* sparse *if it is* n*-sparse for some* $n \in \mathbb{N}$. *If* X *is a* d_1*-dimensional subshift and* $d_2 > d_1$, *we define* $X^{\mathbb{Z}^{d_2-d_1}}$ *as the* d_2*-dimensional subshift where the contents of every* d_1*-dimensional hyperplane* $\{\sum_{i=1}^{d_1} n_i \boldsymbol{e}_i \mid \boldsymbol{n} \in \mathbb{Z}^{d_1}\} \subset \mathbb{Z}^{d_2}$ *are independently taken from* X.

An n-sparse subshift is one where at most n symbols 1 may occur, and the sunny side up subshifts are the ones with no additional constraints. The name sunny side up subshift is from [13]. We called the n-sunny side up subshift *the* n-sparse subshift in [14], but feel that the terminology used here is a bit better.

We also use the following variation of the well-known mirror subshift.

Definition 5. *The* d-dimensional mirror subshift $X_{\mathrm{mirror}}^d \subset \{0,1\}^{\mathbb{Z}^d}$ *is defined by the following forbidden patterns.*

- *All patterns* P *of domain* $\{0\} \times \{0,1,2\}^{d-1}$ *such that the all-*1 *pattern of domain* $\{\boldsymbol{0}, \boldsymbol{e}_i\}$ *for some* $i \in \{2, \dots d\}$ *occurs in* P, *but* $|P|_0 \neq 0$.
- *All patterns* P *of domain* $\{0,k\} \times \{0,1\}^{d-1}$ *for some* $k > 1$ *with* $|P|_0 = 0$.
- *All patterns* P *of domain* $\{-k,k\} \times \{0\}^{d-1} \cup \{0\} \times \{0,1\}^{d-1}$ *for some* $k > 1$ *where* $P|_{\{0\}\times\{0,1\}^{d-1}}$ *contains no symbols* 0 *and* $P_{(-k,0,\dots,0)} \neq P_{(k,0,\dots,0)}$.

Intuitively, the rules are that if two symbols 1 are adjacent on some $(d-1)$-dimensional hyperplane perpendicular to $\boldsymbol{e}_1$, then that hyperplane must be filled with 1's, and there is at most one such hyperplane, whose two sides are mirror images of each other. In two dimensions, the hyperplane is just a vertical line.

Finally, we define a type of counter machine, which we will simulate by 2- and 3-head automata in the proofs of Proposition 3 and Theorem 5. This is essentially the model MP1RM (More Powerful One-Register Machine) defined in [15]. We could also use any other Turing complete machine with a single counter which supports multiplication and division, such as John Conway's FRACTRAN [5].

Definition 6. *An* arithmetical program *is a sequence of commands of the form*

- *Multiply/divide/increment/decrement* C *by* m,
- *If* $(C \bmod m) = j$, *goto* k,
- *If* $C = m$, *goto* k,
- *Halt,*

where $j, m \in \mathbb{N}$ *are arbitrary constants and* $k \in \mathbb{N}$ *refers to one of the commands.*

To run such a program on an input $n \in \mathbb{N}$, we initialize a single counter C to n, and start executing the commands in order. The arithmetical commands work in the obvious way. We may assume the program never divides by a number unless it has checked that the value in C is divisible by it, and never subtracts m unless the value in C is at least m. Thus, C always contains a natural number. In the goto-statements, execution continues at command number k. The halt command ends the execution, and signifies that the program accepts n. It is well-known that this model is Turing complete; more precisely, we have the following.

Lemma 1 ([15]). *If a set* $L \subset \mathbb{N}$ *is recursively enumerable, then* $\{2^n \mid n \in L\}$ *is accepted by some arithmetical program.*

5 Results

Our first results place the class S_1^d between SFT^d and sofic^d.

Lemma 2. *In all dimensions* d, *we have* $(X_1^1)^{\mathbb{Z}^{d-1}} \in S_1^d \setminus \mathrm{SFT}^d$.

Proof. Note that $X = (X_1^1)^{\mathbb{Z}^{d-1}}$ is the d-dimensional subshift where no row may contain two symbols 1. First, we show X is not an SFT: Suppose on the contrary that it is defined by a finite set of forbidden patterns with domain $[0, n-1]^d$ for some $n \in \mathbb{N}$. Consider the configurations $x^0, x^1 \in \Sigma^{\mathbb{Z}^d}$ where $x^i_{(0,0)} = x^i_{(n,i)} = 1$ and $x^i_{\boldsymbol{v}} = 0$ for $\boldsymbol{v} \in \mathbb{Z}^d - \{(0,0), (n,i)\}$. Since any pattern with domain $[0, n-1]^d$ occurs in x^0 if and only if it occurs in x^1, we have $x^0 \in X$ if and only if $x^1 \in X$, a contradiction since clearly $x^0 \notin X$ and $x^1 \in X$.

To show that $X \in$ 1PWDFA, we construct a one-head automaton for X. The idea is that the head will walk in the direction of the first coordinate, and increment a counter when it sees a symbol 1. If the counter reaches 2, the automaton rejects. More precisely, the automaton is $A_1 = (\{q_0, q_1, q_2\}, \{0,1\}, \delta, \{q_0\}, \{q_2\})$, where $\delta(q_0, a) = (q_a, \boldsymbol{e}_1)$, $\delta(q_1, a) = (q_{1+a}, \boldsymbol{e}_1)$ and $\delta(q_2, a) = (q_2, \boldsymbol{0})$ for $a \in \{0,1\}$. If there are two 1's on any of the rows of a configuration $x \in \Sigma^{\mathbb{Z}^d}$, say $x_{\boldsymbol{v}} = x_{\boldsymbol{w}} = 1$ where $\boldsymbol{w} = \boldsymbol{v} + n\boldsymbol{e}_1$ for some $n \geq 1$, then the run of A_1 on x from $(q_0, \boldsymbol{v})$ is not accepting, as the rejecting ID $(q_2, \boldsymbol{w} + \boldsymbol{e}_1)$ is entered after $n+1$ steps. Thus, $x \notin S(A_1)$. On the other hand, it is easy to see the if no row of $x \in \Sigma^{\mathbb{Z}^2}$ contains two symbols 1, then $x \in S(A_1)$. □

Theorem 1. *In all dimensions d, we have $S_1^d \subset \mathrm{sofic}^d$, with equality if $d = 1$.*

Remark 2. For all dimensions $d_1 < d_2$, all k, and all subshifts $X \in S_k^{d_1}$, we have $X^{\mathbb{Z}^{d_2 - d_1}} \in S_k^{d_2}$, since a d_2-dimensional kPWDFA can simply simulate a d_1-dimensional one on any d_1-dimensional hyperplane. In particular, if $X \subset \Sigma^{\mathbb{Z}}$ is sofic, then $X^{\mathbb{Z}^{d-1}} \in S_1^d$ for any dimension d.

Of course, since multidimensional SFTs may contain very complicated configurations, the same is true for the classes S_1^d. In particular, for all $d \geq 2$ there are subshifts in S_1^d whose languages are co-RE-complete. However, just like in the case of SFTs, the sparse parts of subshifts in S_1^d are simpler.

Theorem 2. *Let the dimension d be arbitrary, and let $X \in S_1^d$. For all k, the intersection $X \cap X_k^d$ is recursive.*

Proof. Let $X = S(A)$ for a 1PWDFA $A = (Q, \Sigma, \delta, I, R)$ that only takes steps of length 0 and 1. First, we claim that it is decidable whether a given configuration y with at most k symbols 1 is in Y. We need to check whether there exists $\boldsymbol{v} \in \mathbb{Z}^d$ such that started from $\boldsymbol{v}$ in one of the initial states, A eventually rejects y.

To decide this, note first that if A does not see any symbols 1, then it does not reject – otherwise, the all-0 configuration would not be in Y. Define $W = \{\boldsymbol{v} \in \mathbb{Z}^d \mid \|\boldsymbol{v}\| \leq |Q|\}$, and denote $\mathbb{Z}W = \{n\boldsymbol{w} \mid n \in \mathbb{Z}, w \in W\}$. Let $E \subset \mathbb{Z}^d$ be the convex hull of $D = \{\boldsymbol{v} \in \mathbb{Z}^d \mid y_{\boldsymbol{v}} = 1\}$, and let $F = E + W + W$. Note that no matter which initial state A is started from, the only starting positions from which it can reach one of the symbols 1 are those in

$$W + \mathbb{Z}W + W + D \subset \mathbb{Z}W + F.$$

Namely, whenever A takes $|Q|$ steps without encountering a symbol 1, it must repeat a state. Thus, if A is at least $2|Q|$ cells away from the nearest symbol 1, then it must be ultimately periodically moving in some direction $\boldsymbol{v} \in \mathbb{Z}^d$ with $\|\boldsymbol{v}\| \leq |Q|$, repeating its state every $s \leq |Q|$ steps. If we denote by $(q_n, \boldsymbol{v}_n)_{n \leq N}$ the (finite or infinite) sequence of states and coordinates that A visits before encountering a symbol 1, then there are $a < b \leq |Q|$ with $q_a = q_b$. This implies that $\boldsymbol{v}_{a+k(b-a)+\ell} = \boldsymbol{v}_a + k(\boldsymbol{v}_b - \boldsymbol{v}_a) + \boldsymbol{w}_\ell$ for all $k \in \mathbb{N}$ and $\ell \leq b - a$ for which the coordinate is defined, where $\|\boldsymbol{v}_a - \boldsymbol{v}_0\|, \|\boldsymbol{w}_\ell\| \leq |Q|$. The claim follows, since A must enter the domain D in order to encounter a 1.

Next, we show that we only need to analyze the starting positions in $G = W + W + W + F$. Namely, if A enters the set F for the first time after $a + k(b-a) + \ell$

steps and $k > 2|Q|/\|\boldsymbol{v}_b - \boldsymbol{v}_a\|$, then the distance of the coordinate $\boldsymbol{v}_n$ from F is at least $|Q|$ for all $n \leq a$. This means that if we initialize A at the coordinate $\boldsymbol{v}_0 + \boldsymbol{v}_b - \boldsymbol{v}_a$ in the same state $q_0 \in Q$, then it will also enter F for the first time in the state $q_{a+k(b-a)+\ell}$ and at the coordinate $\boldsymbol{v}_{a+k(b-a)+\ell}$.

From each starting position in the finite set G and each initial state, we now simulate the machine until it first enters F or exits $W + G$ (in which case it never enters F). Now, we note that if the machine re-exits F after the first time it is entered, then it does not reject y. Namely, $F = E + W + W$ is convex and contains a 0-filled border thick enough that A must be in an infinite loop, heading off to infinity. Thus, if A ever rejects y, it must do so by entering F from G without exiting $W + G$, then staying inside F, and rejecting before entering a loop, which we can easily detect. This finishes the proof of decidability of $y \in Y$.

Now, given a pattern P with domain $D \subset \mathbb{Z}^d$, we need to decide whether it occurs in a configuration of Y. If $|P|_1 > k$, the answer is of course 'no' since Y is k-sparse, so suppose $|P|_1 \leq k$. Construct the configuration y with $y|_D = P$ and $y_{\boldsymbol{v}} = 0$ for $\boldsymbol{v} \in \mathbb{Z}^d \setminus D$. If $y \in Y$, which is decidable by the above argument, then we answer 'yes'. If $y \notin Y$ and $|P|_1 = k$, then we can safely answer 'no'.

If $y \notin Y$ and $|P|_1 < k$, then we have found a rejecting run of A that only visits some finite set of coordinates $C \subset \mathbb{Z}^d$. If there exists $x \in Y$ such that $x|_D = P$, then necessarily $x_{\boldsymbol{v}} = 1$ for some $\boldsymbol{v} \in C \setminus D$. For all such $\boldsymbol{v}$, we construct a new pattern by adding $\{\boldsymbol{v} \mapsto 1\}$ into P, and call this algorithm recursively on it. If one of the recursive calls returns 'yes', then we answer 'yes' as well. Otherwise, we answer 'no'. The correctness of this algorithm now follows by induction. □

For the previous result to be nontrivial, it is important to explicitly take the intersection with a sparse subshift instead of assuming that X is sparse, for the following reason.

Proposition 1. *For all dimensions $d \geq 2$, the class S_1^d contains no nontrivial sparse subshifts.*

Proof. Let A be a 1PWDFA such that $S(A)$ is sparse and contains at least two configurations. We may assume that $X_1^d \subset S(A)$ by recoding if necessary. Recall the notation of the proof of Theorem 2. It was shown there that if A can reach a position $\boldsymbol{v} \in \mathbb{Z}^d$ from the origin without encountering a 1, then $\boldsymbol{v} \in W + W + \mathbb{Z}W$. Let $V \subset \mathbb{Z}^d$ be an infinite set such that $\boldsymbol{v} - \boldsymbol{w} \notin \mathbb{Z}W + W + W$ for all $\boldsymbol{v} \neq \boldsymbol{w} \in V$. One exists since $d \geq 2$. Define $x \in \Sigma^{\mathbb{Z}^d}$ by $x_{\boldsymbol{v}} = 1$ if and only if $\boldsymbol{v} \in V$. Then A accepts x, since it encounters at most one symbol 1 on every run on x, contradicting the sparsity of $S(A)$. □

Next, we show that two heads are already quite powerful in the one- and two-dimensional settings, and such results do not hold for them. In two dimensions, some type of searching is also possible with just two heads.

Proposition 2. *The k-sunny side up shift X_k^2 is in S_2^2 for all k.*

The following proposition gives the separation of the classes S_1^d and S_2^d for $d \leq 2$. It can be thought of as an analogue of the well-known result that two counters are enough for arbitrarily complicated (though not arbitrary) computation.

Proposition 3. *For $d \leq 2$, there is a 2-sparse co-RE-complete subshift $X \in S_2^d$.*

Proof. We only prove the case $d = 2$, as the one-dimensional case is even easier. Let X be the subshift of X_2^2 where either the two symbols 1 are on different rows, or their distance is not 2^n for any $n \in L$, for a fixed RE-complete set $L \subset \mathbb{N}$.

To prove $X \in S_2^2$, we construct a 2PWDFA A for it. The heads of A are called the 'zig-zag head' and the 'counter head'. Since S_2^2 is closed under intersection, Proposition 2 shows that we may restrict our attention to configurations of X_2^2. First, our machine checks that it is started on a symbol 1 and another symbol 1 occurs on the same row to the left, by doing a left-and-right sweep with the zig-zag head. Otherwise, A runs forever without halting. The rightmost 1 is ignored during the rest of the computation, and from now on, we refer to the leftmost 1 as the *pointer*. Since the heads never leave the row on which they started, they can keep track of whether they are to the right or to the left of the rightmost 1.

We think of the distance of the counter head from the pointer as the value of a counter C of an arithmetic program accepting the language $L' = \{2^n \mid n \in L\}$ (which exists by Lemma 1). We simulate this program using the two heads as follows: The finite state of the zig-zag head will store the state of the program. If the counter of the arithmetical program contains the value C and the pointer is at $\boldsymbol{v} \in \mathbb{Z}^2$, then both heads are at $\boldsymbol{v} + (C, 0)$ (except for intermediate steps when a command of the program is being executed). See Fig. 1. To increment or decrement C by m, the zig-zag head and the counter head simply move m steps to the left or right, staying together. To check $C = m$, the zig-zag head moves m steps to the left and looks for the pointer, and to check $(C \bmod m) = j$, the zig-zag head makes a left-and-right sweep, visiting the pointer and returning to the counter head, using its finitely many states to compute the remainder.

Multiplications and divisions are done by standard signal constructions. For example, to move the zig-zag head and the counter head from $\boldsymbol{v} + (C, 0)$ to $\boldsymbol{v} + (C/2, 0)$ (assuming it has been checked that C is even), the counter head starts moving left at speed 1, and the zig-zag head at speed 3, bouncing back from the pointer, and the two meet at exactly $\boldsymbol{v} + (C/2, 0)$. It is easy to construct such pairs of speeds for multiplication or division by any fixed natural number.

If the arithmetical program eventually halts, then A rejects the configuration, and otherwise it simulates the program forever. Now, let $x \in X_2^2$ be arbitrary. If A is not started on the rightmost 1 of a row of x that contains two 1's, then it does not reject x. Suppose then that this holds and let $\ell \in \mathbb{N}$ be the distance between the two 1's, so that A starts simulating the arithmetical program as described above, with input value ℓ. If $\ell \in L'$, then the program eventually halts and the automaton rejects, and we have $x \notin X$. Otherwise, the program and thus the automaton run forever, and $x \in X$ since A does not reject x from any starting position. This shows that $S(A) = X$. □

We do not believe that *all* 2-sparse co-RE-complete subshifts are in S_2^d for $d \leq 2$, but we cannot prove this. In three or more dimensions, however, we obtain the following analogue of Proposition 1, which is proved similarly.

Theorem 3. *For all dimensions $d \geq 3$, the class S_2^d contains no nontrivial sparse subshifts.*

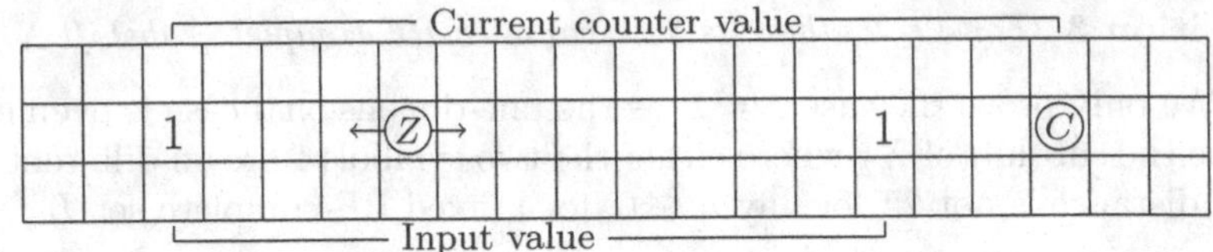

Fig. 1. Simulating an arithmetical program with two heads, labeled Z for zig-zag and C for counter. The leftmost 1 is the pointer, and empty squares contain 0-symbols.

Proof. Let A be a 2PWDFA taking only steps of length 0 or 1 such that $S(A)$ is sparse and contains at least two configurations. We may again assume that $X_1^d \subset S(A)$. As in the proof of Theorem 2, it is easy to see that there exists some $p \in \mathbb{N}$ such that, denoting $W = \{\boldsymbol{v} \in \mathbb{Z}^d \mid \|\boldsymbol{v}\| \leq p\}$ and $\mathbb{Z}W = \{n\boldsymbol{w} \mid n \in \mathbb{Z}, \boldsymbol{w} \in W\}$, we have the following. Let the two heads of A be initialized on some coordinates $\boldsymbol{v} = \boldsymbol{v}_0 \in \mathbb{Z}^2$ and $\boldsymbol{w} = \boldsymbol{w}_0 \in \mathbb{Z}^2$ in any states, and denote by $(\boldsymbol{v}_n)_{n \leq N}$ and $(\boldsymbol{w}_n)_{n \leq N}$ their itineraries up to some timestep $N \in \mathbb{N}$. If we have $\|\boldsymbol{v} - \boldsymbol{w}\| \leq p$ ($\|\boldsymbol{v} - \boldsymbol{w}\| > p$), then $\boldsymbol{v}_n \in \boldsymbol{v} + \mathbb{Z}W + W$ and $\boldsymbol{v}_n \in \boldsymbol{v} + \mathbb{Z}W + W$ until either head sees a symbol 1 (either head sees a symbol 1 or the heads meet each other, respectively). In the former case, note that the heads may travel together, so that their 'combined state' can have a period greater than $|Q|$.

Analogously to the proof of Proposition 1, let $V \subset \mathbb{Z}^d$ be an infinite set such that $\boldsymbol{v} - \boldsymbol{w} \notin \mathbb{Z}W + \mathbb{Z}W + W + W$ for all $\boldsymbol{v}, \boldsymbol{w} \in V$. Define $x \in \Sigma^{\mathbb{Z}^d}$ by $x_{\boldsymbol{v}} = 1$ if and only if $\boldsymbol{v} \in V$. We prove that x is accepted by A, contradicting the sparsity of $S(A)$. We may assume that A is started at some position $\boldsymbol{w} \in \mathbb{Z}^d$ and encounters a 1 at the origin after some number of steps.

By the first paragraph, both heads stay in the region $\boldsymbol{w} + \mathbb{Z}W + W$ until the origin is found, say by the first head. Then $\boldsymbol{w} \in \mathbb{Z}W + W$, so the second head stays in the domain $\mathbb{Z}W + \mathbb{Z}W + W + W$ until it encounters the origin or the first head. The first head is restricted to the domain $\mathbb{Z}W + W$ until it meets the second head, so the heads cannot reach any coordinate $\boldsymbol{v} \in V \setminus \{\boldsymbol{0}\}$ before this. But if the heads meet, they must do so in a coordinate of $\mathbb{Z}W + W$, and after this, they are confined to the domain $\mathbb{Z}W + \mathbb{Z}W + W + W$ until one of them reaches the origin again. Thus, the heads never reach a symbol 1 other than the origin, and since $X_1^d \subset S(A)$, the configuration x must be accepted. □

There are no nontrivial restrictions for sparse sofic shifts.

Theorem 4. *For all dimensions $d \geq 2$, every sparse co-RE subshift is in* sofic^d.

Combining Theorems 3, 4 and Proposition 1, we obtain the following.

Corollary 1. *For all dimensions $d \geq 2$, we have $S_1^d \subsetneq \text{sofic}^d$, and for all dimensions $d \geq 3$, we have $S_2^d \not\subset \text{sofic}^d$.*

While Theorem 4 shows that all sparse S_2^d subshifts are sofic, we can show that this is not true in general. In particular, the next result shows that S_1^d is properly contained in S_2^d for all $d \geq 2$.

Proposition 4. *In all dimensions $d \geq 2$, we have $X^d_{\text{mirror}} \in S^d_2 \setminus \text{sofic}^d$.*

Proof. The proof of $X^d_{\text{mirror}} \notin \text{sofic}^d$ is completely standard both in the theory of subshifts and in the theory of picture languages, although we do not have a direct reference for it. The same argument is applied in [12, Example 2.4] to a slightly different subshift.

To show that $X^d_{\text{mirror}} \in S^d_2$, we describe a 2PWDFA for it. Using the fact that S^d_2 is closed under intersection, we restrict to the SFT defined by the first point of Definition 5. We can also assume there is at most one hyperplane of symbols 1, as this is checked by a 1PWDFA that walks in the direction of the first axis from its initial position, and halts if it sees the pattern $\{\mathbf{0} \mapsto 1, \boldsymbol{e}_2 \mapsto 1\}$ twice.

Under these assumptions, the mirror property is easy to check. One of the heads memorizes the bit in the initial position in its finite memory. Then, one of the heads starts traveling to the direction $\boldsymbol{e}_1$, and the other to $\boldsymbol{e}_1 + \boldsymbol{e}_2$. If the latter sees a hyperplane of symbols 1, it turns to the direction $\boldsymbol{e}_1 - \boldsymbol{e}_2$. If the heads meet, they check that the bit in the initial position matches the bit under the current position, and if not, the configuration is rejected. □

Finally, we collapse the hierarchy. This can be thought of as an analogue of the well-known result that three counters are enough for *all* computation.

Theorem 5. *In all dimensions d, the classes S^d_k for $k \geq 3$ coincide with the class of co-RE subshifts.*

Proof. We only need to show that S^d_3 contains all Π^0_1 subshifts. Namely, $S^d_k \subset S^d_{k+1}$ holds for all $k > 0$, and since a Turing machine can easily enumerate patterns supporting a rejecting computation of a multihead finite automaton, every S^d_k subshift is also Π^0_1.

Let T be a Turing machine that, when started from the initial configuration c_0 with empty input, outputs a sequence $(P_i)_{i \in \mathbb{N}}$ of patterns by writing each of them in turn to a special output track, and visiting a special state q_{out}. We construct a 3PWDFA A_T accepting exactly those configurations where no P_i occurs. The heads of A_T are called the *pointer head*, the *zig-zag head*, and the *counter head*. The machine has a single initial state, and when started from any position $\boldsymbol{v} \in \mathbb{Z}^d$ of a configuration x, it checks that no P_i occurs in x at $\boldsymbol{v}$. Since A_T is started from every position, it will then forbid all translates of the P_i.

The machine simulates an arithmetical program as in the proof of Proposition 3, but in place of the 'leftmost symbol 1', we use the pointer head. The crucial difference here is that unlike a symbol 1, the pointer head can be moved freely. This allows us to walk around the configuration, and extract any information we want from it. The arithmetical program simulates Algorithm 1, which finally simulates the Turing machine T.

The algorithm remembers a finite pattern $P = x|_{D(P)+\boldsymbol{v}}$, where $\boldsymbol{v} \in \mathbb{Z}^d$ is the initial position of the heads, and a vector $\boldsymbol{u} \in \mathbb{Z}^d$ containing $\boldsymbol{w} - \boldsymbol{v}$, where

Algorithm 1. The algorithm that the three-head automaton A_T simulates.

$c \leftarrow c_0$ ▷ A configuration of T, set to the initial configuration
$\boldsymbol{u} \leftarrow \mathbf{0} \in \mathbb{Z}^d$ ▷ The position of the pointer head relative to the initial position
$P : \emptyset \to \{0,1\}$ ▷ A finite pattern at the initial position
loop
  repeat
    $c \leftarrow \textsc{NextConf}_T(c)$ ▷ Simulate one step of T
  until $\textsc{State}(c) = q_{\text{out}}$ ▷ T outputs something
  $P' \leftarrow \textsc{OutputOf}(c)$ ▷ A forbidden pattern
  while $D(P') \not\subset D(P)$ **do**
    $\boldsymbol{w} \leftarrow \textsc{LexMin}(D(P) \setminus D(P'))$ ▷ The lexicographically minimal vector
    while $\boldsymbol{u} \neq \boldsymbol{w}$ **do**
      $\boldsymbol{d} \leftarrow \textsc{NearestUnitVector}(\boldsymbol{w} - \boldsymbol{u})$ ▷ Nearest unit vector in $\mathbb{Z}^d$
      $\textsc{MoveBy}(\boldsymbol{d})$ ▷ Move the heads of A_T to the given direction
      $\boldsymbol{u} \leftarrow \boldsymbol{u} + \boldsymbol{d}$
    $b \leftarrow \textsc{ReadSymbol}$ ▷ Read the symbol of x under the pointer head
    $P \leftarrow P \cup \{\boldsymbol{u} \mapsto b\}$ ▷ Expand P by one coordinate
  if $P|_{D(P')} = P'$ **then halt** ▷ The forbidden pattern P' was found

$\boldsymbol{w} \in \mathbb{Z}^d$ is the current position of the pointer. The machine T is simulated step by step, and whenever it outputs a forbidden pattern P', the algorithm checks whether $D(P)$ contains its domain. If so, it then checks whether $x|_{D(P')+\boldsymbol{v}} = P'$. If this holds, then the algorithm halts, the arithmetical program simulating it halts, and the automaton A_T moves all of its heads to the pointer and rejects. If P' does not occur, the simulation of T continues.

If $D(P')$ is not contained in $D(P)$, then the algorithm expands P, which is done in the outer **while**-loop of Algorithm 1. To find out the contents of x at some coordinate $\boldsymbol{w} + \boldsymbol{v}$ for $\boldsymbol{w} \in D(P')$, the algorithm chooses a unit direction (one of $\pm \boldsymbol{e}_i$ for $i \in \{1, \ldots, d\}$) that would take the pointer head closer to $\boldsymbol{w} + \boldsymbol{v}$, and signals it to A_T via the arithmetical program. In a single sweep of the zig-zag head to the pointer and back, A_T can easily move all of its heads one step in any unit direction. Then the simulation continues, and the algorithm updates $\boldsymbol{u}$ accordingly. When $\boldsymbol{u} = \boldsymbol{w}$ finally holds, the algorithm orders A_T to read the symbol $x_{\boldsymbol{v}+\boldsymbol{u}}$ under the pointer, which is again doable in a single sweep. The bit $b = x_{\boldsymbol{v}+\boldsymbol{u}}$ is given to the algorithm, which expands P by defining $P_{\boldsymbol{u}} = x_{\boldsymbol{v}+\boldsymbol{u}}$.

For a configuration x and initial coordinate $\boldsymbol{v} \in \mathbb{Z}^d$, the automaton A_T thus computes the sequence of patterns $(P_i)_{i \in \mathbb{N}}$ and checks for each $i \in \mathbb{N}$ whether $x|_{D(P_i)+\boldsymbol{v}} = P_i$ holds, rejecting if it does. Since $\boldsymbol{v}$ is arbitrary, we have $x \in S(A_T)$ if and only if no P_i occurs in x. Thus S_3^d contains an arbitrary Π_1^0 subshift. □

The basic comparisons obtained above are summarized in Fig. 2.

6 The Classes S_2^1 and S_2^2

A major missing link in our classification is the separation of S_2^d and S_3^d in dimensions $d \leq 2$. We leave this problem unsolved, but state the following conjecture.

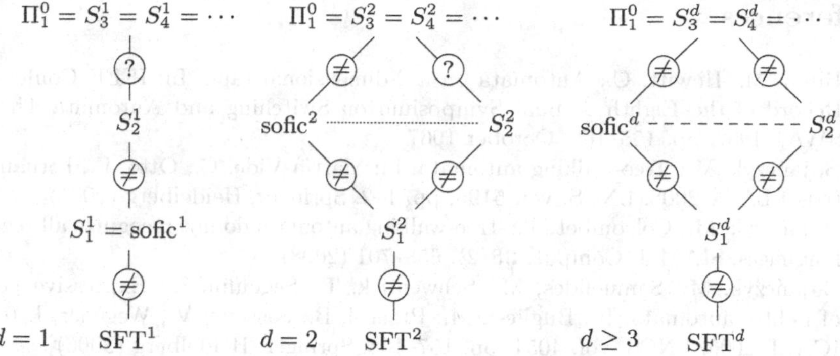

Fig. 2. A comparison of our classes of subshifts. The solid, dashed and dotted lines denote inclusion, incomparability and an unknown relation, respectively, as we only know $S_2^d \not\subset \text{sofic}^d$ for $d = 2$.

Conjecture 1. For $d \leq 2$, there exists a sparse co-RE subshift which is not in S_2^d. In particular we have $S_2^d \subsetneq S_3^d$, and sofic^2 and S_2^2 are incomparable.

Recall from the proof of Proposition 3 that two counters are enough for a plane-walking automaton to simulate any arithmetical program in a sparse subshift. It is known that two-counter machines (which are basically equivalent to arithmetical programs by [15]) cannot compute all recursive functions, and in particular cannot recognize the set of prime numbers [9]. A natural candidate for realizing Conjecture 1 in the one-dimensional case would thus be the subshift $X \subset X_2^1$ where the distance of the two 1's cannot be a prime number.

However, instead of simply simulating an arithmetical program, the automaton may use the position of the rightmost 1 in the middle of the computation, and a priori compute something an ordinary arithmetical program cannot. In some sense it thus simulates an arithmetical program that remembers its input. Conversely, we also believe that a run of a 2PWDFA on a 2-sparse subshift can be simulated by such a machine. All currently known proof techniques for limitations of two-counter machines break down if one is allowed to remember the input value, which raises the following question.

Question 1. Can arithmetical programs (or two-counter machines) that remember their input (for example, in the sense that they can check whether the current counter value is greater than the input) recognize all recursively enumerable sets? In particular, can they recognize the set of prime numbers?

Other tools for separating classes of multihead automata are diagonalization, where an automaton with much more than k heads can analyze the behavior of one with k heads, and choose to act differently from it on some inputs, and computability arguments, where algorithms of certain complexity can only be computed by machines with enough heads. Unfortunately, these approaches cannot separate S_2^d from S_3^d, since both are capable of universal computation.

References

1. Blum, M., Hewitt, C.: Automata on a 2-dimensional tape. In: IEEE Conference Record of the Eighth Annual Symposium on Switching and Automata Theory, SWAT 1967, pp. 155–160, October 1967
2. Bojańczyk, M.: Tree-walking automata. In: Martín-Vide, C., Otto, F., Fernau, H. (eds.) LATA 2008. LNCS, vol. 5196, pp. 1–2. Springer, Heidelberg (2008)
3. Bojańczyk, M., Colcombet, T.: Tree-walking automata do not recognize all regular languages. SIAM J. Comput. **38**(2), 658–701 (2008)
4. Bojańczyk, M., Samuelides, M., Schwentick, T., Segoufin, L.: Expressive power of pebble automata. In: Bugliesi, M., Preneel, B., Sassone, V., Wegener, I. (eds.) ICALP 2006. LNCS, vol. 4051, pp. 157–168. Springer, Heidelberg (2006)
5. Conway, J.H.: Fractran: a simple universal programming language for arithmetic. In: Cover, T.M., Gopinath, B. (eds.) Open Problems in Communication and Computation, pp. 4–26. Springer-Verlag New York Inc., New York (1987)
6. Giammarresi, D., Venezia, F., Restivo, A.: Two-dimensional languages (1997)
7. Holzer, M., Kutrib, M., Malcher, A.: Multi-head finite automata: characterizations, concepts and open problems. ArXiv e-prints, June 2009
8. Hsia, P., Yeh, R.T.: Marker automata. Inform. Sci. **8**(1), 71–88 (1975)
9. Ibarra, O.H., Trân, N.Q.: A note on simple programs with two variables. Theor. Comput. Sci. **112**(2), 391–397 (1993)
10. Inoue, K., Takanami, I.: A survey of two-dimensional automata theory. Inform. Sci. **55**(1–3), 99–121 (1991)
11. Kari, J., Salo, V.: A survey on picture-walking automata. In: Kuich, W., Rahonis, G. (eds.) Algebraic Foundations in Computer Science. LNCS, vol. 7020, pp. 183–213. Springer, Heidelberg (2011)
12. Kass, S., Madden, K.: A sufficient condition for non-soficness of higher-dimensional subshifts. Proc. Amer. Math. Soc. **141**(11), 3803–3816 (2013)
13. Pavlov, R., Schraudner, M.: Classification of sofic projective subdynamics of multidimensional shifts of finite type (submitted)
14. Salo, V., Törmä, I.: Commutators of bipermutive and affine cellular automata. In: Kari, J., Kutrib, M., Malcher, A. (eds.) AUTOMATA 2013. LNCS, vol. 8155, pp. 155–170. Springer, Heidelberg (2013)
15. Schroeppel, R.: A two counter machine cannot calculate 2^N (1972)

Author Index

Printed in the United States
By Bookmasters